RESEARCH ON EXEMPLARY SCHOOLS

EDUCATIONAL PSYCHOLOGY

Allen J. Edwards, Series Editor
Department of Psychology
Southwest Missouri State University
Springfield, Missouri

A complete list of titles in this series is available from the publisher.

RESEARCH ON EXEMPLARY SCHOOLS

Edited by

GILBERT R. AUSTIN
HERBERT GARBER

Center for Educational Research and Development
University of Maryland Baltimore County
Catonsville, Maryland

With a Foreword by Wilbur Brookover

Michigan State University

1985

ACADEMIC PRESS, INC.

(Harcourt Brace Jovanovich, Publishers)

Orlando   San Diego   New York   London
Toronto   Montreal   Sydney   Tokyo

ACADEMIC PRESS, INC.
Orlando, Florida 32887

United Kingdom Edition published by
ACADEMIC PRESS INC. (LONDON) LTD.
24–28 Oval Road, London NW1 7DX

LIBRARY OF CONGRESS CATALOGING-IN-PUBLICATION DATA

Main entry under title:

Research on exemplary schools.

   Includes indexes.
   1. Education—United States—Evaluation—Addresses,
essays, lectures.   2. Public schools—United States—
Evaluation—Addresses, essays, lectures.   3. Private
schools—United States—Evaluation—Addresses, essays,
lectures.   4. Education and state—United States—
Addresses, essays, lectures.   I. Austin, Gilbert R.
II. Garber, Herbert.   III. University of Maryland,
Baltimore County. Center for Educational Research
and Development.
LA217.R47   1985   370'.973   85-3966
ISBN 0-12-068590-6 (alk. paper)
ISBN 0-12-068591-4 (paperback)

PRINTED IN THE UNITED STATES OF AMERICA

85 86 87 88   9 8 7 6 5 4 3 2 1

CONTENTS

PART III. RESEARCH IMPACT ON POLICY AND PRACTICE

CONTRIBUTORS

Numbers in parentheses indicate the pages on which the authors' contributions begin.

Susan Abramowitz (31), Office of Planning, The New York Hospital, New York, New York 10021

Carolyn S. Anderson (97), Crete-Monee School District, Crete, Illinois 60417

Gilbert R. Austin (65), Center for Educational Research and Development, University of Maryland Baltimore County, Catonsville, Maryland 21228

David C. Berliner (127), Department of Educational Psychology, College of Education, University of Arizona, Tuscon, Arizona 85721

Dale C. Carlson (83), California Assessment Program, California Department of Education, Sacramento, California 95814

John D. Donovan (47), Department of Sociology, Boston College, Chestnut Hill, Massachusetts 02167

Mark E. Fetler (83), Division of Planning, Evaluation, and Research, California Department of Education, Sacramento, California 95814

Herbert Garber (201), Center for Educational Research and Development, University of Maryland Baltimore County, Catonsville, Maryland 21228

Jane Hannaway (31), Woodrow Wilson School of Public and International Affairs, Princeton University, Princeton, New Jersey 08544

Stephen P. Holowenzak (65), University of Maryland, European Division, APO, New York 09102

Kenneth A. Leithwood (155), Ontario Institute for Studies in Education, Toronto, Ontario M5S 1V6, Canada

George F. Madaus (47), School of Education, Boston College, Chestnut Hill, Massachusetts 02167

Stephen K. Miller (3), Foundations of Education, University of Louisville, Louisville, Kentucky 40292

Deborah J. Montgomery (155), Ontario Institute for Studies in Education, Toronto, Ontario M5S 1V6, Canada

Stewart C. Purkey[1] (181), Wisconsin Center for Education Research, University of Wisconsin, Madison, Wisconsin 53706

Marshall S. Smith (181), Wisconsin Center for Education Research, University of Wisconsin, Madison, Wisconsin 53706

[1] Present address: Lawrence University, Mursell Center, Appleton, Wisconsin 54912

FOREWORD

I recommend this collection of articles on exemplary schools to all researchers and practitioners who would improve the outcomes of all students in our schools. Readers will find no magic formula or specific recipes for making their schools more effective, but the history of the effective schools movement and much of the relevant research is reviewed in this volume. Knowledge of the research and numerous suggestions should help facilitate changes in educational practice.

The chapters in this volume reflect a major shift in the areas of educational research emphasis. Two decades ago, success or failure in school learning was seldom attributed to the effectiveness or ineffectiveness of the school. There was great emphasis on identifying and analyzing a student's abilities and characteristics on the assumption that student learning was primarily determined by differences in individual potential and needs. The chapters in this volume all, in one way or another, derive from the assumption that the characteristics of the school learning environment may explain the extent to which students master the outcomes desired from the school teaching–learning experience.

Although there is no comprehensive theoretical statement for the research in the reviews provided here, a general theoretical frame of reference characterizes all the chapters. That is a general social-psychological theory that the nature of the school social system, including its organization and culture or climate, largely determines the learning that occurs in the school. Thus, contrary to much prior belief, *schools can make a difference.* Several of the chapters in various degrees reflect the fact that schools are complex social systems that involve both the total school organization and culture, as well as classroom subunits.

We have only begun to analyze the nature of these school social systems, so definitive formulas for making schools more effective in producing both excellent and equitable outcomes for all the students are not yet available. However, this volume makes a significant contribution to our knowledge.

WILBUR BROOKOVER

Michigan State University
East Lansing, Michigan

PREFACE

America's schools are scapegoats par excellence. When political–economic crises arise, the nation often turns to its public schools to solve the problem. When the crisis subsides, the public discovers that the schools added little to the solution. Moreover, the schools get blamed periodically for causing such problems as declining Scholastic Aptitude Test (SAT) scores, illiterate high-school graduates, incompetent beginning workers in factories and stores, and inequality of economic outcomes between racial groups.

Researchers and others have tried to understand and to explain the schools to society for generations. The researchers, unlike public personalitites, need to work from data and a reasonable research design. The time-honored techniques they have used come and go, while trouble for and from the schools persists. Recently, a new movement has emerged that intends to use new sets of data in quite different ways. It is called effective or exemplary schools research.

This book attempts to describe this movement or cause in some depth. The book is divided into three parts: Scope and Content, Research Approaches, and Research Impact on Policy and Practice. In Chapter 1, the history of the movement receives thorough treatment by Stephen K. Miller. Chapters 2 and 3 by Jane Hannaway and Susan Abramowitz, and by John D. Donovan and George F. Madaus, respectively, describe and discuss research findings and policy implications concerning the relationships between private and public education, both Catholic and nonsectarian.

Part II includes chapters on methods for identifying exemplary schools (Chapter 4 by Gilbert R. Austin and Stephen P. Holowenzak, and Chapter 5 by Mark E. Fetler and Dale C. Carlson), the existing literature on school climate (Chapter 6 by Carolyn S. Anderson), and research on the roles of the teacher and the school principal (Chapter 7 by David C. Berliner, and Chapter 8 by Kenneth A. Leithwood and Deborah J. Montgomery).

In Part III, Chapter 9 by Stewart C. Purkey and Marshall S. Smith describes and explores the policy issues emerging from effective schools research. Finally, Herbert Garber summarizes in Chapter 10 and offers some critical thoughts on the movement as he sees it from the perspective of an educational psychologist whose specialities are educational measurement and instructional design.

The contributors come from various disciplines: sociology, political science, and educational administration, as well as psychology. The editors know of no other book that addresses the specific issues covered here. Others deal with policy formation, teacher and administrator training, and quasi-biographies of individual exemplary schools. This book, rather, should enable the reader to understand better the purposes and aims of the effective–exemplary schools research movement. It does this by describing at some length the findings from several research models on how such schools are identified, how they differ from ordinary schools, and how this knowledge may or may not be applicable generally.

The editors acknowledge with gratitude the support they received from the University of Maryland at Baltimore County and many individuals. Special thanks are extended to Richard F. Neville, Hugh D. Graham, and William R. Johnson of that university for their kind support. Due acknowledgment is made to Shirley Alonso, Eleanor Austin, Joanne Calderone, Audrey Mahoney, and Doris Garber for the parts they played in helping complete this work.

PART I

Scope and Content

CHAPTER 1

Research on Exemplary Schools: An Historical Perspective*

Stephen K. Miller

INTRODUCTION

The existence of exemplary schools and their study lies at the heart of the effective schools research movement. While the movement has now spawned one of the most productive and commonly used research strategies for understanding schools and applying reforms, studies of exemplary schools were virtually nonexistent until the early 1970s. Why?

As is demonstrated by this book and other research in this field, considerable knowledge has accrued from investigating exemplary schools. The clear advantages of studying unusually successful schools for comparison to schools not so successful are now widely recognized. But the history of research in American schools suggests that in fact there was nothing obvious about this strategy.

Why was the concept of exemplary schools so difficult to discover? Historically, what was the focus of educational research? Is there a connection between the focus of early educational research and the apparent inability of researchers to discover and use so obvious (to us, today)

* Support for this research came originally from a Title IV-C Grant through the Michigan Department of Education. The author acknowledges his debt to Wilbur B. Brookover throughout the development of this work. Edward Berman provided critical feedback and Herbert Garber contributed significantly to the current form of the chapter. Any inaccuracies remain the responsibility of the author.

3

a strategy as comparing good to bad schools? What have been the major factors that eventually led to the development of the study of exemplary schools? These questions form the central thrust of this chapter and raise basic issues concerning school effectiveness, educational reform, national manpower needs, individual success, and social mobility. Answers help illuminate how educational research and practice have been influenced by the economic and political system and how the presumed relationships among schooling, success, and individual ability help legitimate inequality in American society.

More generally, the answers to these questions can be better explained if it is possible to understand the historical and economic context within which educational research has been framed. Accordingly, this chapter also focuses on the prevailing ideas that have developed with regard to education as they pertain to explanations of individual differences and stratification in society. Particular attention is given to beliefs that those in higher social classes are considered superior in terms of biological, mental, and moral attributes and, conversely, to the prevalence in American folklore of the "poor are dumb, lazy, and morally decrepit" beliefs (see Moore, 1981). Tracing the origins of the folklore, ideologies, and myths that constitute commonsense everyday explanations of basic inequalities requires the insight that certain values, theories, and beliefs are differentially associated with different social strata (Mannheim, 1936, 1956). Going full circle, we must follow that insight with the further question, Why is it that the beliefs of the higher classes have become the prevailing ideas in society?

Subsequent to this question, further attention is given to the Social Darwinist "survival of the fittest" explanations of the English sociologist Herbert Spencer. These Social Darwinist ideas were consistent with beliefs of American business elites of the late 1800s and were incorporated into the evolving model of the American schools. Based on IQ, individual differences, and grouping structures, the resultant schools functioned to differentiate between the fortunate few and the masses. The rationale for this division was the existence of extreme differences in individual ability. These innate differences required the provision of a differentiated education that was appropriate for the different abilities of the masses and those who were destined to be leaders. Thus the emphasis on the needs and abilities of the individual, thought to be widely variant, came to dominate educational thought and explanations of success or failure in both the school and the wider society.

This chapter relates these early conceptions of education to the seeming inability of researchers to discover the strategy of studying exemplary schools. In so doing, much of what follows is a critique of the ways in which the psychology of individual differences is conceived and implemented in American schools. There is no intent to suggest that individual differences do not exist. Rather, the thesis is developed that emphasis on innate, individual differences in students, tracing back to the Social Darwinism of the late 1800s, has resulted in an exaggerated importance for individual differences at the expense of underestimating human similarities and the impact of social structure on individuals.

FRAME OF REFERENCE

All social research and analysis make certain basic assumptions about the nature of humanity and the relationship between the individual and society. Unfortunately, these assumptions are often not made explicit. Karabel and Halsey (1977) suggest that intellectual history should help make explicit the underlying assumptions in a given model and should increase our understanding of the assumptions and biases that are inherent in analyses using different models or theories. A parallel could be made to the content in high school civics classes. Whether they are taught in the United States, Japan, or Russia, these classes reflect the patriotic heritage and ideology of the society of which they are a part. In other words, civics classes in different countries, like different educational theories, reflect differing assumptions about human motivation, ability, government, and economic systems.

Intellectual history, with an emphasis on unmasking unstated assumptions and unrecognized bias, requires an explication of the assumptions in the researcher's own frame of reference. This work is based on Harris' (1968, 1979) model of cultural materialism. Derived from anthropological studies of sociocultural phenomena and change, Harris' work suggests specifically that economic, technological, and ecological factors form the primary determinants of a people's response to producing the goods and services necessary for the continued survival of that society. Energy requirements, food (primarily protein needs), and population pressures are among the driving forces that influence the economic response. In turn, social structures and a complex of beliefs, values, ideologies, and intellectual perspectives develop. Such ideas, including theories of education, help explain and justify the particular economic response a society has adopted. At the same time these ideas and structures form the basis of the society's efforts to expand its economic and technological productivity (or function to negate these efforts in stagnant societies).

Harris provides a rationalizing explanation of humanity rather than the rational conception that is prevalent among more common psychological or idealistic versions of culture and history (see Perrow, 1982). This perspective suggests that in the long run, over decades and even centuries, values and beliefs gradually change to reflect and explain (justify) the economic system. For example, changes from agricultural to industrial to electronic–computer eras brought about fundamental changes in values and beliefs. In the short run, people decide (or at least think they do) what they want and how to go about getting it. But these decisions are shaped and framed within a set of constraints—economic and technological givens, political structures, sociofamilial patterns, and prevailing modes of thought, values, and education—of which the typical person is unconscious and unaware. And it is precisely this larger framework of economic constraints and givens, which varies from society to society and through history, that is the source of change and social development.

Harris' materialist position does not imply that ideas and the spokespersons for these ideas have no role in changing technology and values. There are always competing ideas in the marketplace of public opinion. The real question is why some ideas rather than others are accepted and become the conventional wisdom. Perhaps even more important, Why do some ideas receive so much more exposure and support than contrasting ideas?

For example, a few women have long worked to articulate and to popularize the feminist cause. But not until the early 1960s, when large numbers of working women began to experience the discrimination of the workplace, did these ideas find a sufficient number of receptive ears to become a movement. Significantly, it was the changing economic structure that necessitated the increased number of working women (Harris, 1981).

AMERICAN EDUCATION IN PERSPECTIVE

The framework developed by Harris (1968, 1979) has a close parallel in education. Since the 1960s, a somewhat loosely bound group of scholars, known collectively as revisionists, have conducted studies that focus on the ties between the educational system and the development of industrialism. The revisionists, using historical, economic, and sociological perspectives, have related the changes and reforms in the schools to the predominant business values and elite interests of the nascent corporate capitalism. Some of the more prominent themes include studies of scientific management, the development of "objective, scientifically developed" IQ tests, the urbanization of schools, the "upgrading" of school boards by replacing the working class politics of the ward with business persons and professionals, and the introduction of vocational education for the masses (Bowles & Gintis, 1977; Callahan, 1962; Karier, Violas, & Spring, 1973; Katz, 1968, 1971; Tyack, 1974; Violas, 1978). These works collectively attempt to demonstrate that a major function of school reform has been to meet and serve the interests of the economic system and the wealth-owning elites.

The sweeping changes in the American schools during the late nineteenth and early twentieth centuries (the Progressive Era) have been aptly chronicled by Cremin (1964). This overall historical treatment, coupled with the more economically based analyses of the revisionists, is helpful in thinking about the problems of social control during the period following the Civil War. Marks (1980) helps frame the problem by focusing on the central dilemma for the developing industrial–capitalist economy, as viewed from the perspective of the elites who were faced with maintaining power and stability in a turbulent period.

Marks (1980) notes that during the eighteenth and nineteenth centuries, America was the land of opportunity in a country of rugged individualists. Hard work, perserverance, and ability were to be rewarded (the ethos of the Protestant Ethic); always the perceived route to this success was via the expanding western frontier. During the 1800s, the common schools developed, with the focus of providing an identical educational background for all. Perkinson (1977) suggests that this was intended to perform a leveling or equalizing function to reduce the advantages of inherited wealth. The shortage of labor and the developing economy encouraged, and the country needed, the maximization of the full potential of everyone.

But industrialization and the gradual closing of the frontier changed this. The tremendous inequalities of wealth could no longer be justified satisfactorily based on the nostrums of the Protestant Ethic and land of opportunity. Increasingly, workers were forced into monotonous, alienating, low-paying factory jobs with no chance of advancement. Now that the workers were faced with this drudgery and the obvious reality that they were not sharing in the wealth that industrialization was producing, the Protestant Ethic came under attack. More important, the supply of stable, complaisant workers who fed the industrial machine with their labor was threatened by a growing militancy. Worker unrest, strikes, and violence in Europe and America were the source of grave concern. A new means of legitimating the inequalities of the American economic system was needed as the nineteenth century drew to a close.

A major part of the solution to this problem lay in the schools. Various forms of segregation between the elites and the masses were coming into use, ranging from neighborhood schools based on residential distinctions, to private academies, to tracking or grouping. But as greater numbers of students went beyond eighth grade, more objective means were needed for determining the few who would be selected for the college preparatory curriculum and the many who would receive manual and vocational training.

Enter the IQ test. Brought to America just after the turn of the century, it was not until the army utilized a form of IQ tests for sorting large numbers of inductees in World War I that the full potential of testing was realized. Soon after the war, IQ testing flourished in the schools. With the advent of objective measurement, the science of individual differences was born (Blum, 1978; Gould, 1981; Karier, 1973; Marks, 1980).

The full impact of this movement must be seen in the context of the period. "Survival of the fittest" was the slogan of the Social Darwinists of the late nineteenth century; this philosophy and the license it allowed individual entrepreneurs had helped produce the fortunes of the industrial magnates, the so-called robber barons (Hofstadter, 1944; Moore, 1981; Wasserman, 1972). The belief in the predominance of heredity fed the eugenics movement, which influenced research and theory (Besag, 1981) and encouraged the general climate of acceptance for IQ testing. Perhaps even more to the point was the substantial funding and support for research on IQ provided to E. L. Thorndike, the acknowledged leader of the movement, by the Carnegie Foundation (Marks, 1980). Selective funding of intellectuals whose ideas and research are consistent with the needs and beliefs of the ruling elites, as opposed to intellectuals with countervailing positions, is one way that the ideas of the ruling elites become the ruling ideas (Arnove, 1980).

The problem of legitimating industrial capitalism was solved. "Land of opportunity" had been changed to "equality of educational opportunity." The science of genetically based individual difference explained the vast inequalities in wealth, education, social status, and physical drudgery. The public schools were to allow true talent to emerge by providing equal opportunity to everyone. That the vast majority of the poor and working classes had low IQs merely reinforced the common folklore "poor are dumb" theories. Horatio Alger success stories, which always receive publicity far beyond the limited number of such exceptional cases, continued to highlight the belief that America was still the land of opportunity. Education, however, was to be the major vehicle for social mobility.

SCHOOLS, RESEARCH, AND INDIVIDUAL DIFFERENCES

In light of these developments, the issue of research in the schools takes on new meaning. The school, its structure, and the curriculum were all designed to meet and foster individual differences in students. Developments in American schools during the twentieth century invariably reflect this basic assumption, including such practices and innovations as differentiated curriculum, vocational counselors and programs, standardized norm-referenced tests, competitive grading on the curve, reading groups associated with basal readers, individualized instruction, special education, and gifted–talented programs. In short, schooling has been transformed from providing a common education to acting as a selection agency for the stratified economic system.

Without question, differentiating programs and concepts, all based on the psychology of individual differences, are the prevailing norm in American schools. Belief in the concept of individual differences is ingrained in the schools and society; this belief is a part of the American Dream, generally accepted at an unconscious level without awareness or understanding of the possible effects on educational theory, practice, or outcomes.

A major effect of this belief has been the adoption of the medical model as the prevailing approach to learning and instruction: When students are not learning adequately the problem lies within the individual student, based on differences in ability from a variety of causes. The typical solution is to provide a battery of diagnostic tests to identify the particular problem. Once the problem is identified, the student can be labeled and placed in an appropriate treatment program that fits the student's needs. Thus, programs are differentiated based on presumed differences in types of problems. That the differentiated outcomes may be due to the differential quality and quantity of instruction provided by these programs themselves is seldom considered. Rather, differentiated outcomes are expected, tautological though it may be, because of the existence of the individual differences in abilities or deficits that the battery of tests have already identified.

Several major functions are accomplished by this process. First, the "needs" of individual students are met. Second, schools avoid responsibility for students who are not learning. The normal curve dictates that there will always be a substantial number of students who are not capable of achieving at grade level. Forgotten or ignored is the process of item analysis used in standardized test construction in which only items that contribute to a normal curve are retained (other items are revised or discarded). Similarly unrecognized is the process of choosing a large standard deviation on IQ tests and then developing test questions that reflect that a priori decision (Green, 1981, Appendix B). The implicit assumption and obvious result of this process is the belief that the range of individual differences in ability is large and inevitable. In reality, this process masks the fact that researchers do not know the natural standard deviation of IQ, let alone intelligence; the standard deviation of height or weight stems from natural variation in human populations, while the standard deviation of IQ tests is based on individual differences, cultural differences, and the procedures of test construction. The actual proportion of variance due to each of these factors is not known.

Third, research in education focuses on the individual student and is deflected from middle range or macro level theoretical solutions that might provide alternative answers to why students are not learning (e.g., the school as an organization or the economic system and society itself). Fourth, the manpower needs of society can be met by a talent pool that coincides with a few elites and large numbers of workers whose aptitude is suited for doing manual labor, consistent with the distribution of jobs in an expanding industrial economy.

This analysis suggests that individual differences have been socially constructed (Berger & Luckmann, 1967) by practices in society and in the schools that differentiate students consistent with presumed genetic individuality. However, Marks (1980) points out that most educators no longer take seriously the excessive emphasis on genetic traits of the early IQ researchers, many of whom were leading proponents of the eugenics movement. Yet, the many programs that differentiate studies into tracks and groups make sense only if the differences are genetic. Differences that are primarily environmental are presumably amenable to correction by enriched instructional quality. Even a strong hereditarian like Jensen (1980) has recommended that heterogeneous grouping makes far more sense than ability grouping. Ironically, educators have continued to accept the notion of programs differentiated to accommodate genetically based individual differences even as they have moved toward a recognition of the environment in producing those very differences. The inference, of course, is a massive self-fulfilling prophecy that exaggerates the small degree of individual differences that students bring with them to primary school, regardless of the source of those differences—genetic or environmental.

THE TENSION BETWEEN SELECTION AND
EQUALITY

America has never been completely comfortable with the inequalities in society. The American Dream exemplifies this: The individual can become rich and successful, surpassing his neighbors, if only he (gender used intentionally) has the ability and the willingness to adhere to the values of hard work, frugality, and perseverance, and if everyone has the same opportunity to achieve this. Schools generally have been invoked as the assurance that equal opportunity is available. The transformation of schooling (from approximately 1880 to 1920) from common school to selection agency based on individual differences provided a new rationale for inequality, but the system never really worked properly. Instead, schools reproduced the existing inequalities over generations, irrespective of ability (Bowles & Gintis, 1977). Thus, a tension is produced by this opposition between grim reality and the rhetoric of equality of educational opportunity.

How this tension has been dealt with has been the subject of several works (e.g., Collins, 1979; Perkinson, 1977; and revisionist historians such as Greer, 1972; Katz, 1971; and Karier et al., 1973). The nuances of this treatment lie beyond the scope of this chapter, but awareness of the gap between rhetoric and reality and the changing nature of that awareness are central to both the belated and eventual development of an exemplary schools approach to research and reform.

Pertaining to the actual efficacy of schooling relevant to equality of opportunity, numerous studies, spread over several decades, conducted primarily from a sociological framework and concerned with the existing social-class structure of American communities, produced consistent evidence that schools function primarily to reproduce the existing social-class structure (e.g., Hollingshead, 1949; Lynd & Lynd, 1929, 1937; Sexton, 1961; Warner, Havighurst, & Loeb, 1944). Despite evidence that schools provided neither equity nor opportunity, they continued to utilize structural means to duplicate inequalities by differentiating students into ability groups and curriculum tracks.

An important question is why educators continued to maintain beliefs and practices consistent with the psychology of individual differences, given mounting, conflicting evidence. A major factor in this belief is the training of teachers and educational researchers primarily from a psychological perspective (see Hill, 1971; Persell, 1976, 1977; Stein, 1971). This not only reinforces the prevailing model of individual differences, but also inhibits exposure of educators to countervailing research that demonstrates the myth of equality of educational opportunity. Furthermore, at the secondary level, the curriculum tracking occurred within the context of the comprehensive school, which was designed to provide for a common heritage and civic responsibility, even as different career needs were being met. Perkinson (1977) suggests that, for educators, emphasis on this common heritage was a major factor in mitigating the tension between equality and differentiation. So far had the schools moved toward this civic education during the post–World War II boom that the "life adjustment" curriculum became the major target of criticism by the likes of Admiral Hyman Rickover and the Council for Basic Education. In the early 1950s, these critics declared that the schools had gone soft and were not adequately selecting for talent and ability (Broudy, 1972; Spring, 1976).

The changes in schools that occurred in the 1950s can be seen as adjustments to the changing economic conditions, again consistent with a materialist explanation. Perceived by many to be the finest hours of the schools, public and governmental trust in education was reflected in a variety of ways such as the GI Bill for veterans, the intimate connection between "good" schools and the growth of suburbia, and the increasing number of high school and college graduates.

What was perhaps not so clearly seen was the connection between these trends and the evolving service economy wherein industrial workers were to gradually give way to the white-collar, organization men who worked increasingly for large service-oriented corporations (see Mills, 1951; Whyte, 1957). From this perspective, the life adjustment curriculum reflected manpower needs for a rapidly growing college-educated workforce who were able to function in organizations based on their communication and "people" skills. The social orientation of the upwardly mobile suburbs reinforced this trend. However, there is evidence that the softness of the curriculum in the early 1950s was overstated (Franklin, 1984). Clearly, schools had not stopped tracking and sorting students, although the proportion of students in different tracks apparently was changing to reflect the increasing and decreasing proportion, respectively, of the service and industrial sectors of the economy.

Any actual tendency toward greater equality and less selection was short lived. Russia orbited Sputnik in 1957 and the challenge to assert our military and technical superiority was placed on the schools. Congress responded with the National Defense Education Act of 1958; major works in education touted increased academic excellence in math, science, and foreign language with greater emphasis on the top 25% of the population (Bruner, 1960; Conant, 1959). The message was still clear: To fix the schools, the solution was to further differentiate programs to fit the widely divergent abilities of students.

Schools still maintained their credibility with the public and policymakers. Disillusionment was not far off, however. The 1960s were to bring a series of events that resulted in the conclusion that schools do not make a difference. Foreshadowings of that discontent were visible back in the 1950s, chiefly school desegregation (*Brown v. Board of Education*, 1954) and the beginnings of the civil rights movement. With the early 1960s came the discovery of poverty and growing awareness of the plight of the disadvantaged pupil, examined in a series of influential works (e.g., Harrington, 1963; Hoffman, 1964a, 1964b; Moynihan, 1965; Passow, 1963; Riessman, 1962). The poverty movement, reflecting a shift in the tension between equality and social efficiency, was an integral factor in changing how schools were perceived.

SCHOOLS DO NOT MAKE A DIFFERENCE

The message of current research on exemplary schools is that a few schools have overcome the effects of low social class, with the obvious implication that others could too if they adopted practices consistent with the characteristics of exemplary schools. This message counters the conventional wisdom that schools do not make a difference, meaning that schools simply reproduce and magnify the differences that children of different social status bring with them to their educational experience.

Yet the conventional wisdom must be set in historical context. This reality-based message, beginning in the mid-1960s and continuing up to the present, was a product of the turbulence and disillusionment that accompanied the events of the 1960s, in particular the publishing of *Equality of Educational Opportunity* (Coleman *et al.*, 1966), commonly known as the Coleman Report. The Coleman Report, commissioned by the Civil Rights Act of 1964 with the intent of demonstrating the inequalities of resources between segregated black and white schools in the south, received public scrutiny and policy debate that far exceeded the attention of earlier academically oriented studies on social class and schooling that had likewise demonstrated the limited efficacy of the schools in overcoming inequality. The controversy and publicity of the Coleman Report and the questioning of various social institutions that was generated by the civil rights, student, and women's movements, the Vietnam War and draft resistance, the spread of counterculture values, and the growing awareness of poverty went a long way toward dashing the naive faith in the schools that had been a hallmark of this country. Policymakers and educators were no longer so quick to profess the undying belief that schools provided access to social mobility for all, the so-called instrumental meritocracy (Persell, 1977).

But just as critics of the schools in the early 1950s may have overstated the case regarding changes in the ways that schools operate, so did the public rhetoric about the ineffectiveness of schools in the 1960s exaggerate any actual changes in the functioning of schooling. In fact, despite the new conventional wisdom, a strong case could be made that the public, educators, and policymakers continued to believe in the efficacy of schooling. If anything, it was faith in the performance of schools to do what they were supposed to that was questioned as opposed to a lessening of the belief that schooling and education were the cornerstones of the American Dream and individual success.

Throughout this era of political flux, schools continued to sort and select students consistent with the stratified economic structure. What changed was the interpretation of the basis for this selection rather than the nature of the selection itself. With the awareness of poverty came a new surge of interest in the attainment of equity, somewhat countering the push for social efficiency that was brought about by the post-Sputnik crisis.

Once again the shifts in tension betwen these two opposing values— equity and efficiency—can be associated with changes in the economic structure. Following the recession of the late 1950s, a period of dramatic growth resulted from the economic recovery of the early 1960s, coupled with the superheating of the economy brought about by the escalating Vietnam involvement. Social comparison and relative deprivation theory (Festinger, 1954; Howard, 1974; Katz, 1967; Runciman, 1966) suggest that people will be more magnanimous toward those less fortunate at those times when their own fortunes are rising and they perceive little threat to their livelihood from those below them; conversely, in a shrinking economy or a protracted period of little or no growth, uncertainty over their own future and security leads to increased suspicion and hostility toward those below themselves, who are now viewed as a real or potential threat. These perceptions, which comprise one of the factors leading to the cyclical swings in the public mood from liberal to conservative consciousness, also have their effects on how schools are viewed.

CHANGING THEORETICAL PERSPECTIVES ON THE SCHOOLS

From the 1940s through the 1960s, the predominant theoretical perspective in sociology was structural-functionalism, a model that explains society by the correspondence between form and purpose of the organizations, institutions, groups, and values that comprise a given society. Merton (1957) furnishes a seminal treatment of the ways in which structure shapes and is shaped by function. Parsons (1959) provides an explicit statement of the relation between structure and function in education: Schools select for talent based on individual ability and equal opportunity in accordance with the stratified needs of society. Furthermore, this selection process is a hallmark of advanced industrial countries and is a significant advance over traditional means of selection based on ascriptive characteristics. This process assumes that educational performance is grounded in natural ability.

Until the early 1960s the genetic assumptions of structural–functionalism or some variant thereof dominated education. Alternative explanations for individual differences were few and received little if any attention in the schools. Events were soon to change this. In 1964, aided by the martyrdom of President Kennedy, Johnson's honeymoon with Congress, and a rising tide of prosperity, a coalition of blacks and northern liberals passed a set of social legislation that included the Elementary and Secondary Education Act (ESEA) of 1965 (the origin of the compensatory education title programs), launching President Johnson's Great Society War on Poverty. Central to the assumptions of the War on Poverty was a fundamental change in the explanation of individual differences. The genetic position (nature) gave way to an environmental emphasis (nurture) that was characterized by such phrases as the *pathology of the black, lower-class family* (Moynihan, 1965) or the *culture of poverty* (Lewis, 1966).

For the schools, this change translated into the policies of compensatory education. Disadvantaged children were to receive extra help to overcome the effects of growing up in a deprived neighborhood and home. As suggested above, however, the rhetoric of change was greater than the reality. Ryan's (1976) *Blaming the Victim* notes the underlying assumption of the War on Poverty: The fault still lies within the individual, now environmentally produced rather than genetic in origin, but nevertheless a deficit to be cured. The strategy focuses on compensatory assistance to the individual, while leaving unchanged the structure of the school or the wider economic system in which the relative advantage and disadvantage occurs. Consistent with this view, tracking, grouping, and differentiation for instructional purposes remained the basis of the structural organization of most schools. Paradoxically, a theoretical model that focused explicitly on environmentally produced differences continued to utilize a structural model of stratified schooling designed to accommodate genetic differences.

The irony may be exaggerated. Intolerable irony would follow from a situation in which there is full agreement for the environmental explanation at the same time that policy and practice support the genetic position. Although there was a shift toward the culture of poverty thesis, the evidence suggests that by no means was the genetic position dead, then or now. Indeed, a materialist explanation of economic and cultural change, in combination with relative status deprivation, would predict a shift back toward the genetic side under conditions of economic decline, "stagflation" (the economic doldrums of the 1970s), or massive dislocations and uncertainty (the rise of the computer-service sector and the decline of the smokestack industries). Confirmation of this hypothesis can be seen in the subsequent resurgence of the meritocratic position (Bell, 1972) and the IQ argument (Jensen, 1969; Herrnstein, 1971), as well as in the development of sociobiology (e.g., Barash, 1977; Wilson, 1975, 1978), a theory that frequently has been touted as a new biological determinism to justify the status quo in terms of hierarchy, inequality, and economic efficiency (Caplan, 1978; Gould, 1981; Green, 1981; Harris, 1979).

In education various theoretical models include a significant ability factor; studies based on these models produced the "schools-don't-make-a-difference" conclusions. In most instances the ability factor was construed as genetic in origin. Prominent work includes the status attainment literature (Blau & Duncan, 1967; Haller & Portes, 1973), which focuses on the role of education in the social mobility process and the school effects studies (see Averch, Carroll, Donaldson, Kiesling, & Pincus, 1972; Centra & Potter, 1980; Glasman & Biniaminov, 1981), which investigate the relative effects of demographic background variables versus schools on student outcomes.

Results of the work in both fields consistently indicated that schools have little effect on achievement when social class is held constant. Furthermore, the research seemed to suggest that it made little difference whether the ability factor was genetic or environmental. Either way, schools seemed not able to overcome the initial differences in the students who attend different schools. Thus, in retrospect, the poverty movement of the 1960s significantly altered thinking about the source of individual differences (greater awareness of environmental influence), but the outcomes of school practice and the conclusions of the research remained unchanged: Schools still functioned as selection agencies and provided very little in the way of equity.

CHALLENGING THE "NO-SCHOOL-EFFECTS" CONCLUSION

Although the 1960s brought greater awareness that schools were not providing equity, many Americans were unwilling to accept that conclu-

sion. Most of the public continued to believe in the centrality of education as part of the American Dream, policymakers professed faith in the
programs of compensatory education, and some researchers began to
look for new evidence regarding the effectiveness of schools. Although
educators in general continued instructional practices and beliefs based
on individual differences, there were many teachers and even a few
schools that were making a difference. Unfortunately, researchers had
still not developed an explicit strategy of looking for and studying these
exemplars.

The seeds of an exemplary schools model had been sown, however.
As is true of research and theory in general, exemplary schools research
did not just materialize out of nowhere. Several related but independent
strands of inquiry such as self-concept and school climate investigated
various aspects of the larger question of school effectiveness. The
Coleman Report, and the controversy it generated, gave rise to
extensive reanalyses and further investigations. The federal government contracted for extensive evaluations of the 1965 ESEA compensatory education programs, notably Head Start and Title I. The theoretical assumptions of the cultural deprivation thesis were strongly
criticized.

All of these efforts eventually were to contribute to exemplary schools
studies. Although they were conducted from a variety of research perspectives, they were not based on the causal assumptions of individual
differences as had been typical of previous research. Collectively, these
studies provided evidence that challenged the conventional wisdom.
Yet these efforts, individually, were not future-directed toward studies
on exemplary schools. Advances in science build incrementally on previous results. Researchers were not able to focus explicitly on exemplary
schools until political events and research evidence had progressed sufficiently to turn attention from the psychology of individual differences (the problem is within the student) to the school as a uniquely
functioning social system (why do some schools function better than
others?).

TRENDS IN THE RESEARCH

A complete review of the trends just noted is not possible in this
chapter (see Miller, 1983a), but a brief accounting of these studies is
necessary to help understand the findings and events that allowed researchers to shift focus from the individual to the school.

One of the first attempts[1] to study the social system rather than the educability of individual students was the work on school climate. A few highlights are addressed here, since Chapter 6 in this book by Carolyn S. Anderson covers the topic thoroughly. The landmark development was the Organizational Climate Description Questionnaire (OCDQ) by Halpin and Croft (1963). Although the OCDQ is among the most commonly used scales in education, it actually contributed to the exemplary schools movement only indirectly. Its major contribution was a focus on the collective climate of the faculty and a recognition that teachers are influenced by group norms that vary in emphasis and intensity among schools. The relative lack of direct influence on the study of school effectiveness stems from the origin of the school-climate literature. Part of the human relations movement, the OCDQ was a measure of affect for staff–principal relations. Seldom were student outcomes even measured (Lezotte, Hathaway, Miller, Passalacqua, & Brookover, 1980; Miller, 1983b). School-climate research has gradually merged with the exemplary schools studies and is now more likely to investigate the learning climate as it affects student outcomes.

Another early influence was the work on self-concept. Although considerable research has been done on a global definition of self-esteem (Coopersmith, 1967; Rosenberg, 1965), more pertinent to education are the studies on self-concept of academic ability (Brookover, Paterson, & Thomas, 1962; Brookover, LePere, Hamachek, Thomas, & Erickson, 1965; Brookover, Erickson, & Joiner, 1967). Derived from the work of Cooley (1902) and Mead (1934), the notion of self-concept is framed on the assumptions of symbolic interactionism: that generalized expectations for appropriate behavior are communicated through interactions, role definitions, and surveillance of significant others in the context of primary and secondary groups (see Brookover & Erickson, 1975; Rose, 1962). In simplified terms, the self-concept develops within the context of organizations and groups through which individuals learn to behave appropriately, consistent with societal expectations.

Closely related to the self-concept research is the self-fulfilling prophecy literature. Popularized by *Pygmalion in the Classroom* (Rosenthal &

---

[1] Actually jounalistic surveys of individual schools with exemplary reputations had occurred much earlier during the progressive education era. *Schools of To-Morrow* by John and Evelyn Dewey (1915) is the most widely known. The 8-year study of 30 high schools that adopted progressive education philosophy and techniques from 1932 to 1940 was the subject of several evaluation reports of considerable sophistication (see Cremin, 1964, Chapters 5 & 7). Yet these schools and studies were on the romantic fringe of the progressive movement and never had the lasting influence of the scientific differentiation based on IQ and ability that was the enduring legacy of progressivism.

Jacobsen, 1968), the issue is the extent to which teacher expectations produce corresponding levels of student outcomes. Despite considerable debate over methodological procedures, studies focus not on the existence of the effect, but rather how it is communicated to students and why teachers form different expectations. Research on exemplary schools consistently shows that teacher expectations constitute one of the most powerful factors in accounting for student achievement. Numerous reviews are available including Cooper and Good (1983), Brophy and Good (1974), and Persell (1977).

While the three bodies of literature just noted were all reasonably independent from the political milieu, other developments in research were closely tied to the events of the 1960s. One of these was the growing critique of the culture of poverty. Numerous researchers had realized that the deficit model still placed the locus of the problem within the student, despite the more liberal attribution of cause to environmental forces. A variety of work was produced to show that cultural deprivation was overstated and did not necessarily lead to low achievement, poor moral character, and the like (see Baratz & Baratz, 1970; Leacock, 1971; Stein, 1971; Valentine, 1968, 1971).

The Coleman Report, which became a political document, also generated substantial research specific to its findings that was independent yet generally cognizant of the various strands just described (McIntosh, 1968; Mosteller & Moynihan, 1972). Although the original results of the Coleman Report are generally accepted as valid, the interpretation of those findings has changed with the insights that accrued from advances in methodology. Important issues, explained in more detail in Miller (1983a), include the ways in which achievement is measured, the existence of contextual effects, whether individual students, classrooms, or the school become the unit of analysis, the relationship between achievement variance and school effectiveness (Brown & Saks, 1975; Lark, Blust, & Coldiron, 1984), and the substantive issue of how to measure school effects. The latter problem represented perhaps the most important long-term finding of the Coleman Report, that is, that resources expended in a school do not have as much influence on achievement as the social-psychological processes and norms that characterize interactions between staff and students within the school. Retrospectively, much of the impetus for the exemplary schools movement can be seen as a search for the social-psychological factors that make a difference in outcomes between schools.

Finally, the evaluation studies of the compensatory education programs of the ESEA of 1965 must be recognized. The political use of these studies is undeniable. For many districts, Title money represents significant resources. Congress has been keenly interested in studies that could justify not only a highly popular program, but also one that is clearly symbolic of government support for equality of educational opportunity. Often these studies are methodologically sophisticated due to the complexities involved in answering questions such as, Do children in compensatory education perform better, over a range of time lines, than similar children not in compensatory education? No consensus exists on the answer although it is typically accepted that compensatory education has beneficial potential. For an overview of this research, see Mullin and Summers (1983), Plunkett (1985), and Stickney and Plunkett (1983).

What is not controversial is the fact that not all compensatory education programs are of equal effectiveness. Dyer (1966, 1972) conceptualized an approach to identifying and studying programs and schools that were differentially successful. Austin (1979, 1981) reviews other early studies of this type. With the understanding that not all programs are equally effective, it was only a matter of time until Dyer's strategy would be applied to schools themselves (Klitgaard & Hall, 1973).

EXEMPLARY SCHOOLS

Case studies of disadvantaged schools that are identified a priori as particularly successful have been most commonly regarded as exemplary schools research. Weber's (1971) *Inner-City Children Can Be Taught To Read: Four Successful Schools* is generally depicted as the prototype of this kind of study and can be regarded as the symbolic beginning of the movement. At the time Weber did his work, the conventional wisdom that schools don't make a difference was almost universally believed. Weber's landmark research can be considered a counterexample, demonstrating that at least one school did make a difference. But research on exemplary schools is not limited to case studies, and it is difficult to determine the exact beginning of research in this area.

In addition to the related work noted in the previous section, two other types of early studies contributed a more direct part of the exemplary schools research. Both go back a considerable distance, clearly adding to the knowledge base that eventually led to the exemplary schools approach, and yet were not thought of, at that time, as explicitly a part of the exemplary schools movement. The first type is the investigation of the effects of gross time and isolation on achievement. Perhaps the best example of this is the analysis of Prince Edward County, Virginia (Green, Hofman, Morse, Hayes, & Morgan, 1964). Because the county decided to close its schools rather than comply with a desegregation order, the black children had no formal schooling for 4 years while the white children attended private "county" schools. The results showed that not only did achievement for the black children decline precipitously, as was expected, but so did the supposedly stable IQ scores (from 15 to 30 points). The bridge between gross studies of time in school and micro-level measures of time-on-task (Anderson, 1981) is demonstrated by Wiley and Harnischfeger (1974). The second type of early research is the study of social-psychological learning climates. The influence of several of these studies contributed to the development of the exemplary schools approach, especially measurement of high school academic climates (McDill, Meyers, & Rigsby, 1967) and classroom climates (Walberg, 1974, 1979). Further discussion of both learning climates and measures of time is presented in Miller (1983a). Anderson (Chapter 6, this volume) deals at length with this important topic.

CURRENT WORK

Exemplary schools research is also known by other terms, often used interchangeably, for example, effective schools, atypical schools, or school effectiveness. Other types of related research include these: (1) evaluation studies of intervention projects designed to implement an exemplary schools model, and (2) outlier studies[2] in which high-achieving, low-income schools and low-achieving, high-income schools are identified by computer. These contrasting pairs are then subjected to the usual case study techniques.

The first priorities of exemplary schools research have been to ascertain if any truly exemplary schools exist after controlling for socioeconomic status, to determine what characteristics of these exemplars differentiate them from average or negative outlying schools, and to discern if these exemplary schools have a consistent and generalizable pattern that accounts for their distinguishing characteristics. (See Chapter 5, this volume, for a detailed description of this technique.) This last point is important because exemplary schools are, by definition, not typical of schools in general. Work in the field has now progressed to the point that most researchers agree that exemplars exist and that there are some common characteristics. Scientists do not yet agree on precise

---

[2] *Outliers* is a statistical term indicating certain units (in this case, schools) that score or measure much higher or much lower than would be typically expected. For schools, achievement is highly associated with the average level of income of the students attending the school, that is, "expected" achievement ranges from low for low-income schools to high for high-income schools. Exemplary schools are positive outliers; low-achieving, affluent schools—negative outliers—also exist.

listings of those characteristics nor on a scheme for classifying the findings.

It is not possible nor necessary to review the literature on school effectiveness here. Numerous reviews and special issues of journals have appeared, some scholarly (e.g., Bickel, 1983; Miller, 1983a; Purkey & Smith, 1983), some advocacy-based and oriented to practitioners (e.g., Brookover *et al.*, 1982; Gartner, 1984; MacPhail-Wilcox, 1983), and some devoted to the problems of change and implementation (e.g., Cuban, 1984; Lieberman, 1984). The most widely known work is Edmonds' (1979a, 1979b) summary of the five factors of exemplary schools and concomitant moral appeal for using exemplary schools research as the basis of school improvement programs.

Current research focuses on several areas, among them problems of defining an exemplary school, deciding on the appropriate goals and objectives, measuring objectives other than basic achievement, improving the quality of empirical studies, understanding processes of educational and organizational change, establishing causal relationships among variables, and refining the theoretical models used to explain the why and how of school effectiveness. Collectively these questions are being referred to as second generation research, following the earlier priority of identifying and studying the characteristics of exemplars. The types of questions suggested here also raise certain issues germane to the earlier historical perspective on equity versus social efficiency.

SOCIAL IMPLICATIONS

It would be a serious mistake to believe that knowledge of the practices and beliefs of exemplary schools has dramatically changed the face of American education. Although a few individual schools perform well for disadvantaged children, the vast majority of schools still do not make a difference. School improvement projects in districts around the country are becoming commonplace, and several large cities and state departments of education now have school effectiveness programs. There is evidence that these programs have had some success in improving achievement. But change is usually slow and the total number of schools is far larger than the number that have begun to implement exemplary school projects.

On the other hand, the exemplary schools research has potential for reform that far surpasses previous movements. Supplemented by research on effective teaching (Berliner, 1983; Chapter 7, this volume), the capability to transform schools would now seem to be at hand. But the capability to do so and the political will to accomplish that goal are two different matters. Again, the distinction between the two opposing values of equity and social efficiency is crucial. Most schools typify an economic efficiency model that maximizes individual differences, based on the assumption that human ability is widely variant and that scarce resources should be concentrated on developing the potential of the best and the brightest. Exemplary schools represent an equity-based effectiveness model that develops the full potential of all students, on the assumption that virtually all humans can learn well and that economic resources should be focused on increasing the productivity of everyone in society.[3]

Looking at the opposing value assumptions in these two models helps explain several trends affecting education and exemplary schools research. Foremost of these is the oft-noted dramatic growth of the exemplary schools field. Clearly, the concept appeals tremendously to policymakers, educators, and the public (How can anyone be against an "exemplary" school?). The research is quickly being converted into a reform movement. Considering the fact that education has always served both as a panacea for the nation's problems and as a scapegoat for our failure to solve those problems, it is not surprising that the positive message, schools can make a difference, has been well received, especially given the negative image and public criticisms of our schools in recent years, for example, drug problems, declining scores, poor discipline, violence, and the like. In this instance, the good news has reaffirmed American faith in the primacy of the schools as a part of the American Dream. The danger is that schools continue simultaneously to function as societal scapegoats. If things do not get better, the likelihood exists that exemplary schools research will be tagged as the latest fad and educators will once again be labeled mediocre and complacent.

Another issue concerns the considerable criticism that exemplary schools research has received. Harry Miller (1981) contends that the belief that schools can overcome the effects of social class is Pollyannaish and ignores the considerable evidence stressing the relative immutability of early childhood experiences. Tomlinson (1982) suggests that effective schools should expand the amount of variance between students of different ability rather than increasing learning for all students. Ralph and Fennessey (1983) suggest that there is little more to the movement than ideological reformers' zeal. Implicit in these positions is a support-

---

[3] See Brookover, Gigliotti, Henderson, Niles, and Schneider (1974) for a major discussion of the issue of economic efficiency versus equity-based effectiveness as alternative school values.

ing justification of the status quo: The effects of individual differences in ability and early environment are impervious to efforts of the schools to effect change.

The unstated assumption of this position seems to support a model of inequality based on the psychology of individual differences. That model, it must be remembered, is the basis of prevailing ideas about the American Dream. The processes of socialization, of which the grouping practices and selection procedures of the school are among the most important (see also Della Fave, 1980), ensure that most Americans will act on and believe in the tenets of social mobility, tying together ability, schooling, and individual success. Continued public acceptance of this predominant ideology obviously receives powerful support from elites who have the greatest stake in the status quo and from many professional–technical upper-middle-class individuals who ostensibly "made it" on their own.

Finally, there has been renewed talk about excellence. Various commission reports, the challenge of the Japanese, concern over declining productivity—all these reflect a growing belief that America has slid toward mediocrity. Much of the rhetoric seems to imply that programs of affirmative action, open admissions, and other efforts to increase opportunity are responsible for the decline of America and the loss of excellence. These arguments assume that differences in individual ability are sufficiently great that efforts to open up the system can only come through lowering overall standards.

This is not the place to debate such assertions, either explicit or implicit. However, it is consistent with the theme of this chapter that such attacks on equity are likely to coincide with changes in economic well-being. As noted above, declining economic conditions are likely to foster support of greater inequalities with justifications based on differences in ability. On one hand the exemplary schools movement is celebrated for its potential for affecting school improvement and for restoring trust in the efficacy of education. On the other hand, the exemplary schools model is equity-based and as such is a threat to a stratified economic system.

It is perhaps worth pondering the effects on society if all schools managed to become exemplary, thus raising every child's learning significantly. Given the extent to which political decisions are influenced by economic interests, there seems a strong likelihood that powerful forces will continue to support greater selection in the name of economic efficiency. Perhaps the question is not whether exemplary schools are possible educationally, but whether economic and political elites will support and encourage equity in schools. That would be tantamount to an assault on the very educational inequalities that form the current justification of the economic inequalities from which the elites benefit. It is hard to imagine any group knowingly working against its own self-interest.

Such conjecture indicates that ultimately the fate of the exemplary schools movement may depend on its appeal to a broad populist base, which in turn depends on the success of the movement in reaching the public with the message of exemplary schools: Some successful disadvantaged schools exist, and improvement programs based on exemplary schools research are currently producing more.

REFERENCES

Anderson, L. W. (1981). Instruction and time-on-task: A review. *Journal of Curriculum Studies, 13*, 289–303.

Arnove, R. F. (Ed.). (1980). *Philanthropy and cultural imperialism: The foundations at home and abroad.* Bloomington, IN: Indiana University Press.

Austin, G. R. (1979). Exemplary schools and the search for effectiveness. *Educational Leadership, 37*(1), 10–14.

Austin, G. R. (1981). Exemplary schools and their identification. *New Directions for Testing and Measurement, 10*, 31–48.

Averch, H. A., Carroll, S. J., Donaldson, T. S., Kiesling, H. J., & Pincus, J. (1972). *How effective is schooling? A critical review and synthesis of research findings.* Santa Monica, CA: Rand.

Barash, D. P. (1977). *Sociobiology and behavior.* New York: Elsevier North-Holland.

Baratz, S. S., & Baratz, J. C. (1970). Early childhood intervention: The social science base of institutional racism. *Harvard Educational Review, 40*, 29–50.

Bell, D. (1972, Fall). On meritocracy and equality. *Public Interest, 29*, 29–68.

Berger, P. L., & Luckmann, T. (1967). *The social construction of reality: A treatise in the sociology of knowledge.* New York: Doubleday Anchor.

Berliner, D. C. (Ed.). (1983). Research on teaching [Special issue]. *Educational Psychologist, 18*(3).

Besag, F. P. (1981). Social Darwinism, race, and research. *Educational Evaluation and Policy Analysis, 3*(1), 55–69.

Bickel, W. E. (Ed.). (1983). Effective schools [Special issue]. *Educational Researcher, 12*(4).

Blau, P., & Duncan, O. D. (1967). *The American occupational structure.* New York: Wiley.

Blum, J. M. (1978). *Pseudoscience and mental ability: The origins and fallacies of the IQ controversy.* New York: Monthly Review Press.

Bowles, S., & Gintis, H. (1977). *Schooling in capitalist America.* New York: Basic.

Brandt, R. S. (Ed.). (1979). Effective schools, effective teaching [Special issue]. *Educational Leadership, 37*(1).

Brandt, R. S. (Ed.). (1982). Toward more effective schools [Special issue]. *Educational Leadership, 40*(3).

Brookover, W. B., Beamer, L., Efthim, H., Hathaway, D., Lezotte, L., Miller, S., Passalacqua, J., & Tornatzky, L. (1982). *Creating effective schools: An inservice program for enhancing school learning climate and achievement.* Holmes Beach, FL: Learning Publications.

Brookover, W. B., & Erickson, E. L. (1975). *Sociology of education.* Homewood, IL: Dorsey.

Brookover, W. B., Erickson, E. L., & Joiner, L. M. (1967). *Self-concept of ability and school achievement, III.* East Lansing, MI: Human Learning Research Institute, Michigan State University.

Brookover, W. B., Gigliotti, R. J., Henderson, R. D., Niles, B. E., & Schneider, J. M. (1974). Quality of educational attainment, standardized testing, assessment, and accountability. In C. W. Gordon (Ed.), *Uses of the sociology of education: The seventy-third yearbook of the National Society for the Study of Education* (Part II, pp. 161–191). Chicago: University of Chicago Press.

Brookover, W. B., LePere, J., Hamachek, D., Thomas, S., & Erickson, E. (1965). *Self-concept of ability and school achievement, II.* East Lansing, MI: Human Learning Research Institute, Michigan State University.

Brookover, W. B., Paterson, A., & Thomas, S. (1962). *Self-concept of ability and school achievement.* East Lansing, MI: College of Education, Michigan State University.

Brophy, J. E., & Good, T. L. (1974). *Teacher-student relationships: Causes and consequences.* New York: Holt, Rinehart, and Winston.

Broudy, H. S. (1972). *The real world of the public schools.* New York: Harcourt Brace Jovanovich.

Brown, B. W., & Saks, D. H. (1975). The production and distribution of cognitive skills within schools. *Journal of Political Economy, 83,* 571–593.

Brown v. Board of Education of Topeka, 347 U.S. 483 (1954).

Bruner, J. S. (1960). *The process of education.* New York: Vintage.

Callahan, R. (1962). *Education and the cult of efficiency.* Chicago: University of Chicago Press.

Caplan, A. L. (Ed.). (1978). *The sociobiology debate.* New York: Harper and Row.

Centra, J. A., & Potter, D. A. (1980). School and teacher effects: An interrelational model. *Review of Educational Research, 50,* 273–291.

Coleman, J., Campbell, E., Hobson, C., McPartland, J., Mood, A., Weinfeld, F., & York, R. (1966). *Equality of educational opportunity.* Washington, DC: U.S. Government Printing Office.

Collins, R. (1979). *The credential society: An historical sociology of education and stratification.* New York: Academic.

Conant, J. B. (1959). *The American high school today.* New York: McGraw-Hill.

Cooley, C. H. (1902). *Human nature and the social order.* New York: Charles Scribner's.

Cooper, H., & Good, T. (1983). *Pygmalion grows up: Studies in the expectation communication process.* New York: Academic.

Coopersmith, S. (1967). *Antecedents of self esteem.* San Francisco: W. H. Freeman.

Cremin, L. A. (1964). *The transformation of the school: Progressivism in American education 1876–1957.* New York: Vintage.

Cuban, L. (1984). Transforming the frog into a prince: Effective schools research, policy, and practice at the district level. *Harvard Educational Review, 54,* 129–151.

Della Fave, L. R. (1980). The meek shall not inherit the earth: Self-evaluation and the legitimacy of stratification. *American Sociological Review, 45,* 955–971.

Dewey, J., & Dewey, E. (1915). *Schools of to-morrow.* New York: Dutton.

Dyer, H. S. (1966). The Pennsylvania plan. *Science Education, 50,* 242–248.

Dyer, H. S. (1972). The measurement of educational opportunity. In F. Mosteller & D. P. Moynihan (Eds.), *On equality of educational opportunity* (pp. 513–527). New York: Vintage, Random House.

Edmonds, R. (1979a). Effective schools for the urban poor. *Educational Leadership, 37*(1), 15–24.

Edmonds, R. (1979b). Some schools work and more can. *Social Policy, 9,* 28–32.

Festinger, L. (1954). A theory of social comparison processes. *Human Relations, 7,* 117–140.

Franklin, B. (1984, April). *The secondary school curriculum in Minneapolis, 1930–1980: "A nation at risk" and the issue of quality education.* Paper presented at the American Educational Research Association Annual Meeting, New Orleans.

Gartner, A. (Ed.). (1984). School effectiveness [Special issue]. *Social Policy, 15*(2).

Glasman, N. S., & Biniaminov, I. (1981). Input-output analyses of schools. *Review of Educational Research, 51,* 509–539.

Gould, S. J. (1981). *The mismeasure of man.* New York: W. W. Norton.

Green, P. (1981). *The pursuit of inequality.* New York: Pantheon.

Green, R. L., Hofman, L. J., Morse, R. J., Hayes, M. E., & Morgan, R. F. (1964). *The educational status of children in a district without public schools.* East Lansing, MI: Bureau of Educational Research, Michigan State University, Cooperative Research Project No. 2321.

Greer, C. (1972). *The great school legend: A revisionist interpretation of American public education.* New York: Basic.

Haller, A., & Portes, A. (1973). Status attainment processes. *Sociology of Education, 46,* 51–91.

Halpin, A. W., & Croft, D. B. (1963). *The organizational climate of schools.* Chicago: Midwest Administration Centre, The University of Chicago.

Harrington, M. (1963). *The other America: Poverty in the United States.* Baltimore, MD: Penguin.

Harris, M. (1968). *The rise of anthropological theory: A history of theories of culture.* New York: Thomas Y. Crowell.

Harris, M. (1979). *Cultural materialism: The struggle for a science of culture.* New York: Random House.

Harris, M. (1981). *America now: The anthropology of a changing culture.* New York: Simon and Schuster.

Herrnstein, R. J. (1971, September). I.Q. *Atlantic Monthly,* pp. 43–64.

Hill, S. I. B. (1971). *Race, class, and ethnic biases in research on school performance of low income youth.* Unpublished doctoral dissertation, University of Oregon.

Hoffman, M. L. (Ed.). (1964a). Current research in infant development [Special issue]. *Merrill-Palmer Quarterly of Behavior and Development, 10*(2).

Hoffman, M. L. (Ed.). (1964b). Papers from the Arden House Conference on Pre-School Enrichment [Special issue]. *Merrill-Palmer Quarterly of Behavior and Development, 10*(3).

Hofstadter, R. (1944). *Social Darwinism in American thought.* Boston: Beacon.

Hollingshead, A. B. (1949). *Elmtown's youth.* New York: Wiley.

Howard, J. R. (1974). *The cutting edge: Social movements and social change in America.* Philadelphia: J.B. Lippincott.

Jensen, A. R. (1969). How much can we boost IQ and scholastic achievement? *Harvard Educational Review, 39,* 1–123.

Jensen, A. R. (1980). *Bias in mental testing.* New York: Free Press.

Karabel, J., & Halsey, A. H. (1977). Educational research: A review and an interpretation. In J. Karabel & A. H. Halsey (Eds.), *Power and ideology in education* (pp. 1–85). New York: Oxford University Press.

Karier, C. J. (1973). Testing for order and control in the corporate liberal state. In C. J. Karier, P. Violas, & J. Spring (Eds.), *Roots of crisis: American education in the twentieth century* (pp. 108–137). Chicago: Rand McNally.

Karier, C. J., Violas, P., & Spring, J. (Eds.). (1973). *Roots of crisis: American education in the twentieth century.* Chicago: Rand McNally.

Katz, I. (1967). The socialization of academic motivation in minority group children. In D. Levine (Ed.), *Nebraska symposium on motivation* (Vol. 15, pp. 133–191). Lincoln, NE: University of Nebraska Press.

Katz, M. B. (1968). *The irony of early school reform: Educational innovation in mid-nineteenth century Massachusetts.* Cambridge, MA: Harvard University Press.

Katz, M. B. (1971). *Class, bureaucracy and schools.* New York: Praeger.

Klitgaard, R. E., & Hall, G. R. (1973). *A statistical search for unusually effective schools.* Santa Monica, CA: Rand.

Lark, H. N., Blust, R. S., & Coldiron, J. R. (1984, April). *An investigation of the variation in student scores for effective and ineffective schools.* Paper presented at the American Educational Research Association Annual Meeting, New Orleans.

Leacock, E. G. (Ed.). (1971). *The culture of poverty: A critique.* New York: Simon and Shuster.

Lewis, O. (1966, May). The culture of poverty. *Scientific American,* pp. 19–25.

Lezotte, L. W., Hathaway, D. V., Miller, S. K., Passalacqua, J., & Brookover, W. B. (1980). *School learning climate and student achievement: A social systems approach to increased student learning.* Tallahassee, FL: National Teacher Corps, Florida State University Foundation.

Lieberman, A. (Ed.). (1984). School improvement: Research, craft, and concept [Special issue]. *Teachers College Record, 86*(1).

Lynd, R., & Lynd, H. (1929). *Middletown.* New York: Harcourt, Brace.

Lynd, R., & Lynd, H. (1937). *Middletown in transition.* New York: Harcourt, Brace.

MacPhail-Wilcox, B. (Ed.). (1983, October). In pursuit of school effectiveness [Special section]. *NASSP Bulletin, 67*(465).

Mannheim, K. (1936). *Ideology and utopia: An introduction to the sociology of knowledge.* New York: Harvest Book.

Mannheim, K. (1956). *Essays on the sociology of knowledge.* London: Routledge and Kegan Paul.

Marks, R. (1980). Legitimating industrial capitalism: Philanthropy and individual differences. In R. F. Arnove (Ed.), *Philanthropy and cultural imperialism: The foundations at home and abroad* (pp. 87–122). Bloomington, IN: Indiana University Press.

McDill, E. L., Meyers, E. D., Jr., & Rigsby, L. C. (1967). Institutional effects on the academic behavior of high school students. *Sociology of Education, 40,* 181–189.

McIntosh, R. G. (Ed.). (1968). Equality of educational opportunity [Special issue]. *Harvard Educational Review, 38*(1).

Mead, G. H. (1934). *Mind, self, and society, from the standpoint of a social behaviorist* (C. W. Morris, Ed.). Chicago: University of Chicago Press.

Merton, R. K. (1957). *Social theory and social structure* (rev. ed.). Glencoe, IL: Free Press.

Miller, H. L. (1981). Pollyanna in the policy patch: A response to Frederick Wirt. *Educational Evaluation and Policy Analysis, 3*(5), 83–93.

Miller, S. K. (1983a, April). *The history of effective schools research: A critical overview.* Paper presented at the American Educational Research Association Annual Meeting, Montreal, Canada. (ERIC Document Reproduction Service No. ED 231 818)

Miller, S. K. (1983b, February). *Thinking about school climate: Past and present.* Paper presented at the National Association of Secondary School Principals Annual Meeting, Dallas.

Mills, C. W. (1951). *White collar: The American middle classes.* New York: Oxford University Press.

Moore, J. H. (1981). Plutocratic perspectives on class and intelligence in America. In M. S. Collins, I. W. Warner, & T. A. Bremmer (Eds.), *Science and the question of human equality* (pp. 37–69). Boulder, CO: Westview.

Mosteller, F., & Moynihan, D. R. (Eds.). (1972). *On equality of educational opportunity.* New York: Vintage.

Moynihan, D. P. (1965). *The Negro family: The case for national action.* Washington, DC: U.S. Government Printing Office.

Mullin, S. P., & Summers, A. A. (1983). Is more better? The effectiveness of spending on compensatory education. *Phi Delta Kappan, 64*(5), 339–347.

Parsons, T. (1959). The school class as a social system: Some of its functions in American society. *Harvard Educational Review, 29,* 297–318.

Passow, A. H. (Ed.). (1963). *Education in depressed areas.* New York: Teachers College Press, Columbia University.

Perkinson, H. J. (1977). *The imperfect panacea: American faith in education, 1865–1976* (2nd ed.). New York: Random House.

Perrow, C. (1982). Disintegrating social sciences. *Phi Delta Kappan, 63*(10), 684–688.

Persell, C. H. (1976). *Quality, careers and training in educational and social research.* New York: General Hall.

Persell, C. H. (1977). *Education and inequality: The roots and results of stratification in America's schools.* New York: Free Press.

Plunkett, V. R. L. (1985). From Title I to Chapter 1: The evolution of compensatory education. *Phi Delta Kappan, 66*(8), 533–537.

Purkey, S. C., & Smith, M. S. (1983). Effective schools—A review. *Elementary School Journal, 84,* 427–452.

Ralph, J. H., & Fennessey, J. (1983). Science or reform: Some questions about the effective schools model. *Phi Delta Kappan, 64*(10), 689–694.

Riessman, F. (1962). *The culturally deprived child.* New York: Harper and Row.

Rose, A. M. (1962). A systematic summary of symbolic interaction theory. In A. M. Rose (Ed.), *Human behavior and social processes* (pp. 3–19). Boston: Houghton-Mifflin.

Rosenberg, M. (1965). *Society and the adolescent self-image.* Princeton, NJ: Princeton University Press.

Rosenthal, R., & Jacobson, L. (1968). *Pygmalion in the classroom.* New York: Holt, Rinehart, and Winston.

Runciman, W. G. (1966). *Relative deprivation and social justice.* Baltimore: Penguine.

Ryan, W. (1976). *Blaming the victim* (rev. ed.). New York: Vintage.

Sexton, P. C. (1961). *Education and income.* New York: Viking.

Spring, J. (1976). *The sorting machine: National educational policy since 1945.* New York: David McKay.

Stein, A. (1971). Strategies of failure. *Harvard Educational Review, 41,* 158–204.

Stickney, B. D., & Plunkett, V. R. L. (1983). Closing the gap: A historical perspective on the effectiveness of compensatory education. *Phi Delta Kappan, 65*(4), 287–290.

Tomlinson, T. M. (1982). Review of "Creating Effective Schools." *Educational Leadership, 40*(3), 72–73.

Tyack, D. (1974). *The one best system.* Cambridge: Harvard University Press.

Valentine, C. A. (1968). *Culture and poverty.* Chicago: University of Chicago Press.

Valentine, C. A. (1971). The "culture of poverty": Its scientific significance and its implications for action. In E. Leacock (Ed.), *The culture of poverty: A critique* (pp. 193–225). New York: Simon and Schuster.

Violas, P. (1978). *The training of the urban working class.* Chicago: Rand McNally.

Walberg, H. J. (Ed.). (1974). *Evaluating educational performance: A sourcebook of methods, instruments, and examples.* Berkeley, CA: McCutchan.

Walberg, H. J. (Ed.) (1979). *Educational environments and effects: Evaluation, policy, and productivity.* Berkeley, CA: McCutchan.

Warner, W. L., Havighurst, R. J., & Loeb, M. B. (1944). *Who shall be educated?* New York: Harper.

Wasserman, H. (1972). *Harvey Wasserman's history of the United States.* New York: Harper and Row.

Weber, G. (1971). *Inner-city children can be taught to read: Four successful schools* (Occasional Paper No. 18). Washington, DC: Council for Basic Education.

Whyte, W. H., Jr. (1957). *The organization man.* Garden City, NY: Doubleday Anchor.

Wiley, D. E., & Harnischfeger, A. (1974). Explosion of a myth: Quantity of schooling and exposure to instruction, major educational vehicles. *Educational Researcher, 3*(4), 7–11.

Wilson, E. O. (1975). *Sociobiology: The new synthesis.* Cambridge, MA: Harvard University Press.

Wilson, E. O. (1978). *On human nature.* Cambridge, MA: Harvard University Press.

CHAPTER 2

Public and Private Schools: Are They Really Different?

Jane Hannaway and Susan Abramowitz

INTRODUCTION

One way to improve public schools that has been suggested in the last few years is to "privatize" them; that is, subject them to market pressure through the introduction of competition and consumer choice. Vouchers and tuition tax credits are two of the ways proposed to accomplish privatization. Proponents claim that more effective and more efficient schools would result; opponents claim it would mark the death of the American common school.

Debate over privatization proposals intensified when the Coleman, Hoffer, and Kilgore (1981) study showed that nonpublic schools were, in fact, more efficient and more effective. This research claimed that public schools were limited in their ability to educate, overwhelmed by state and federal regulation, and unable to cope with student disruption. Private schools, on the other hand, not only created environments conducive to learning and generally promoted student achievement but, the study alleges, they did so while being more integrated than public schools.

Caveats in the professional literature abound about the Coleman results as initially reported (e.g., Cronbach, 1981; Goldberger, 1981;

31

Heyns & Hilton, 1982; Page & Keith, 1981). One major criticism suggests that differences in student achievement may be due to the selection of students into private schools, both through self-selection by students and through school admission procedures, rather than to the school's educational program (Bryk, 1981). Questions also remain about the validity of the public and private school images presented in the study, yet little has been done to identify distinguishing ways in which public and private schools actually function.

This chapter aims to provide a better understanding of the public–private school debate by analyzing school processes, that is, by looking at what public and private schools actually do. It does not compare the two sets of schools in terms of their academic outcomes. The longitudinal analyses produced by the National Center on Education Statistics, that will succeed the Coleman cross-sectional study, will provide a more definitive answer to that issue. The question addressed here is more basic: Do public and private schools behave differently? If they do, the results may offer some plausible reasons for differences in achievement. If they do not, it should increase suspicion that selection biases account for achievement differences.

Two areas specifically chosen for comparing the two sets of schools are school management practices and school culture. These were selected because both directly affect the behavior of in-school participants, and both have been related in the literature to school effectiveness.

The results show that there were substantial differences between public and private schools in both management practices and school culture. Schools in the public sector exercised greater levels of formal management control over the school's teaching and learning process. Private schools, on the other hand, were characterized by a greater sense of commitment and involvement among school participants, particularly the parents. Management differences were not associated with school achievement, but school culture factors significantly discriminated between high- and low-achieving schools in each of the sectors.

The results suggest a couple of things. First, attempts to reform schools by using tighter management practices may have only a minimal effect. Certainly, some base level of management control is necessary, but that is not what distinguishes high-achieving schools. Second, the distinction commonly made by researchers between "in-school" factors and "out-of-school" factors may not be well conceived. The findings here suggest the two are integrally related in the schooling process. The implications of these findings for school reform are discussed at the end of the chapter.

SCHOOL MANAGEMENT PRACTICES AND SCHOOL CULTURE

Management practices refers primarily to bureaucratic means of control, for example, the use of rules and supervision. Research on school effectiveness.has concluded that school management practices, especially the behavior of the principal, are important determinants of school effectiveness (Austin, 1978; Edmonds, 1979; Murnane, 1975; Rutter *et al.*, 1979). The research suggests that in order to promote higher levels of school effectiveness, principals should (1) exhibit assertive, instructionally oriented leadership, (2) establish rules and guidelines that promote an orderly school climate, (3) have high expectations for the performance of staff and students, and (4) design a system of instructional objectives and evaluation (Shoemaker & Fraser, 1981). While most of this research was conducted in elementary schools, it is reasonable to expect that close management control in high schools also is related to school effectiveness.

School culture refers to the common set of values, beliefs, and practices operating within a school. Unlike management practices that are premised on formal bureaucratic and usually hierarchical means of control, a school's culture acts as a social control mechanism directing behavior through institutionalized norms generally subscribed to by organizational participants. The importance of culture has received considerable attention in the organizational literature (Deal & Kennedy, 1982; Jelinek, Smircich, & Hirsch, 1983). Strongly held common values are viewed as critical contributors to organizational effectiveness (Peters & Waterman, 1983), in large part due to the commitment they engender among organizational employees.

The intent here is not to determine the precise relationship between these dimensions of the school and its effectiveness. Even if their effect on student achievement were insignificant, any discernible differences between public and private schools would still be important, if only because many parents behave as if public–private differences are consequential. If, however, differences are important in determining the effectiveness of schools, then our findings suggest avenues of reform.

THE DATA

The data used in this study are a subset of the data collected by the National Institute of Education for two studies, *High School '77* (Abramowitz & Tenenbaum, 1978) and *The Private High School Today* (Abramowitz

& Stackhouse, 1980). These studies were intended to provide general descriptive information on the students, staff, and programs of high schools in the United States. The particular subset used here is the responses of school principals to fact questions and their perceptions of student, staff, and parent opinions and needs.

The public school sample of 2000 schools and the private school sample of 600 schools both represent approximately 12% of their respective secondary school populations. Vocational, continuation, and alternative schools and schools for the handicapped were not included. A total of 1448 usable public school and 454 usable private school responses were received—a 72.4% and 75.6% response rate, respectively. The private school sample included 358 Catholic schools and 96 other private schools.

The indicators of school management practices in this study are limited to those that directly relate to the school's teaching and learning activities on the assumption that these have the greatest impact on the effectiveness of the school. They include measures of the frequency of classroom observations by the principal, the extent to which they value working with teachers, and the frequency of formal teacher evaluations within the school.

The items selected to indicate a school's culture, that is, the common set of attitudes, values, and behaviors operating in the school, are the following: the parents' and principal's goals; the commitment and interest of parents, students, and teachers; the types and severity of school problems; and the level of conflict among participants.

THE RESULTS

The results show that public schools exhibit management characteristics associated with effective schools to a greater extent than do private schools; that is, public schools employ more instructionally oriented management practices. This finding may surprise many who assume that private organizations are more tightly run than public ones. However, because the management practices of the high-achieving schools in each of the sectors were not substantially different from those of other schools in the same sector, the results suggest that management practices, by themselves, may not be critically important to secondary school achievement. In terms of school culture, the results show that the dominant culture of private schools is very different from that of public schools. And, unlike management practices, these differences do seem to be associated with greater school achievement in each of the sectors, suggesting that a school's culture is an important ingredient for school success. The implications of these findings for public policy are discussed later in the chapter.

MANAGEMENT PRACTICES

An Avis model provides an apt characterization of public school principals and their manner of running the instructional program of a school: They try harder. They conduct actual classroom observations and formal teacher evaluations with considerably greater frequency and place a higher value on working closely with teachers than do private school heads.

Of the public secondary school principals, 43% report they engage in classroom observations several times a week while the proportion of Catholic school principals who do the same is 15%, and for other nonpublic school heads it is 12%. Public school principals also make a greater effort to obtain feedback on teacher performance. The difference on this measure between public schools and other nonpublic schools is particularly striking, with 39% of the other nonpublic schools and 15% of the Catholic schools reporting that teacher evaluations are rarely conducted. Only 5% of the public school principals report the same. Of the public schools, 32% conduct formal teacher evaluations more than once a year, compared to only 16% of the other nonpublic schools.

This instructionally oriented behavior of school principals is consistent with the value they place on working closely with teachers. Public school principals were more likely to feel that working closely with teachers was an important part of their job, with 83% of public school principals compared to 69% of the Catholic heads and 50% of the nonpublic principals considering this part of their work very important.

Public schools also seem to "try harder" in establishing an orderly school climate. They are more likely to have rules requiring hall passes and formal rules for dealing with students who are disruptive in class (Abramowitz and Stackhouse, 1980).

SCHOOL CULTURE

Contrary to the findings about management practices, differences that favor private schools emerge in the analysis of school culture differences. The dominant culture in private schools is one that is more likely to foster an environment of student achievement.

Private schools are different from public schools in (1) the goals principals perceive parents value, (2) the goals valued by the principals, (3) the commitment and interest of parents, students, and teachers, (4) the types and severity of school problems, and (5) the level of conflict among participants. These results suggest a different way of approaching public–private school differences, an approach that considers the parent–child–school nexus. Focusing solely on student characteristics and issues of in-school management and discipline results in an incomplete picture of the determinants of the behavior of school participants and subsequent school effectiveness. The boundaries between in-school and out-of-school factors may, in fact, not be clear.

An examination of principal reports of parent goals for education supports this view. The reports suggest that parents of private school students are very different from parents of public school students. Private school parents value most educational goals more highly than public school parents, and the value they place on goals such as moral citizenship, individual responsibility for learning, college preparation, and aesthetic appreciation is considerably higher. For example, about twice the proportion of private school parents (30% of Catholic, 34% of other private, and 16% of public) feel that individual responsibility for learning is a very important educational goal. Private school principals also attach a higher value to each of these goals than do public schools principals.

A stronger sense of community in private schools may also contribute to school effectiveness. One indication of a community atmosphere is the level of conflict reported in schools in each of the sectors. Greater levels of conflict in public schools were reported among students, among teachers, between teachers and students, between teachers and principals, between teachers and parents, between administrators and parents and between schools and central offices. The greatest difference between public and private schools in levels of conflict concerned parents: specifically, conflict between teachers and parents. Of the Catholic and other private school administrators, 72% and 75%, respectively, reported this a rare event, while only 44% of the public school heads reported parent–teacher conflict as rare.

A related pattern emerges when the incidence and severity of problems that principals report is examined. The greatest differences between the problems faced by public and private schools concern the attitudes or behaviors of the major participants in the school—teachers, students, and parents—not issues related to school resources, such as the number of counselors and teachers or the availability of instructional materials. Teacher lack of commitment is considered a serious or very serious problem by over 15% of public school principals, while only 1.7% of Catholic school principals and none of the other private school principals call it a serious problem. Similarly, over 40% of principals in public school think student apathy is a serious or very serious problem, while only 9% of Catholic leaders and 5% of other school leaders consider student apathy serious. Public school heads also reported more severe problems with parents. Parent lack of interest was reported as a serious problem by 36.2% of public school principals, while only 7.4% and 2.2% of Catholic and other nonpublic school heads, respectively, thought it was serious.

Next, we attempted to discover whether differences between public and private schools were significant and, if so, which factors distinguished them most strongly. We also used the same analytic technique (discriminant analysis) to determine if the same logically derived variables that distinguished public from private schools could also distinguish high-achieving schools (those sending 80% or more of their graduates on to further education) from low-achieving schools within the same public–private sector. These analyses were performed using the following variables:

Close Management (Close Instructional Management)—an additive index combining a 4-point scale on the frequency of classroom observation by the principal and a 4-point scale on the frequency of formal teacher evaluation.

Participant Problem (Problem Associated with School Participants)—an additive index combining 4-point scales on the degree of severity of the following problem areas associated with school participants: teacher absenteeism, lack of commitment or motivation, and incompetence; student absenteeism, class-cutting, and apathy; and parental lack of interest and/or lack of involvement.

Participant Conflict (Conflict Associated with School Participants)—an additive index combining 4-point scales on the frequency of the following conflict areas: among students, among teachers, between teachers and students, between teachers and school heads, and between teachers and parents.

Goal Differences—an index based on the sum of the squared difference between the school head and parents in the importance of different goals.

Size—school enrollment

Table 2.1 shows that, on average, *Close Management* in public schools is practiced to a significantly greater degree than in the private schools,

Table 2.1

Means and Standard Deviations of Scores on Five Variables from Public, Catholic, and Other Private High Schools[a]

Variable	Public		Catholic		Other private	
	M	SD	M	SD	M	SD
Close management	4.22	1.27	3.50	1.44*	2.89	1.39
Participant problem	9.40	3.32	5.42	2.78*	3.74	2.55*
Participant conflict	4.96	3.67	2.29	2.46*	2.15	2.73*
Goal differences	5.24	4.68	3.91	3.90*	3.11	2.36*
Size	954	653	486	337*	385	352*

[a] From data in Abramowitz and Tenenbaum (1978); Abramowitz and Stackhouse (1980).
* Differs from public school at or beyond .001 level (could occur by chance fewer than one time in 1000).

Table 2.2

Standardized Canonical Discriminant Function Coefficients[a] Distinguishing Public from Catholic and Other Private High Schools, Respectively

Variable	Public vs. Catholic ($n = 1193$) ($n = 292$)	Public vs. other ($n = 81$)
Size	.36	.30
Close management	.36	.50
Participant problem	.65	.69
Participant conflict	.29	.15
Goal differences	.05	.09

[a] The larger the coefficient, the more important, statistically, the variable for distinguishing the two school types. From data in Abramowitz and Tenenbaum (1978); Abramowitz and Stackhouse (1980).

and it was the second most important variable discriminating public schools from schools in the other two sectors (see Table 2.2).

But how do management differences relate to school achievement? Although we do not have the proper achievement measures to address this question directly, we can conduct an informative preliminary analysis. For example, one would expect a greater proportion of high-achieving schools to exhibit valued management practices to a greater extent if instructional management is a critical contributor to school achievement. Management practices in high-achieving schools across the three types of schools would also tend to be more alike. By asking these questions, we are, in effect, controlling for school achievement and looking for associated changes in management practices. Even if one did not believe there to be a causal connection, one might still expect to find this systematic relationship since management practices might correspond to the nature of the school program, for example, a college preparatory program.

Surprisingly, very few differences between the management practices of the high-achieving schools and low-achieving schools emerged. In neither the public school sample nor in the Catholic school sample, was the difference in *Close Management* between the high-achieving and low-achieving schools significant (see Table 2.3). The standardized coefficients resulting from the discriminant analysis show some mixed results. *Close Management* contributes almost nothing ($-.04$) to discriminating high-achieving and low-achieving public schools (see Table 2.3). It makes a modest contribution in the Catholic school sample ($-.27$) where it is associated with high-achieving schools. In the other private school sample, however, it is the most important variable distinguishing high achievers from low achievers (.68), but there it is associated with low-achieving schools.

The findings seem somewhat contradictory when we try to relate them to achievement, possibly because management practices are more closely associated with school type than with school effectiveness. The differences among the three sectors are considerably greater than the differences within them. That is, school management practices differ significantly by school type, public or private, but they do not seem to be affected by whether the school is high achieving or low achieving. High-achieving and low-achieving schools within the same sector are managed similarly. The results suggest that reformers who argue that public schools should become more like private schools in the way they are managed do not have a full understanding of the relationship between management and school achievement. This is not to say the practices that were outlined earlier are unimportant. On the contrary, common sense tells us systematic attention to instructional objectives and an orderly environment are necessary conditions for school achievement, evidently attainable in both public and private systems. What the results do suggest is that management practices are probably not the primary determinant of achievement differences between public and private schools.

Why might management practices differ by school type? The most likely explanation probably lies in the very nature of private schools. Clients and private schools join together through choice. Clients make an active choice in selecting a school and then schools apply admission standards to determine which clients will actually attend. (Clients may also exercise choice of residence in attending a public school, but this

Table 2.3

Standardized Canonical Discriminant Function Coefficient[a] Distinguishing High- from Low-Achieving High Schools by Type of School

Variable	Public		Catholic		Other	
	High (n = 111)	Low (n = 953)	High (n = 170)	Low (n = 94)	High (n = 58)	Low (n = 21)
Size		-.80		-.09		.34
Close management		-.04		-.27		.68
Participant problem		.74		.74		.50
Participant conflict		-.16		.09		.20
Goal differences		.15		.42		.33

[a] The larger the coefficient (regardless of sign) the more important, statistically, the variable for distinguishing a high- from a low-achieving school type. From data in Abramowitz and Tenenbaum (1978); Abramowitz and Stackhouse (1980).

form of choice is more limited.) The result is that clients attend a school they desire (as opposed to one to which they are assigned) and schools work with a preferred clientele. Under such conditions many formal supervisory management practices may be completely unnecessary (see Salganik and Karweit, 1982, for further discussion of this view). No doubt this process generates a greater degree of value congruity between schools and clients than a process where clients are assigned and schools are legally obligated to accept them. An underlying set of shared values can be very forceful in directing behavior, perhaps more forceful than formal rules and regulations in the school setting where there is still considerable uncertainty about the technology associated with teaching and learning. The findings on school culture support this view.

The results related to school culture factors provide a better explanation for achievement differences. This is particularly true of *Participant Problem*, which was both the most important variable distinguishing public schools from both Catholic and other private schools, .65 and .69, respectively (see Table 2.2), and a significant discriminator between high- and low-achieving schools in all three groups of schools (see Table 2.3).

Given the central nature of *Participant Problem* in the results, the components associated with different participants were analyzed separately in order to assess their relative importance, that is, parent problems, teacher problems, and student problems (See description of *Participant Problem* index for specific problems for each participant group.) The stepwise method of discriminant analysis was used. Consistent with earlier descriptive findings, the most important participant group was parents. Problems associated with parents was the only factor that significantly discriminated between high- and low-achieving schools in all three school types and was the most important discriminator for both public schools and Catholic schools.

The predominant role parental interest and involvement plays in our results should not be surprising. The importance of family background characteristics on student achievement is well known. But there is an important distinction between the background measures commonly used—parental education and income—and the measures used here, generally, parental values. While the two may be correlated, the relationship is far from perfect. Parental interest in a child's education, and the lack of it, knows no class barriers. When comparing public and private schools, parental interest is particularly salient because, by definition, all private school parents are interested and involved as evidenced by their active choice about their child's school. Making that choice may be what distinguishes them in a critical way from their public school counterparts. The Coleman study made a great effort to control for family background, using objective and subjective family background measures. It then reported that students in private schools had fewer behavior problems, higher attendance rates, and higher achievement than students in public schools and credited the schools with these results. But the family measures used in the Coleman study were only the readily observable background differences. What may be the most important background difference—whatever values led private school parents to choose a private school—was not controlled. This process is what researchers call self-selection, where the subjects of study have selected themselves (as opposed to being randomly assigned into a *treatment* group), and it is unclear how to control for the effects of this. (See *Evaluation Studies Review*, 1980, for articles on self-selection biases.) While controls are difficult to implement when comparing these populations, parental interest is generally accepted as an important factor affecting school achievement. Part of the effect is probably direct, affecting the values and motivation of the child toward school work. Another part of its effect is probably indirect, affecting student achievement through an effect on the behaviors of teachers and administrators. Interested parents may motivate teachers while apathetic parents may contribute to teacher apathy. Parental interest and appreciation is one of the few sources of external rewards for teachers. If this view is correct, then school norms and school cultures may be significantly influenced by parental values. This has important implications for studying school effectiveness because it suggests that in-school factors and out-of-school factors are difficult, if not impossible, to distinguish. Any claims that one set of schools is better than another set and that do not take into account the contribution of clients to its effectiveness are questionable.

In summary, what we are arguing here and what our findings suggest is simple: The commitment and involvement of school participants makes a significant difference in a school's success. And the difference it makes is greater than what can be achieved through formal management techniques. More specifically, we are arguing to bring the parents back in; they seem to be central. Not only do they affect the behavior and attitudes of their children, but their commitment may also be a very forceful motivating force for school level personnel.

AN OBSERVATION ON SCHOOL SIZE

Although public–private differences in the effect of school size were not hypothesized, school size showed up as a significant discriminator of high- and low-achieving schools in the public, but not in the private, sector. Reducing school size is often suggested as a way to improve schooling outcomes (Barker & Gump, 1964; Chambers, 1981; Erikson & Nault, 1978; Murnane, 1975). Because most research findings on the effect of size are more directly associated with the affective outcomes of schooling, school size was expected to have an important effect on school culture, on the attitudes and values of school participants, and ultimately on other school outcomes.

The effect of school size was examined by dividing schools into size categories and looking for differences in the severity of problems associated with different school participants. In general, size made a consistent difference in the severity of problems for public schools, but not for Catholic and other private schools. The rate at which public school principals reported almost all problem areas as serious increased with size. Some of these were substantial. For example, only 4% of the public school principals in schools of 250 or fewer thought student absenteeism was a serious problem, while 12% in schools with larger enrollments (500–1000) thought it was serious. Similarly, 12% of the smaller school principals reported student cutting as serious, while twice that proportion in larger schools thought it was serious. The problem rate associated with Catholic and other private schools, however, did not change with size according to any clear pattern. A possible explanation for this is that choice may dominate size in determining school culture in private schools, but in public schools where choice is not available, school size may be an important contributor to a school culture supportive of educational achievement.

SUMMARY AND CONCLUSION

The implications of the findings provide no easy solutions for those interested in improving schools. What the findings do suggest is that public school principals have a particularly difficult job and they seem to do more of the right things in trying to manage their schools. But the degree to which any management practices, beyond some base level, can impact on student achievement is questionable. Loose-coupling theories of educational organizations would support this view (March & Olsen, 1976; Meyer & Rowan, 1977; Weick, 1976).

The findings regarding school culture provide more insight into public–private differences and perhaps also into school achievement. But if school culture is a primary determinant of school achievement, how does one develop a supportive school culture? While it is no doubt easy to control a school's culture through selection, that is, choose students whose parents have the "right" values, this is not an option open to public schools. There are reforms, however, that might affect parental interest. For example, much of social psychology suggests that choice alone engenders greater commitment, and reform such as vouchers and magnet schools, despite other limitations associated with them, do encourage active parent–student choice.

School culture is an aspect of a school that is difficult to manipulate. But its intractability should not lead policymakers to ignore it as a possibly fruitful focus in the consideration of various reforms for school improvement. Perhaps it is time for schools to put less reliance on costly formal supervisory practices and explore other ways to encourage school participants to behave productively. Certainly, the relationship among parent choice, commitment, and a productive school culture is one that merits serious research attention.

REFERENCES

Abramowitz, S., & Stackhouse, E. A. (1980). *The private high school today.* Washington, DC: Government Printing Office.

Abramowitz, S., & Tenenbaum, E. (1978). *High school '77.* Washington, DC: Government Printing Office.

Austin, G. (1978). *Process evaluation: A comprehensive study of outliers.* Baltimore, MD: Maryland State Department of Education. (ERIC:ED 160 644)

Barker, R. G., & Gump, P. V. (1964). *Big school, small school.* Stanford, CA: Stanford University Press.

Byrk, A. (1981). Disciplined inquiry or policy argument: *Harvard Education Review, 51*(4), (pp. 497–509).

Chambers, J. G. (1981). Analysis of school size under a voucher system. *Educational Evaluation and Policy Analysis, 3*(2), (pp. 29–40).

Coleman, J. A., Hoffer, T., & Kilgore, S. (1981). *Public and private high schools.* A Report to the National Center for Education Statistics, National Opinion Research Center.

Cronbach, L. J. (1981, April). Remarks in response to an invited address by James Colman on *Public and private schools.* Annual Meeting of American Educational Research Association, San Francisco

Deal, T. E., & Kennedy, A. A. (1982). *Corporate cultures.* Reading, MA: Addison-Wesley.

Edmonds, R. (1979). Effective schools for the urban poor. *Educational Leadership,* (pp. 15–24).

Erikson, D. A., & Nault, R. L. (1978). *Currency, choice, and commitment: An exploratory study of the effects of public money and related regulation on Canadian catholic schools.* San Francisco: University of San Francisco.

Evaluation Studies Review Annual, Volume VI. New York: Sage, 1980.

Goldberger, A. (1981). *Coleman goes private (in public).* Unpublished manuscript, University of Wisconsin, Madison.

Heyns, B., & Hilton, T. L. (1982). The cognitive test for high school and beyond: An assessment. *Sociology of Education, 55*, 89–102.

Jelinek, M., Smircich, L., & Hirsch, P. (1983). Special issue of *Administrative Science Quarterly* on Organizational Culture, *28*:3.

March, J. G., & Olsen, J. (1976). *Ambiguity and choice in organizations.* Bergen, Norway: Universitiesforlaget.

Meyer, J., & Rowan, B. (1977). Institutionalized organizations and formal structure as myth and ceremony. *American Journal of Sociology, 83*:340–363.

Murnane, R. (1975). *The impact of school resources on the learning of inner city children.* Cambridge, MA: Balliner.

Page, E. B., & Keith, T. Z. (1981). Effects of U.S. private schools: A technical analysis of two recent claims. *Educational Researcher, 10*, 7–17.

Peters, T., & Waterman, R. (1983). *In search of excellence: Lessons from America's best-run companies.* New York: Harper and Row.

Rutter, M. *et al.* (1979). *Fifteen thousand hours.* Cambridge: Harvard University Press.

Salganik, L. H., & Karweit, N. (1982). Voluntarism and government in education. *Sociology of Education, 55*, 152–161.

Shoemaker, J., & Fraser, H. W. (1981, November). What principals can do: Some implications from studies of effective schooling. *Phi Delta Kappan, 63*, 178–182.

Weick, K. (1976). Educational organizations as loosely coupled systems. *Administrative Science Quarterly, 21*, 1–19.

CHAPTER 3

The Problems of Public Schools: The Catholic Connection

John D. Donovan and George F. Madaus

INTRODUCTION

In recent years the problems of public schools in America have been highlighted by the Coleman Report's invidious comparison of the achievement performances of public and private, including Catholic, school pupils (Coleman, Hoffer, & Kilgore, 1982). This chapter is a kind of intermission in what critics will succeed in making a long-run methodological drama. Consequently, it does not address either the Coleman analysis or its policy implications directly. Suffice it to say that Coleman's findings are not unexpected. The fact that Catholic school norms on standardized tests are consistently higher than those of the total national sample has been known for a number of years (Madaus & Linnan, 1973). It also has been recognized that such direct comparisons cannot be taken at face value because of institutional and individual selectivity associated with Catholic schools. Further, Coleman's measures are generalized achievement measures and as such may be considered as surrogates for home and community background factors (Madaus, Airasian, & Kellaghan, 1980). This complicates any attempts to control for selectivity factors in comparative analyses. A more interesting comparison of public and parochial–private school achievement involves using curricular sensitive measures with specific subpopulations. For example, a comparison of the achievement of public and parochial

47

school students taking physics or second year algebra would make more sense. So much for the Coleman Report at this time.

The focus of this chapter is restricted to one sector of the American private education system, Catholic elementary schools. The question raised is to what degree, if at all, is the existence and the goals of Catholic schools connected to the continuing problems of public schools?

Unfortunately, this question may be read or heard as an indictment. This absolutely is not the intent. Neither bad faith nor bad intentions are imputed to Catholic schools in their relationship with the public sector. Catholic schools did not cause the problems of public schools. But once these problems were recognized, Catholic connections to them did occur. These connections vary by and within regions, but they do, nonetheless, make Catholic schools a part of the problem of America's public schools. Moreover, the connections will continue to be affected by educational policy decisions the Catholic church and its members are forced to make. These policy decisions emerge from the necessary reassessment by the church of her ecclesiastical and educational goals and priorities in the midst of a changing socioeconomic, cultural and religious world.

In summary, therefore, the chapter describes Catholic connections to the problems of public schools in the contexts of (1) the changed situation of Catholic schools after 1965, (2) the sources of the crisis of confidence experienced by public schools during the late 1970s, (3) the exemplary image of the Catholic schools, and (4) the policy questions confronted by Catholic schools that have significant implications for the future status of public schools.

THE CHANGED SITUATION OF CATHOLICS: POST-1965

If Catholic schools are now somehow a part of the problem of America's public schools it should be recalled that the parochial school system emerged as a response to the anti-Catholic orientation of the public schools of an earlier era. Expressed in the more positive policy language of church leaders, parochial schools were to be built and to be staffed by religious teachers in order to protect and enrich the religious faith and ethnic identity of the children of Catholic immigrants. Inasmuch as these schools were financed by church members, useful in segregating some of the suspect immigrant population, and eventually seen as helpful in the Americanization process, they posed no problems for the

Table 3.1

Data on Increase or Decrease in Number of Catholic Schools, Enrollment, and Number of Religious Teachers, 1920–1980[a]

Year	No. schools	Inc./dec. in no. schools from year to year (%)	No. of enrollments	Inc./dec. in enrollments from year to year (%)	No. of religious teachers	% of staff
1920	6,551		1,795,673		38,592	93.8
1940	7,944	+17.53	2,035,182	+11.77	56,438	94.9
1960	10,501	+24.35	4,373,422	+53.46	79,119	73.0
1967–68	10,350	−1.44	4,105,805	−6.12	64,562	59.0
1968–69	10,113	−2.23	3,859,709	−5.99	61,071	55.0
1969–70	9,695	−4.13	3,607,168	−6.54	56,157	51.0
1970–71	9,366	−3.39	3,359,311	−6.87	52,190	47.0
1971–72	8,982	−4.10	3,076,000	−8.43	47,369	44.0
1972–73	8,761	−2.46	2,871,000	−6.66	44,020	42.0
1973–74	8,550	−2.41	2,714,000	−5.57	40,369	39.0
1974–75	8,418	−1.56	2,602,000	−4.30	37,306	37.0
1975–76	8,340	−0.93	2,525,000	−3.05	34,750	35.0
1976–77	8,281	−0.71	2,483,000	−1.69	33,089	33.0
1977–78	8,204	−0.93	2,421,000	−2.50	33,888	31.0
1978–79	8,159	−0.55	2,365,000	−2.30	28,453	29.0
1979–80	8,100	−0.72	2,293,000	−1.30	26,868	28.0
1980–81	8,043	−1.08	2,269,000	−1.05	24,454	25.0

[a] From National Catholic Educational Association, 1970, 1971, 1972, 1974, 1981.

public school system. Quite the opposite, they symbolized the American principles of both freedom and pluralism, and more practically, reduced the financial drain on the taxpayers.

In such a setting the Catholic school system, not insignificantly supported by continuing immigration, a high fertility rate, and growing financial resources, expanded rapidly to the point where by 1960 approximately one out of seven students nationwide was enrolled in parochial schools. To capsule the facts of this growth and to establish its distinctive character, the data of Table 3.1, taken from National Catholic Education Association (NCEA) reports, tell a remarkable story. Between 1920 and 1960 there was a 62% increase in the number of elementary schools, a 41% increase in enrollments and a 49% increase in the number of religious teachers. By 1960, the peak year in the expansion of Catholic elementary schools, there were 10,501 schools in which 4,373,422 children were instructed by a staff of 108,160 teachers of whom 73.1%, or 79,119, were religious. At this point in time nonpublic education was dominated by Catholic schools. At the combined elementary and secondary levels Catholic schools constituted 86.9% of all private schools in the United States (NCEA, 1981).

By the mid-1960s, however, the expansion in Catholic education was in reverse. By 1965 a numerical decrease in enrollments and in the numbers of teaching religious had occurred (see Table 3.1), and this trend continued steadily until about 1975 when the rate of decline dropped appreciably and appeared to stabilize. By 1980, compared to 1960, 2458 elementary schools had closed and there were 2,104,422 fewer students and 55% fewer teaching religious. Simple division shows that school closings accounted for only a part of the student loss. Schools that remained open also experienced declines in enrollments. In spite of these dramatic losses, as an alternative to the public school system, Catholic schools still constituted an important proportion of private sector schools—65% in 1976–1977 (NCEA, 1981). However, a conspicuous change in the character of those schools can be found in the evidence that the religious teachers who constituted 93% of the total staff in 1940, and 73.1% of the staff in 1960, had declined by 1980 to minority status constituting only 25% of Catholic elementary school teachers (NCEA, 1981).

The reasons for the sharp reversal in the growth of parochial schools over the past 20 years are clearly complex. The decline in the birthrate, the nonreplacement of immigrant Catholic populations, the movement of large numbers of Catholics to the suburbs, and the spiraling costs of education at all levels, were significant discrete factors (Donovan, Erickson, & Madaus, 1971). However, two fairly general interactive factors loom as most significant in explaining this withdrawal pattern and the attendent crisis of confidence in parochial schools. Simply put, the crisis in Catholic schools was the product of two change patterns that had been merging for some years but intersected (more or less) in the mid-1960s. The first of these was a change in ethnic, class, and educational composition of the Catholic population. This resulted in an identity shift from American Catholic to Catholic American. What was a noun became an adjective; what was an adjective became a noun. The second factor interacting with the identity change was the complex of altered religious perspectives formalized by the church's Vatican Council II, and the resultant shift from a closed, authoritarian system toward a more open democratic set of values and structures. Widespread dissent on the part of large numbers of laity and clergy to the strictures of *Humanae Vitae* (Pope Paul VI's 1968 encyclical opposing birth control) contributed to this shift, which is by no means yet complete.

The detailed description of these crisis-causing changes cannot here detain us. Suffice it to say that the nineteenth-century goals of protecting the faith that had inspired the church's policy of establishing and staffing schools could no longer be sold to a more socially mobile, more educated, more religiously ecumenical, and more democratically oriented Catholic population. And this was compounded when priests, brothers, and nuns in large numbers either sought official laicization or simply left the religious life.

The crisis of parochial schools preoccupied Catholic ecclesiastical and educational leaders throughout the decades of the 1960s and the 1970s. It also was a crisis important to public officials and public school educators who had to absorb students opting out of parochial schools or those forced out by school closings. In Catholic circles retrenchment was the byword. Feverish, sometimes intemperate, political lobbying by church officials for federal or state financial support alternated with policy decisions not to build new schools or to phase out those schools with either declining enrollments or fewer religious teachers. Nationally, there was pressure to increase tuitions and parish subsidies. It was a time of rearguard action. Ecclesiastical and educational leaders of Catholic schools now had to call into question the relevance and the viability of the goals that had for so long not only justified but undergirded the existence and the growth of Catholic schools. The long-term perspective became one of how a vastly reduced parochial system might meet the educational, social, and religious realities of the new era. The shorter-term perspective was that of a school system in need of a lifeline.

THE PUBLIC SCHOOL CRISIS OF THE LATE 1970s: THE CATHOLIC CONNECTIONS

The lifeline needed by the parochial schools came from an unexpected source—a growing sense of dissatisfaction with public schools. The empty spaces that for very pragmatic reasons needed to be filled in many parochial schools coalesced with the needs of disaffected public school parents who sought alternatives. For many Catholics this new crisis in public education provided a basis for some optimism regarding the future of parochial schools. The misfortunes of public schools were omens of good luck for Catholic schools.

Statistical reports by the NCEA indicate that over a 5-year period, 1977–82, there has been a significant deceleration in the rate of decline in both enrollments and in the number of Catholic school closings. Considering the smaller number of school-age children, Catholic elementary school enrollments have remained at a relatively constant level (NCEA, 1981). The rate of decline in Catholic schools during this period is about equal to the national rate of decline of school-age children. Up until 5 years ago the rate of decline was much sharper than could be explained solely on the basis of demographic declines in the number of school-age children. A few figures from Table 3.1 illustrate this point. Until about 1976 the annual rate of decline in the number of pupils ran between 6 and 8%; for schools closing, the rate ran between 2 and 4%. Starting in 1976–77 the rate of decline for enrollment was about 2%, and for schools the rate of closing was under 1%.

The stabilizing or leveling off of enrollments in Catholic schools despite huge losses in the number of religious teachers (down, as Table 3.1 shows, from 75% of the staff in 1960 to 25% in 1980) can be explained in part by the availability of space in Catholic schools at the very time when parents were, often frantically, seeking alternatives to public education.

A combination of factors led to the growing crisis of confidence with the public schools, particularly with those schools located in the urban areas. The factors contributing to the malaise are several, interactive, and by and large perceptual. There is not time to trace these factors in any detail (we return to them briefly, later) nor is it productive to raise questions about the validity of these negative perceptions of public education. The objective facts are that these negative perceptions, often faulty and overgeneralized, were nonetheless widespread and became the basis for parental actions that resulted in a self-fulfilling prophecy. Bailey (1981) touches on this point when he says, "Quiet progress in education does not make news; raucous conflict and humiliating failures do. Surely some of the loss of public support for education has been caused or abetted by colorful, but often simplistic, coverage of educational matters by the media"(p. 37). A recent dramatic example is afforded by the cover of *Boston* magazine, which depicts two young children in school uniforms under the headline "Public School? Are You Crazy?" As W. I. Thomas (1923) observed, if men define situations as real, they are real in their consequences.

Empirically the evidence shows that a number of different factors moved public school parents to seize the transfer opportunities afforded by available space in parochial schools. First, among these is the growing belief that public school academic standards have fallen and that students are promoted from grade to grade solely on the basis of seat time. This perception about standards was fueled by widespread TV and print publicity and by complaints from businesses, colleges and the military that public schools were graduating pupils badly deficient in basic skills. Additional fuel came from the decade of decline in the SAT scores, the instituting of minimum competency testing programs in more than three out of four of the states and, more recently, from Coleman's findings (1982) about the higher achievement levels of private schools. Second, particularly in urban centers, publicity fed the blackboard jungle image of violence and vandalism in the public schools. Third, and especially significant, was the reality of white flight from public to private schools to avoid court-ordered busing.

Because of the negative factors associated with the public schools, large numbers of parents enrolled or transferred their children into parochial schools. Regarding the numbers who transferred because of perceptions related to qualitative declines and/or to problems of discipline and safety, the evidence is presumptive rather than empirical. But there is hard evidence that forced-busing and its negative connotations did in fact move parents to transfer their children to parochial–private schools. J. Michael Ross of Boston University, testifying before a Senate Subcommittee (1981), offered some startling data on the impact of court-ordered busing on both the public and private schools. He followed families with school-age children from six middle-class neighborhoods in Boston and three comparison groups that were similar in terms of residential and socioeconomic characteristics but were not impacted by court-ordered desegregation. Ross stated that of the Boston public school families (i.e., those with all their children enrolled in public schools prior to the court order), 50% avoided court-ordered school desegregation by either transferring at least one child to a parochial school (37%), or by relocating their families outside Boston (19%). In contrast, only 2.7% of the comparison families transferred children from public to parochial schools. Of a small group of families (20) in Boston with preschool children, none subsequently enrolled their children in the public schools. Ross further found that the rate of parochial school enrollment (35.5%) for the younger prekindergarten students was twice as high as the enrollment in the regular district schools since the implementation period. The year-by-year losses of pupils from public to parochial schools also dramatize how Boston parents perceived the empty parochial school seats as an alternative to forced-busing. The transfer rates of pupils from the Boston public schools to parochial schools were 12.8% in 1974, 9.5% in 1975, 6.2% in 1976, 5.1% in 1977, and 4.9% in 1978.

The significance of the Boston data is highlighted by Ross' findings in a comparable California study. Two facts stand out: (1) the size of the parochial system and the availability of space in that system; and (2) the weight of religious values in parental transfer decisions. Los Angeles, unlike Boston, did not have a well-established parochial–private school system. Despite this fact, 16.7% of Los Angeles students affected by busing transferred to private schools 1 year after the plan was initiated, whereas only 1.2% transferred from schools exempt from busing. Ross pointed out that parents in Los Angeles did not have the parochial school option available to the same degree as did those in Boston, therefore, in Los Angeles private schools grew to meet the demand for alternatives to the public schools. The difference in school options for Boston and Los Angeles is a significant factor that needs to be considered in examining church policy regarding its schools.

Ross also found that the primary motivation for white withdrawals from public schools was opposition to mandatory reassignment to another school rather than opposition to desegregation per se. He found nothing to indicate that the transfers were based on religious values. Evidence supporting Ross' conclusions is provided by the Cunningham and Hirsh (1979) study of white flight in Louisville. The authors interviewed parents who transferred their children to parochial and private schools and concluded that the decision of parents was clearly related to the desegregation plan. They were unable to determine whether it was based on a concern for the welfare of their children, a desire to avoid the inconvenience of busing and provide for a better education for their children, or symptomatic racism. It is interesting to note that in Louisville only one out of five parents who transferred their children to parochial schools mentioned religion as an important consideration in their decision (Cunningham, 1980).

On its face, therefore, public school students who transfer to parochial schools do so for reasons other than those that historically have justified the existence of Catholic schools. The fact that these parochial schools provide an escape route or alternative to public schools should be tempered by Ross' evidence that where parochial schools do not exist other options are found or created. The use of any such options—parochial schools, private schools, and even the Metropolitan Council for Educational Opportunity (METCO) programs—by parents who hitherto were not attracted to them increases the likelihood of undermining public education. Efforts to stabilize and improve public education are neutralized or weakened by the withdrawal of children by their concerned parents. Many of these children have high academic ability and strong motivation and are self-disciplined. Their loss to the public schools is not only a numerical one, but one that exacerbates the crisis of confidence in the public schools. Teachers, administrators, public school students, and parents are all at least indirectly affected by these defections. The initial problems of public schools are in this fashion compounded and seemingly rendered intractable.

CATHOLIC SCHOOLS: THE EXEMPLARY IMAGE

So far we have drawn a connection between the Catholic school and the problem of public education strictly in terms of an historical accident regarding the availability of space in Catholic schools that occurred at a time when parents were desperately seeking an alternative to the public schools. This is, however, only one side of the coin. The other side reveals the image of Catholic schools as exemplary. Catholic schools, because of their perceived quality, are an attractive alternative to Catholic families who traditionally were, or might have become, patrons of the public schools.

Over the years Catholic schools have been stereotyped as consisting of uniformed, no-nonsense nuns, uniformed children, strict discipline codes, and a good solid grounding in the basics. In the late 1970s a group of characteristics, in many ways resembling the stereotypes associated with Catholic schools, emerged in the school effectiveness literature as characteristic of exemplary schools: These include a strong academic press, a high incidence of engagement in academic activities, high educational aspirations on the part of students, good attendance, regular homework, rigorous subjects, and strict disciplinary standards. In fact these same characteristics were identified by Coleman, Hoffer, and Kilgore (1982) as associated with the higher average achievement levels of Catholic school students relative to public school students. Coleman and his associates failed to emphasize that research shows this same set of characteristics also differentiates exemplary public schools from their less successful counterparts. Nonetheless, the point is that these characteristics have long been the hallmark of parochial schools.

There is a structural reason behind the perception that Catholic schools have characteristics that make them exemplary. The hierarchical nature of the church translates itself into school practice in disciplinary standards that have been strict. Traditionally, obedience has been a central value in Catholic religious and family life. Students who broke or disregarded school rules and regulations could be and were easily dismissed. The authoritarian nature of the church also helped insure that the school principal had the necessary authority to make and enforce rules of conduct on the part of staff, as well as students. These factors helped foster the perception that Catholic schools are consistent, strict, well run, no-nonsense places that did not tolerate verbal abuse of teachers, fighting, drugs, vandalism, truancy, and unruly behavior.

Another manifestation of the authoritarian aspect of the church is that the schools enroll only those students they want, leading to a much more homogeneous student body. The institutional church has always had clear goals for its schools. The American church has, since the Council of Baltimore in 1840, seen the parochial schools as the source of a well-educated Catholic elite that would respect and foster the church's position and authority. As a consequence, parochial schools have traditionally had an academic orientation. The schools became the vehicle for developing large numbers of the professional and leadership elite. There was an additional institutional self-interest here in that the church needed not only an educated lay body but recruits for the priesthood and religious life. This need translated into an academic, college preparatory emphasis in its schools, particularly its high schools. This in turn led to an academic selectivity that large city public schools could match only in elite examination schools.

In summary, the Catholic connections to the problems of public schools, however real, should not be exaggerated. They are the results of coincidence and not of design. The church did not publicize the problems of public schools and, unlike some other denominational and nondenominational groups, she neither established nor expanded facilities to capitalize on the market of students looking for options to public schools. The undramatic facts are the following: The parochial schools were there; they had competent staffs and they had a reputation for both disciplined and quality education. The more dramatic fact is that they had real fiscal and enrollment concerns. By any other name the problems of public schools represented a windfall to the Catholic school system; a windfall to be welcomed and perhaps not examined too critically.

THE POLICY DIMENSIONS

The availability of the parochial schools alternative and the perception that embodied exemplary characteristics combined to insert the parochial schools into the analysis of the problems of public schools. While regional and other factors influence the importance of Catholic connections, the extent to which they are a part of the public school problem gives policy decisions confronting Catholic school officials significant implications for the public sector.

Initially it is important to note that in their decision to establish parochial schools, American Catholics not only exercised a Constitutional right but also provided educational alternatives that both witness our social and cultural pluralism as a society and provide an educationally competitive model for public schools. The relevant policy decisions, therefore, are not directed to the issues of either the existence or the quality of parochial schools. They are policy questions rooted in the realities of the changing American Catholic scene, realities of large proportions that have both indirect and direct connections to the problems of public schools.

Probably the most important and most immediate policy decision confronting American Catholics is that capsuled in Mary Perkins Ryan's (1964) *Are Parochial Schools the Answer?* This timely question does not challenge the Catholic church's institutional responsibility to socialize its members to the values, attitudes, and patterns of behavior expressive of its religious belief system. It does raise policy questions about the priority status of the parochial school system in the contemporary Catholic American scene and its relationship to the church's educational mission. These are complex issues that involve considerations of principle and practicality as they relate directly to the future of parochial schools and indirectly to the problems of public education.

On the level of principle at least, three policy decisions confronting Catholic Americans have significance for the problems of public schools. The most general of these decisions involves the declining priority status of parochial schools vis-à-vis other system needs. Issues such as peace, poverty, and social justice are increasingly highlighted as priority concerns among almost all strata of the church membership. Their prominence in episcopal statements and in the apostolates of priests, religious and laity, are clear evidences of a broader, more ecumenical and international orientation. The Catholic elementary and secondary schools still have their defenders, but even they recognize the changed conditions and the changing order of priorities. Uncertainty concerning the priority to be given to parochial schools complicates any projections regarding their future status and their relationship to the problems of public schools. In policy terms the dilemma is deepened by pragmatic considerations. The social and religious sources of the enrollment crisis during the 1960s and 1970s have not gone away. In addition, the exodus of religious teachers from parochial schools not only has eliminated a powerful symbol of religious education but also has forced the hiring of more highly paid lay teachers. The resulting higher tuition costs, declining birthrate, and inflation have all worked to reduce the market for parochial schools. These factors have emerged in a context that no longer equates parochial schools with religious education and provides further substance to the question of whether parochial schools can and should be maintained.

At a more specific level, another dilemma is posed when both Catholic and non-Catholic children, presumably seeking to escape integrated public schooling, apply for admission as transfer students to parochial schools. The official position of the church leadership is to resist such transfer requests. Typical of this position is the statement by the Archdiocesan Board of Education of St. Paul, Minnesota. It reads:

> Catholic schools must be responsive to their role in intergrating communities by forcefully attacking the racist attitudes and actions of society so as to bring about the desired structural and attitudinal changes. It is incumbent therefore on every board of education to examine their policy of school admissions in the light of the social teachings of the Church. Any action which furthers racial segregation is in opposition to the very essence of the Christian School. (National Catholic Bishops Conference, 1972, p. 389)

Such statements often prefaced guidelines on admission to parochial schools. The Saint Paul guideline again is typical when it flatly states, "When a student seeks to transfer to a Catholic school solely to avoid integration, such admission should be denied"(p. 389).

Not surprisingly the administrative measures designed to screen out such students have been only partially successful. Some parishes no doubt worked to reduce the numbers transferring into parochial schools. Other parishes under the pressures of rising school costs, empty seats, and pleading parents, interpreted the transfer guidelines more loosely. Thus, in the Boston case, the director of Catholic education is quoted as saying that the entry of students (fleeing the 1974 federal court order desegregating Boston's schools at normal entry points, first or ninth grades) could not be prevented "without announcing that Catholic schools were going out of business" (Franklin, 1983, p. A4).

In this short-term situation the policy options available to the church were neither simple nor attractive. Denying Catholic children the option of transferring from public to parochial schools prevented the opportunity for more intense religious socialization and for a strong financial condition. Accepting them, on the other hand, lent support to racial segregation and drew off some of the more academically talented and responsible students from the public schools.

A third dilemma confronting the Church leadership that has implications for public schools involves the question of where the limited school personnel and financial resources might best be invested. The special problems of central city schools located in areas now largely populated by non-Catholic blacks is a case in point. In many of these areas parochial schools that once served the children of Catholic immigrants have been closed. And public schools in these areas are often rated among the poorest. The National Office for Black Catholics in a statement submitted to the American Catholic Bishop's Conference dramatically describes the policy dilemma:

> It must baffle us, then, and certainly many others, to see the Catholic Church put a "for Catholics only" label on its schools, to give the presence of "non-Catholics" as the reason for not maintaining schools. What church officials must also understand and understand well, is that the dismantling of Catholic educational institutions under this philosophy is to give unmistakably clear notice to all black people—Catholics and non-Catholics—where its priorities are: the white suburban population. In our estimation, that is not even for the good of the Catholic community. (National Catholic Bishop's Conference, 1976, p. 530)

On the other hand, the acceptance by parochial schools of these public school children, Catholic and non-Catholic, has dysfunctional consequences for the public sector. Their acceptance and enrollment may indirectly and unintentionally function to underwrite an immoral racism. It also may deepen the educational and financial plight of the public schools in which the majority of children, Catholic and non-Catholic, are being educated. Furthermore, many Catholic parishioners with children in public schools are unwilling to see their financial contributions used to subsidize the education not only of Catholic children from other parishes but of non-Catholic children as well. The irony that does not escape many parishoners is that their public school sons and daughters receive a dollar value return of about 1 hour a week of religious education.

In sum, the short-term policy questions posed for the Catholic church relative to public schools place her in the position of being "damned if she does and damned if she doesn't." But the decisions arrived at that redefine the priority status of parochial schools, define their relationships to racial segregation, and specify their role in the problem-ridden, non-Catholic, nonwhite central city areas, have direct and indirect implications for many problems of public schools.

The issue of the Catholic connection to the problems of public schools is joined at a more comprehensive policy level in the church's perception and posture toward public education. Historically, the public school as carried a pejorative connotation among many Catholics. In many parishes the Catholic children who attended public school—referred to as the "publics"—were treated as second-class parochial citizens. Today, the very numbers of Catholic children in public schools constitute realities that cannot be denied. Still, public education and public schools seem to constitute a kind of terra incognita for many church officials and Catholic parents. Sporadically, it is true, proposals regarding sex education, school prayer, and religious holidays may provoke clerical and lay reactions. But for the most part public schools seem to be nonexistent or to be the places out of which large numbers of Catholic children appear for their once-a-week religious education training. Parochial school teachers, students, and parents generally maintain a posture of conspicuous nonconcern about public schools.

This nonrecognition of public schools may be the most significant Catholic connection to the problems of public schools. And it is an interesting and selective area for nonchurch involvement. On numerous occasions the pastoral voice of the American Catholic Bishop's Conference has been heard in the exercise of its public responsibility relating to poverty, nuclear arms, housing, crime, racism, and the like. But seldom does that voice express much in the nature of episcopal interest in the problems of public schools in spite of the fact that the vast majority of Catholic children are educated in public school systems. Indeed, atypical in this respect is a statement of the Catholic Bishops of Florida:

> We, the Catholic bishops of the state of Florida, wish to address ourselves briefly to this current problem in a pastoral way expressing great concern for the maintenance of our public-education system and encouraging our Catholic citizens to continue support of their public schools. In view of the problems of the moment it is essential that citizens of every religious persuasion and no religious persuasion unite behind a strong public-education system.
>
> We encourage all our Catholic people and citizens of good will everywhere in our great state to continue to support public schools. It is not likely that there will be a better way in the future of providing for the educational needs of the vast majority of our children. (National Catholic Bishop's Conference, 1980, p. 366)

Such a public endorsement of public schools by a regional body of Catholic church leaders is striking because of its solitary character. Too often a socially responsible interest in the problems of public schools has been deflected by a preoccupation with the in-house problems of parochial schools. A cynic might well say that Catholic parochial schools have a vested interest in the problems of public schools, that they prosper to some degree when the criticism mounts against public education. Such a view overlooks, however, the statistical realities of the public schools as the educational home of the vast majority of Catholic children. From this viewpoint there is reason to conclude that to the degree church officials and Catholic citizens are not concerned with the problems of public schools they are both acting against their own self-interest and defaulting on an important social and moral responsibility. The Catholic nonconnection to the problems of public schools may, indeed, be strategically more significant than the more immediate connections earlier described.

CONCLUSIONS

Against this background two different scenarios with quite different implications for the public schools may be projected. The optimistic scenario in some Catholic circles describes the recent enrollment stabilization as the onset of a new golden age for parochial schools. This image is further enhanced by the anticipated birthrate boom and by hopes for a revival of religious spirit. On the political side, passage of some form of voucher legislation fuels the hopes of many Catholic officials. Clearly, this scenario would compound the problems of public schools. Accordingly, church leaders must give careful consideration to the more immediate consequences on public schools of any support for voucher legislation, and they must not allow any such immediate windfall to obscure more fundamental questions regarding her institutional investment in parochial schools. Catholic Americans in the 1980s must still ask, Does the church have the need, the resources, and the personnel to maintain a parochial school system serving a clear minority of Catholic children?

In other circles the pessimistic scenario recognizes the problems posed for parochial schools by rising inflation, shrinking parish incomes, obsolete buildings, and a continuing decline in religious vocations. In a larger context, even these realities may pale in importance when compared to the multiple theological and ecclesiastical problems confronted by the church. For example, it is projected that in the very near future in some large urban dioceses there will not be enough priests to assign even one priest to every parish.

This possible future confronts church leaders with the need to reevaluate the larger educational apostolate of the church and the question whether the church should and could maintain a parochial school system. Too often Catholic education has been equated with Catholic schools. This equation needs to be examined very critically.

While some parochial schools may survive the fundamental changes outlined in this view, the more likely occurrence is the evolution of parochial schools into private schools with little or no official church connection. In this scenario the public schools may be beneficiaries if they can overcome the factors contributing to their present crises of confidence. In any event it is likely that the Catholic church will be less a part of the problem of American public education.

In conclusion, three points should be emphasized. First, the empirical evidence of parochial school connections to the problems of public schools is in need of more research and elaboration. Second, there are connections between parochial education and the problems of public schools, but this does not constitute an indictment. The connections are the result of coincidences and neglect, not design. Third, these connections raise short- and long-term policy questions regarding the future of Catholic education and its relationship to both parochial and public schools.

REFERENCES

Bailey, S. K. (1981). Political coalitions for public education. *Daedalaus, 110*, 27–43.
Cohen, D. K., & Neufeld, B. (1981). The failure of high schools and the progress of education. *Daedalus, 110*, 69–89.
Coleman, J. S., Hoffer, T., & Kilgore, S. (1982). *High school achievement: Public, Catholic, and private schools compared.* New York: Basic.
Cunningham, G. K., and Hirsh, W. L. (1979, April). *A metropolitan desegregation plan: Where the white students went.* Paper presented at the American Educational Association meeting, San Francisco.
Cunningham, G. K. (1980, April). *Parents who avoid busing: Attitudes and characteristics.* Paper presented at the American Educational Research Association meeting, Boston.
Donovan, J. D., Erickson, D. A., & Madaus, G. F. (1971). *The social and religious sources of the crisis in Catholic schools.* (Report) Washington, DC: President's Commission on School Finance.
Franklin, J. (1983, October 8). Making choices for Boston: Selection of Medeiros studied anew. *Boston Sunday Globe,* p. A4.
Madaus, G. F., Airasian, P., & Kellaghan, T. (1980). *School effectiveness: A reassessment of the evidence.* New York: McGraw-Hill.
Madaus, G. F., & Linnan, R. (1973). The outcome of Catholic education? *School Review, 81*(2), 207–232.
National Catholic Bishop's Conference. (1972). Integration guideline. *Origins, 2*, 389.
National Catholic Bishop's Conference. (1976). The collapse of Catholic schools in the black community. *Origins, 5*, 528–532.
National Catholic Bishop's Conference. (1980). Support expressed for public schools. *Origins, 10*, 366.
National Catholic Educational Association. (1970). *A statistical report on Catholic elementary and secondary schools for the years 1967-68, 1969-70.* Washington, DC: Author.
National Catholic Educational Association. (1971). *A report on U.S. Catholic Schools: 1970-71.* Washington, DC: Author.
National Catholic Educational Association. (1972). *U.S. Catholic schools: 1971-72.* Washington, DC: Author.
National Catholic Educational Association. (1974). *U.S. Catholic schools: 1973-74.* Washington, DC: Author.
National Catholic Educational Association. (1981). *Catholic schools in America: Elementary/secondary.* Englewood, CO: Fisher.
Ross, J. M. (1981). *On court-ordered school desegregation.* Washington, DC: Statement presented at hearings before the Senate Subcommittee on Separation of Powers of the Senate Judiciary Committee.
Ryan, M. P. (1964). *Are parochial schools the answer?* New York: Holt, Rinehart.
Thomas, W. I. (1923). *The unadjusted girl.* Boston: Little, Brown & Co.

PART II

Research Approaches

CHAPTER 4

An Examination of 10 Years of Research on Exemplary Schools

Gilbert R. Austin and Stephen P. Holowenzak

INTRODUCTION

After at least 2000 years of educating young children in the home, in schools, and in the work place, educators still frequently complain that almost nothing is really known about effective education processes. These complaints far too often become a rationalization for the failure of education and an excuse for the quick adoption (and equally rapid rejection) of new educational innovations.

The professional concern of educators since earliest times has been the improvement of knowledge about effectiveness. There is a good deal of evidence to suggest that we are past the age of innocence and can no longer pretend that we are not aware of which things work in education. This chapter documents the fact that we know a great deal about how to educate our children effectively and how to bring about the excellence in education that the researchers seek.

In the chorus of voices criticizing American education today, one of the most prominent themes is the call for excellence. This call is documented in several national studies that have evaluated the status of public school systems throughout the country. Among these studies are the following: *High School* (Boyer, 1983); *A Nation at Risk: The Imperative for National Reform* (National Commission on Excellence in Education, 1983); *Action for Excellence* (Education Commission of the States, 1983);

65

Educating Americans for the 21st Century (National Science Board, 1983); *Making the Grade* (Twentieth Century Fund, 1983); and *The Condition of Teaching* (Feistritzer, 1983). The general tenor of these reports indicates that the nation and the public schools are in trouble.

Bloom (1972) has pointed out repeatedly that under appropriate learning conditions it is only the rate at which most children learn that differs—not the level which the students achieve or the basic capacity to learn. Some theorists would suggest that repeated success in school over a number of years increases the probability of increased self-esteem among students, while repeated failure or low-performance levels increases the probability of negative self-images and low self-esteem.

Human beings are capable of meaningful change; human intelligence is not immutable. Feuerstein, Rand, Hoffman, & Miller (1980), after 30 years of work with children in Israel, are convinced that schools must shift from static measures of ability that encourage giving up on some children to dynamic assessments that point the way to sharpening even the slowest children's mental skills. The research reported in this chapter builds on Feuerstein *et al.'s* concept of mediated learning experiences. Mediated learning experiences are human interactions that facilitate the capacity of an individual to change, to modify him or herself in the direction of greater adaptability. The same belief can be held for school personnel. They, too, can change their behavior. Schools can provide a set of mediated learning experiences for children that will lead to higher levels of achievement than could otherwise be found. Schools that provide this kind of learning experience for children are commonly called effective, or exemplary. These schools are lighthouses of excellence that the reports cited earlier call for.

Much of the research on effective schools has been stimulated by James Coleman's report, *Equality of Educational Opportunity* (Coleman *et al.*, 1966). Prior to the time of this study, people believed that schools were generally effective though there was some concern for equity. The function of educational research was largely to discover methods to fine-tune what was held to be basically sound. Curiously, at least some of the effect of Coleman's report was due to a misinterpretation of his findings. Coleman did not conclude that schools fail to make important contributions to student achievement. Rather, he concluded that schools promote and facilitate great amounts of learning. He also concluded that differences between schools in promoting unusual levels of achievement were not striking, and most of these differences were more readily explained by family background than by the characteristics of schools themselves. The Coleman study resulted from a Justice Department request to identify and document willful discrimination in education.

The findings resulted in far more encompassing and disappointing revelations than were expected.

At about the same time, in England, the Minister of Education called for a comprehensive study of primary education and the transition from primary to secondary education. The resulting Plowden Report, named after the study-group director, Lady Bridgit Plowden, used the volumes of data it collected through interviews, school visits, and questionnaires to conclude essentially the same as Coleman: The strong independent effect of school on the lives of children does not exist (Plowden, 1967).

In the years since the Coleman and Plowden reports, research on education in the United States has taken a roller coaster path in its attempts to identify and understand the characteristics of schooling that will most benefit the nation's children. That journey has ventured from despair over the belief that education has little effect on what happens to children, particularly the disadvantaged, to a more hopeful view that the best of American schools, from all socioeconomic areas, have significant lessons to offer about what makes schooling work.

THE MARYLAND STUDY

This chapter looks at the evolution of research since Coleman and Plowden and at important new findings for the future. It examines exemplary schools research and offers approaches for improving schools at both the elementary and secondary levels. It is based in large part on a longitudinal study of 30 elementary schools in Maryland. The initial report of the study was titled *Process Evaluation: A Comprehensive Study of Outliers* (Austin, 1978). First, we look at how the outlier schools were identified, and then we examine the characteristics that distinguished them. Finally, we give our opinion on how such findings ought to be utilized in other schools.

Data from 3 years of statewide testing (1972–73, 1973–74, and 1974–75) based on the administration of the Cognitive Abilities Test (CAT) and the Iowa Test of Basic Skills (ITBS) were used to identify 30 Maryland outlier schools. Using the school average as the unit of observation, four of the achievement subtest scores (vocabulary, reading comprehension, language total, and mathematics total) on the ITBS were regressed against the school average Standard Age Scores (SAS), a measure of academic ability obtained from the CAT. This regression analysis permitted a transformation of the original distribution of grade equivalents (GE) among the schools to a new "residual" distribution for which the among-school variance in achievement GEs, due to variance in SAS among the schools, had been removed. Given a school's average SAS, that school's position in the residual distribution was determined by finding the school's "expected" or "Maryland norm" GE and subtracting the school's obtained GE from it. The difference is called the school's "residual grade equivalent" and interpreted as an indicator of the school's relative standing in achievement on the subtest, with SAS taken into account or "controlled." In effect, student variation in ability, much of which is usually associated with social class and other out-of-school factors, was removed statistically. Now a school's average achievement was due to school effects.

This residual distribution of GEs formed an important focal point of the process evaluation study. It was the purpose of this study to probe the meaning for a school that finds itself at either extreme of the residual distribution in terms of process quality indicators.

> The word "process" refers to everything which intervenes between inputs and outputs; from curriculum goals and objectives to how teachers conduct their classes; from the nature of the principal's leadership style to the students' classroom behavior. In short, process evaluation considers the entire educational enterprise in action. (Maryland State Department of Education, 1976, p. 653)

The regression model for the research described above came from a proposal by Henry Dyer (1966) and takes into account difficult-to-change socioeconomic status and student-input-performance variables over which the school has little control when predicting student performance. The difficult-to-change conditions include student, home, and community characteristics related to achievement that are not under the direct control of the school. The most common method of applying Dyer's model is regression–residuals analysis, whereby mean values of predictor variables are used to predict mean output achievement.

Dyer (1966) hypothesized that each school develops a set of norms, evaluations, and expectations characterizing the achievement expected of students, in general, and of specific student subgroups within the school. While different norms, expectations, and evaluations for the various groups and individual students within a school account for some variation within the school, Dyer hypothesized that there are differences in the subcultures of schools that also explain differences in achievement between schools.

A study by Klitgaard and Hall (1973) raised important questions about the focus of education research at that time. Noting that large-scale statistical evaluations had failed to identify any important and consistent school effects, they suggested that education researchers look in different places for evidence of school effectiveness. While previous studies generally indicated that school policies did not significantly affect measurable student scholastic and occupational performance, Klitgaard and Hall believed other schools existed that would show different results. The mathematics of prior studies allowed for such a possibility, as long as the number of exceptions to the general findings was not large (Klitgaard & Hall, 1973, p. 147).

To test their theory, Klitgaard and Hall, using Dyer's basic idea, examined six data sets identified by searches for exemplary schools. Using data from Michigan and New York City elementary schools, Project Talent, New York State school districts, New York State schools, and Project Yardstick, the researchers identified groups of overachieving schools that comprised between 2 and 9% of various data samples. They characterized these schools as "statistically unusual." Whether the same schools can also be described as unusually effective depends on one's subjective scale of magnitude. The authors concluded that moving away from average effects in educational research and policy-making was warranted, stating that they had located schools and districts that consistently performed better than their peers.

A learning theory underlying Klitgaard and Hall's research is that the behavior of children in school, including their achievement in academic subjects, is a reflection, in part, of the unspoken expectation of the school. The children learn to behave in ways that the people with whom they interact and who are important to them expect and define as appropriate and proper for them. Individual students thus come to perceive the norms, expectations, values, and beliefs that are considered relevant for them as they interact with others in the social system of the school.

This relatively simple set of assumptions and relationships forms the cornerstone of our research on exemplary schools. The most important assumption is that expectations about achievement and social behavior held by the principal, other administrators, and teachers strongly affect student achievement and social behavior. Too often schools derive their perception of students' achievement from the general nature of the school community, in particular the socioeconomic and racial composition of the student body. Teachers, administrators, and others involved in the school social system communicate their perception of appropriate and proper achievement and their expectations and assessments of students through informal interaction with students and with each other. In turn, the students pick up on the norms and expectations of the school staff and school community and use these in forming their own beliefs about what is appropriate and attainable for them. This interactive process significantly affects the nature of student achievement.

What makes exceptional schools different from average or poorly performing schools is the leadership style, teachers and teaching practices, instructional emphases, and parental and community involvement, and how these resources are used. The author believes that they become mediating structures. Dr. David Elkind (1982) noted that it is (1) the beliefs that children hold about themselves and their abilities, built in those children by the adults with whom they interact, and (2) the mediating structures, the judgments and comments of adults, insights shared with the child, and interpretations of what is being seen and talked about that have the greatest impact on the child. Purkey and Smith (Chapter 9, this volume) identify two broad groups of mediating structures—organization and process. The reader is encouraged to review this chapter with great care since it identifies 13 characteristics under those two categories. The development of personal value systems provides an excellent example of the effects of mediating structures. Children are born without values. They learn values from their parents, other adults, and social systems through adult interpretation of hundreds of situations shared by the adult and child. The child comes into contact with adults who constantly mediate the material that is presented to the child and the situation encountered by the child. A similar process occurs in exceptional schools. A surprisingly high number of mediated learning experiences in exemplary schools are presented to the child in a positive sense, particularly as they reflect on the child's self-concept of his or her ability to interpret the situation and to gain some insight into his or her own competence in a variety of areas.

The authors believe that exemplary school leaders accomplish their mission of schooling using variations of the theories of mediated learning experiences and mediated structures even though those terms may be unfamiliar to them. Summarizing the findings of 10 years of longitudinal study, we would say that great schools are being run as opposed to running. Exceptional schools have a purpose as opposed to being purposeless. If a school is purposeless it doesn't mean that the people aren't working hard; it does mean that they have not gotten together and agreed, "This is the way we do it in our school." It is a creation of a sense of fellowship. There is a sense of being a member of a warm, supportive family that is the hallmark of exemplary or unusually successful schools. You can almost take as a generalization the opposite of that for schools that are not successful. It is important that strong families sometimes strongly disagree, but following the resolution of the disagreement, they continue to work together. How does this happen? How do you create a family feeling in a school?

THE IMPORTANCE OF LEADERSHIP IN
CREATING AN EFFECTIVE SCHOOL

Our research indicates that there is one person who is normally very important in the creation of that atmosphere—commonly the principal, although not always. Because this is a longitudinal study, we have looked at 30 schools over a 10-year period. One school was and continues to be a very good school. We thought that the principal in that school was a real "hotshot." The superintendent moved that principal from the great school to a school that was in trouble, with the mandate to turn the school around. Not only did the principal not turn the school around, but he flunked the job so badly that he is now the director of bus transportation! When you looked at the school more carefully, you found that our generalizations were still true; there was someone in that school who was making it run, but it was the reading specialist, not the principal (Austin, 1984).

It takes a long time to be sensitive to these nuances. Leadership is important and it has to be exerted by someone or a group of somebodies. What is the essence of this leadership? The leaders tend to have very high expectations for themselves, for their teachers, for their children, and for anyone else associated with the school. These high expectations are not transmitted in the form of "You must do better." They are transmitted or mediated always in a positive sense of "I know you can do better, you can help, these children can learn." The major "no-no" in exceptional schools is to assume that it's the child's fault. That is the one thing that the principals of most of these great schools will not accept. It is a challenge to the administration and to the faculty to find out how to succeed with the child rather than saying that it's the child's fault, that he or she cannot succeed. Our longitudinal study repeatedly documents Bloom's (1972) belief that most children can master much more than we believe they can if given more time.

Now, how does a principal do this? He or she doesn't do it by sitting in the back of the class with paper and pencil to do an observation. What he or she does do is to move constantly through the school and observe what is going on and offer to assist. Rarely do these people tell you how to do it. They more commonly say "I think I have some ideas about how we can be more successful with Johnny or Mary in doing this arithmetic lesson; why don't you let me come in and try; then, let's talk about it and work at it together." What a difference from, "I am the principal giving the orders and you're to do it!" It is a relationship where it is all right for the principal or the teacher to fail; it is not a judgmental situation. We note that the best of our principals spend substantial amounts of time—as much as 50%—conferring about instruction with their teachers instead of spending that time in their offices. Our study suggests that the principal can choose to be an instructional leader or an administrative leader. Principals in the exceptionally good schools choose to be instructional leaders first and administrative leaders second. An important question employers ought to be asking candidates for a principalship is "How are you going to win your way into the classrooms of your teachers?" It is in the classroom that the difference is made.

Jane Hannaway and Susan Abramowitz (Chapter 2, this volume) have done a study funded by National Institute of Education, that compares the behavior of principals in private schools and public schools. One of the really key factors is that principals in private schools almost never do formal observations. What they do is spend a great deal of time in the classrooms talking, sharing, and demonstrating their own skills, and helping other teachers become great teachers. They don't sit back and observe a great deal; they are active participants. Through this process of active participation they create great teachers and great students because they transmit to their colleagues and to the students a high level of expectation about what they expect. They expect success and they get it.

These observations of leadership behavior lead us to a theory that explains why exemplary schools are exemplary. We call our theory mediating structures or mediating learning experiences. It draws heavily on the research of Feuerstein et al. (1980) and Elkind (1982). This theory states that most of the beliefs that we hold about ourselves are the result of other people's interpretations of common experiences passed on to us. The best example we can think of is the question of prejudice. We were all born without prejudices. We learned prejudices; in most cases, the prejudices were not taught to us, they were interpreted (mediated) to us. For example, a mother is walking with her children when she is approached on the same side of the street by someone who is a stranger to her. The stranger may be dressed strangely or acting strangely; something about that experience causes the mother some anxiety. She tightens her grip on the child's hand and walks across the street. No words are exchanged but a million messages are transmitted. We believe it is this constant transmission of messages about a person's behavior, particularly by teachers and by the schools, that causes people to believe what they believe to be true about themselves.

A good example in school is the teaching of mathematics. One of the things exemplary teachers at junior and senior high schools work hardest to accomplish is convincing the students that they can master this subject. Earlier teachers have, through mediated experiences, convinced these students that mathematics is challenging and frightening. The students didn't come into the world believing that they were poor mathematicians. It is statistically impossible, for instance, that females should believe themselves to be poor mathematicians as consistently as they do when all the research evidence suggests that genetically they are as able as males. Females believe they are poor mathematicians because in a thousand experiences people have interpreted for them that they cannot excel in mathematics.

Recent technology offers interesting opportunities to provide students with positive mediated learning experiences. Computer-related learning offers great possibilities for more generally rewarding learning experiences. A surprising thing about computers is that everyone thought that they were going to dehumanize education; as a matter of fact, they apparently are having exactly the opposite effect. They have a humanizing effect on education because children are not punished verbally for their incorrect answers. The computer simply says quietly that they got it wrong and offers them another chance without any judgment. In addition, we have found, in terms of computers, that students in groups learn more than single learners. We find that putting two or three children at a computer terminal is more effective than having one child sit there by him or herself in grand isolation. Why? Because the students tend to mediate for each other. The noise level is probably greater in exceptional schools that allow children to work together at terminals and some teachers don't like that, but the learning curves are markedly higher (Austin, 1984).

One of the major factors about exemplary schools, then, is that the teachers in them tend to have very high expectations for the children, for themselves, and for the school. Because they tend to mediate most of the experiences that they share with their colleagues and their students in a positive way, they create a climate in that school that suggests it is a place where you are going to succeed. The people who run these exceptional schools, commonly the principals, tend to be people who hold strong opinions and beliefs about curriculum content. They have advanced degrees in important curriculum areas such as reading or mathematics (Austin, 1978). One difference about these schools is that they tend to recruit their own staffs. We think that one of the best criteria that you might use to judge an exceptional school in your county would be to ask the principal of the school to show you the waiting list they have of people who want to teach at their school. Just as teachers know intuitively who are the really great teachers in their schools, they also know the best schools in the district. Exceptional schools have waiting lists of people who want to transfer into them.

Leithwood and Montgomery (Chapter 8, this volume) describe in some detail a research methodology most useful for finding and describing increasingly effective principal characteristics. The reader will notice certain similarities in what follows.

When we state that exceptional schools frequently have waiting lists, we are told that principals and faculty cannot choose their own staff. In our study we asked two principals how they chose new teachers. The principal of a rather poor school said, "You have little choice in this system. The central administration sends you several candidates and you choose the one you like the most." He said, "They sent me three applicants and I liked the second one, so I hired her." In an exceptional school in the same county, the principal learned he was going to have a vacancy in the third grade. He assembled his second-grade teachers and asked them what characteristics were most needed in a third-grade teacher. He then gathered the third-grade teachers and asked them the same question. He sought to identify present strengths and weaknesses. Subsequently, he met with the parents and shared the list with them. The final list had 17 characteristics. Fourteen teachers were interviewed before they found the one they wanted. Having documented his case well and having the support of his faculty and parent group, this exceptional principal had little difficulty in arguing for the kind of faculty member he sought (Austin, 1978).

In the exceptional schools that we studied, parents play an important and integral part. They feel their opinions are valued and they are involved in important decisions that affect the lives of their children. Principals who have high expectations for parents, teachers, and children must demonstrate this by involving them in meaningful ways.

In the questionnaire that we designed for our study, we asked the children in third through sixth grade, "Do you think you do well in school because of hard work or luck?" The students in the exceptional schools answered that it was because of hard work; children in poorer schools suggested it depended upon luck. It was surprising to us that a child could have internalized the concept as early as third grade that either he controls his destiny or it is in the hands of others. That is a very impressive finding (Austin, 1978).

EXEMPLARY SECONDARY SCHOOLS

The findings described thus far come primarily from research on elementary schools. A primary source of information on secondary schools and their effect is a 5-year study of 12 representative inner-city London schools conducted by Rutter, Maughan, Mortimore, Ousten, and Smith (1979). Most American elementary school research focuses narrowly on achievement in basic skills, primarily reading and mathematics, as both program goals and measures of success. The Rutter team examined a range of secondary school outcomes including attendance, school behavior, and delinquency, as well as academic achievement. They found program objectives in secondary schools more diverse, noting that secondary schools have many purposes for all students and different purposes for different groups of students. Program focus may be on college preparation or vocational training or on a general or terminal academic education. Measuring such different goals presents definition problems in the research.

The overall findings relative to the question of leadership, however, are quite clear. At the secondary school level, leadership is as important as it is at the elementary school level. High expectations on the part of the principal or department chairman were very important; where the expectations were high there were significant correlations between school scores, attendance, and academic outcomes. The Rutter team also reported that all forms of reward, praise, or appreciation tended to be associated with better school outcomes. Positive rewards seemed to be a much stronger mediating influence on students' behavior than negative or punitive reinforcement (Rutter et al., 1979).

A report, City High Schools (Ford Foundation, 1984), comes to a similar set of conclusions about the importance of leadership. It states:

> Schools where faculty and other staff cooperated—acting more like a team than as separate departments or services—were better able to cope with problems and to implement school improvements. Schools with principals who had ongoing training and development in instructional leadership performed better than those where such training was not available. Schools that have been able to sustain systematic and ongoing inservice or staff development programs for teachers demonstrated markedly better efforts in instruction and subsequent achievements in student learning (p. 67).

James Coleman and colleagues (Coleman, Hoffer, & Kilgore, 1982) found that schools do affect student achievement and that some schools are more effective than others. In particular, they concluded that on the average, private schools are more effective in promoting academic achievement than public schools. The distinguishing variables are interesting. Coleman and his colleagues argue that school order, discipline, regular homework, and high levels of teacher involvement as well as high levels of expectation in terms of academic and behavioral success are important attributes of the achieving private high school. These researchers believe such attributes could also improve the performance of public high school students.

This information suggests that leadership on the part of the principal or the administration in secondary schools is as important as it has proven to be in the elementary school. High levels of expectation, positive interpretation of those expectations, and active involvement in the instructional process seem at all levels of schooling to lead to the same result: higher levels of achievement and attainment of positive social behavior on the part of the students.

TEACHERS IN EXEMPLARY SCHOOLS

Now let us turn our attention to exemplary school teachers and their characteristics. (For a broad, general treatment, see Chapter 7, by Berliner, this volume.) Our longitudinal research indicates the following generalizations to be true about the abilities of teachers in exceptional schools. They tend to be among the most able teachers in the school system. They are dedicated to their profession and interested in taking courses associated with higher levels of attainment in their discipline. They generally demonstrate high proficiency in verbal skills, have substantial educational backgrounds, are experienced teachers (i.e., more than 5 years), believe that they have achieved employment status, and have job satisfaction. They have high academic and behavioral expectations for the pupils. These expectations are transmitted or mediated much more commonly in a positive context than in a negative context. The teachers have better class control with less overt effort, they are supported in their expectations by the principal who, as we have already indicated, tends to be an instructional leader rather than an administrative leader. He spends a surprising amount of his time in the classroom acting as a colleague to the teacher in working on educational problems, so the teacher commonly is perceived by the principal as a working colleague and not as one in the traditionally inferior role. Teachers in exceptional schools tend to have good relationships with parents and believe that parent–teacher interaction is important and is to be encouraged. These teachers tend to use grouping procedures that emphasize small instructional groups for reading and mathematics and use the whole group approach for other subjects such as social studies, science, and health.

One of the important factors identified in our research on exceptional schools as it concerned teachers was the question of in-service or staff development training. Exceptionally good schools tend to provide in-service education in a rather different way from that found in less successful schools. The method of in-service education, perhaps not surprisingly, is again developed on a group basis. The principal and his teachers get together and discuss or identify areas where they feel some assistance is needed. Then, having identified the area, they request help from the central administration or other sources to address that specific issue. In-service education is not seen as simply inviting some well-known proponent of a particular point of view to make a presentation. They themselves identify the area of their interest first and then seek help in that area. It is not surprising, therefore, that staff development is seen quite positively in these schools. It addresses needs identified on the part of the teachers themselves.

That this kind of in-service training works at all levels is documented by the fact that across the country one of the most popular things that state departments of education are doing for their administrators at all levels is to create what are commonly called professional development academies. The state of Maryland has one, and it is extremely success-ful. It is successful primarily because it addresses in-service needs that the administrators themselves have identified and about which they are interested in learning additional information. The state department of education solicits this information in the form of questionnaires sent regularly to the principals. It then brings this material together and, cooperatively with the principals' groups, plans the in-service work-shops. A similar phenomenon can be observed in public schools in the United States as it concerns computers and in-service training. The de-mand for assistance in becoming computer literate has primarily come from the faculties in the schools. School systems that have done the best job of responding to that need have identified clearly the in-service and staff development needs of their faculties concerning the computer, and then they have brought together the human and monetary resources to address those needs.

In summary, exceptional elementary school faculties are (1) experi-enced and stable, (2) tend to have higher degrees of education, (3) have taken more training in general elementary education, and (4) come from a greater diversity of educational backgrounds, both socially and geo-graphically, than do teachers in our less successful schools. The faculties of exceptional schools have a more positive concept about themselves, their schools, and their pupils than do teachers in schools that are less successful. Teachers in successful schools seldom have classes with 30 or more children in them. This finding appears to offer support of the often stated concern of teacher groups suggesting that an important relation-ship exists between class size and student learning. Teachers in exceptional schools also tend to have better relationships with their students' parents, holding more conferences with them and seeing them more commonly at PTA meetings.

Unusually large numbers of children in exceptionally good schools develop a positive self-concept or a feeling that they control their own destiny. These beliefs, we assume, are the result of their mediated experience with the principal, teachers, and their parents. All three groups show that they have high expectations for them, that they believe in them, and indicate that they will help in any way possible for the children to be successful. In exceptional schools this concept is fostered by teachers and administrators planning for their children to have a much higher percentage of successful rather than unsuccessful experiences. While it is useful and beneficial for all of us to fail occasionally, we primarily learn to keep trying and to sustain our efforts at difficult tasks because we have had more successes than failures. The same thing is true of children and their views of themselves and their future opportunities. They tend consistently to have an optimistic, positive concept about themselves and beliefs about their future destiny because they have been exposed primarily to people who believe in them and who have demonstrated the capacity to assist them in being successful in their school work.

This, it seems, is one of the most impressive findings in our continuing work with exceptional schools. These findings are also applicable at the secondary school level. In the Ford Foundation study of city high schools, they say it this way:

> Schools that developed clear, simple standards and rules for students—with student and parent participation—and that applied them consistently and fairly had fewer discipline problems . . . Schools that developed solid working relations with such groups as out-of-school volunteers, local business and industry for career training, colleges and universities for assistance to the more academically talented, and social service agencies that help students "at risk" have shown better results in achievement and improvements in the overall climate for learning. (Ford Foundation, 1984, p. 67)

Rutter *et al.* (1979) believe the most important single factor associated with exceptional high schools that they studied was that the administration, faculty, students, and parents had created a positive ethos in the school that was supportive of the students and their efforts to achieve. Again, we believe that this ethos is not created by preaching, it is created by, or through, hundreds of mediated experiences between the administration, the teachers, the students, the parents, and the community in which they live.

The authors of this chapter have been involved not only in an exemplary schools longitudinal research project, but have also been involved in studies for the state of Maryland juvenile justice system, which is primarily concerned with children 12–18 years old. The findings are documented in a 2-year study (Austin, Garber, & Novalis, 1981, 1982) done for the Maryland State Senate. The mediated-structures model that was used for this study of juvenile institutions was similar to that used in the longitudinal study. We were able to identify in the juvenile system the same kinds of characteristics that we observed in the elementary schools; that is, in the most successful institutions there was a real leader, again generally the principal, who took a very real interest in his or her job, the students, and their achievement. Because of this person's high expectations for him or herself and for the teachers, the students made a great deal of progress.

The same kind of findings were documented by Danzig and Austin when they conducted a study of the contribution of honors programs in higher education at the University of Maryland (Danzig & Austin, 1982). Here they identified two groups of equally able students and followed them for 2 years. The students in one group had chosen to be involved in the honors program; the other equally able students did not choose to be involved. Our findings indicate that those students who chose to be involved in the honors program not only obtained higher levels of achievement, but they took more difficult courses within the same time period than their cohorts. The characteristics that we identified in terms of the honors program seem to be similar to those found at the elementary school level and in the juvenile justice system. The people directing the honors programs have very high levels of expectations about themselves and their fellow professors, and the students tend to respond to this very positively. The concept of expectations and the mediated learning experiences seem to be equally evident at the college level. The same findings are true for great universities where the president of the university takes a strong and dynamic leadership role. Where that doesn't happen within institutions, the chairmen of different departments establish preeminence of their department in the university system because of their own dedication to their scholarly pursuits and the level of expectations they hold for their colleagues and the students who are enrolled in their program.

This conclusion about the importance of leadership is reinforced in terms of the number of professional development academies that are being created across the nation, particularly at the state department of education level. It is the authors' conclusion that the single most important characteristic that leads to the creation and the perpetuation of exemplary schools is the leadership function. Therefore, we ought to be

spending a large amount of time and energy attempting to better understand how we can foster the growth and development of exceptional
leaders for future exceptional schools. We should be studying and developing the theory of mediating structures and mediated learning experiences.

CONCLUSION

This chapter has reviewed some of the characteristics of exemplary
schools. It was based on a 10-year longitudinal study of 30 elementary
schools and shorter studies at the junior and senior high school and
university levels. The most important characteristic that has emerged
out of all those identified is leadership. Leadership is an important quality at all levels of schooling from primary school through university.
Leadership style is normally best communicated through performance
rather than words. Leaders of unusually successful schools not only
indicate the desire that the school should be exceptional, but they demonstrate it continually by their own actions and the methods by which
they mediate a hundred different kinds of experiences they encounter
on a daily basis. This kind of behavior we believe is the key to creating
exemplary schools. Because the behavior of these leaders tends to be
site-specific and individually specific, it is difficult to generalize policies
that would be useful for policymakers in creating exemplary schools
where they do not exist.

The authors believe that many of the technological changes that are
taking place in our society will foster the creation of these kinds of
schools because technology and its use will allow schools to become
more decentralized. The use of information technology will allow this
decentralization to occur while at the same time allowing those people
who need central control of things to be kept well informed of what is
happening.

We believe that the research on exemplary schools indicates that self-
help is more important than institutional help and that creativity by
individuals or small groups of individuals in schools is a more effective
way to foster high levels of achievement and positive social behavior
gained in schools than by institutional help. We are entering a period of
greater self-reliance upon individuals and less reliance upon centralized
institutions.

Schools that are unusually successful also seem to stress a kind of
participatory democracy rather than representative democracy. Schools
choose people to represent them at the central administration and in

many cases they do not feel they are well represented. The exemplary schools research seems to suggest that it is active participation within a single school that causes teachers, educational administrators, and parents to believe that they can affect significantly what goes on in that school. As schools move toward greater independence they will also, strangely enough, be moving toward greater dependence. This dependence will be necessitated because of the vast information needs that schools in the future will need to call upon. Therefore, as the school's own control increases, they will build numerous networks by which they will access a wide variety of information that will be used in different ways in different schools.

Accountability, in the authors' opinion, will move from short- to long-term accountability. The central administration will in the future be more careful and demanding in its selection of leaders, but once those leaders are chosen they will be given long periods of time to accomplish their designated tasks. For instance, if a principal is selected to turn a school around, that is, make it a better learning institution than it presently is, the hiring authority ought at the very least to give that person a commitment for about 5 years to accomplish that task. Certainly among the things we have learned in the last few years of the accountability movement is that you cannot plant a seedling in June and pull it up in September to examine the roots to see if there has been significant change. Studies on Head Start (Berrueta-Clement, 1984) have suggested that it has taken 20 years for real demonstrated change to take place in the lives of children based upon their early educational experience.

REFERENCES

Austin, G. R. (1978). *Process evaluation: A comprehensive study of outliers*. Baltimore: Maryland State Department of Education.

Austin, G. R. (1981). Exemplary schools and their identification. In D. Carlson (Ed.), *New Directions for Testing and Measurement* (pp. 31–48). San Francisco: Jossey-Bass.

Austin, G. R. (1984). *Interim report on continuing longitudinal study of 30 exemplary schools*. Unpublished manuscript. University of Maryland, Center for Educational Research and Development, Baltimore.

Austin, G. R., Garber, H., & Novalis, C. (1981). *Report of the Governor's task force to study educational and related needs of children in juvenile residential institutions*. Annapolis: Maryland State Senate.

Austin, G. R., Garber, H. & Novalis, C. (1982). *Final report of the Governor's task force to study educational and related needs of children in juvenile residential institutions*. Annapolis: Maryland State Senate.

Berrueta-Clement, J., Schweinhart, L., Barnett, W. S., Epstein, A., & Weikart, D. (1984). *Changed Lives* Ypsilanti, MI: High Scope Press.

Bloom, B. (1972, May). Innocence in education. *School Review, 80*(3) 3–17.

Boyer, E. (1983). *High school.* New York: Harper & Row.

Coleman, J., Campbell, E., Hobson, C., McPartland, J., Mood, A., Weinfeld, F., & York, R. (1966). *Equality of educational opportunity.* Washington, DC: U.S. Government Printing Office.

Coleman, J., Hoffer, T., & Kilgore, S. (1982) *High school achievement.*New York: Basic Books.

Danzig, A., & Austin, G. (1982). *The contribution of honors programs to excellence in higher education.* Unpublished study. University of Maryland, Center for Educational Research and Development, Baltimore.

Dyer, H. (1966). The Pennsylvania plan. *Science Education, 50,* 242–248.

Education Commission of the States. (1983). *Action for Excellence* Denver, CO: Author.

Elkind, D. (1981, March). *What do we know about the effects of early childhood program planning?* Address to Eleventh Annual Early Childhood Conference, College Park, MD.

Feistritzer, C. E. (1983). *The Condition of Teaching.* New York: The Carnegie Foundation for the Advancement of Teaching

Feuerstein, R., Rand, Y., Hoffman, M. B., & Miller, R. (1980). *Instrumental enrichment: An intervention program for cognitive modifiability.* Baltimore: University Park Press.

Ford Foundation. (1984). *City high schools: A recognition of progress.* New York: Ford Foundation.

Klitgaard, R. & Hall, G. (1973) A statistical search for unusually effective schools. Santa Monica, CA: Rand Corporation.

Maryland State Department of Education. (1976). *Maryland Accountability Report, Year II.* (Rep. No. 3) Baltimore, MD: Author.

National Commission on Excellence in Education. (1983). *A nation at risk: The imperative for educational reform.* Washington, DC: U.S. Department of Education.

National Science Board Commission on Pre-College Education in Mathematics, Science and Technology. (1983). *Educating Americans for the 21st Century.* Washington, DC: National Science Foundation.

Plowden Report. (1967). *Children and their primary schools. Vols. 1 & 2.* London: Central Advisory Council for Education, Her Majesty's Stationery Office.

Rutter, M., Maughan, B., Mortimore, P., Ouston, J., & Smith, A. (1979). *Fifteen thousand hours: Secondary schools and their effects on children.* Cambridge, MA: Harvard University Press.

Twentieth Century Fund Task Force on Federal Elementary and Secondary Education Policy. (1983). *Making the grade.* New York: Wiley.

CHAPTER 5

Identification of Exemplary Schools on a Large Scale

Mark E. Fetler and Dale C. Carlson

INTRODUCTION

John Locke, the philosopher, wrote that all things excellent are as difficult as they are rare. This maxim applies no less in the field of public education than elsewhere. Identification of school excellence is difficult and depends on the availability of information on the school and its environment. If many schools must be assessed, the tasks of data collection and evaluation can be burdensome. Impartial weighing of all relevant evidence by an acknowledged expert would be a desirable way of judging. But where thousands of schools are to be examined, as in California, the method of expert judgment is impractical. In California the need to quickly identify groups of excellent schools necessitates an automatic, computer-driven method of screening, at least as the first stage in an identification process.

The identification of a school as excellent or exemplary presupposes the existence of a standard that can be applied in making an assessment of quality. The standard must be fair and used consistently for all schools. Curricula vary from school to school and among classes in accordance with local needs. Still, to the extent the public has a set of fundamental expectations of schools, it is important to apply uniform standards. The standard must also be relevant to the quality being judged. If school excellence is defined in terms of student achievement,

83

the standard should be based on a reliable and valid measure of achievement. Achievement test scores are valid measures of achievement to the extent that the content of the test corresponds to what is taught. Because instruction varies from school to school and class to class, any one test cannot perfectly measure student achievement in all schools. But to use different tests for different schools would result in a varying standard. This dilemma, the choice between fairness and validity, characterizes any achievement-based standard for excellence.

This study uses achievement data from the annual statewide testing of the California Assessment Program (CAP). CAP is a legislatively mandated program that assesses the achievement of public school students in California, investigates factors related to high or low achievement, and reports the results to the California legislature and involves local schools and districts. The availability of scores from the tests, uniformly administered statewide, provides a means to screen large numbers of schools on the basis of student achievement.

Annually, CAP tests and collects background information from over one quarter million sixth graders in more than 4000 schools. It permits construction of a multiple-year data base of achievement scores and student, school, and community background information. The CAP data base provides an opportunity to examine school achievement in relation to relevant background information and to identify schools with higher than expected mean achievement.

This chapter reports on the use of CAP achievement data to identify exemplary schools. Schools are considered exemplary (1) if they maintained an exceptionally high level of student achievement over a period of 3 years, or (2) if they significantly improved their level of student achievement over 3 years. Improving-schools are of interest because they can serve as models of positive change for low-performing schools.

PERSPECTIVES

The Coleman report (Coleman *et al.*, 1966) implied that, on the average, schools have little effect on student achievement. This implication prompted efforts to locate individual schools that might prove to be exceptions to the rule. One such effort was the *California school effectiveness study* (California State Department of Education, 1977), which set out to identify school factors related to achievement. That study, among others, noted that much of the variation in school mean achievement was related to student, school, and community background factors such as social class.

A problem encountered by researchers in studying school achievement is how to separate school effects from nonschool or background factor effects on achievement. The nonschool effects are those related to social class or other background factors that cannot be changed by schools. Dyer (1966) proposed a statistical solution to the problem. He used a technique called multiple regression to provide estimates of school and nonschool effects. School mean achievement scores are analyzed along with pupil variables describing background characteristics that cannot be manipulated easily by schools. One result that provides an estimate of the nonschool effects on achievement is a prediction of school mean achievement based solely on background factors. The quality of the prediction depends on the background variables. The more accurately the variables measure all relevant nonschool background factors, the better the prediction will be. The difference between the actual score and the prediction is a measure of school effectiveness. A positive difference indicates that school practices are positively related to achievement, after statistically controlling for background factors. Dyer identified and studied schools that scored much better than predicted. Further studies by Dyer, Linn, and Patton (1969), Klitgaard and Hall (1973), and Marco (1974) extended and refined this approach. Austin's (1981) review article provides a thorough discussion of the use of the regression technique in exemplary schools studies.

Historically, the definition of exemplary schools included only those maintaining exceptionally high achievement. Schools with improving achievement were little noticed. However, statistical criteria to evaluate both categories of schools can be specified. Looking at differences between actual and predicted scores it is possible to identify schools that achieve at exceptionally high- as well as exceptionally low-levels. Schools with consistently large positive differences over a period of years are said to be maintaining their exemplary status. A school is said to have improved if over the last 3 years achievement increases from an exceptionally low level to an exceptionally high level. That is, improved schools progress over 3 consecutive years from having large negative differences between actual and predicted scores to having large positive differences. Criteria for what constitutes a large difference are described below.

The primary goal of this study is to identify types of exemplary schools that are either (1) maintaining a high level of achievement or (2) improving their achievement. A related task is to discover whether exemplary performance tends to be isolated in one subject area (reading, mathematics, or language) within a school, or extends across several areas. A final aim is to describe the distributions of student scores in the two types of schools, the extent to which the distributions are similar, and the ways in which they change over years.

METHOD

Data Source

Achievement data is used from three spring administrations of CAP's test, Survey of Basic Skills: Grade Six, between 1979 and 1981. The test assessed performance in reading, language, and mathematics. The reading subtest contained 128 items from four skill areas: word identification, vocabulary, comprehension, and study locational skills. The language subtest contained 128 items that assessed standard English usage, language choices, sentence recognition, sentence manipulation, capitalization, and punctuation. The mathematics subtest contained 160 items covering arithmetic, geometry, measurement, probability, and statistics. The items were distributed among 16 test forms of equal length. The tests were administered under standardized conditions according to a matrix sampling plan with each student responding to 26 reading, mathematics, and language questions on one test form. Roughly equal numbers of each test form were taken in each school.

Background Variables

Along with test forms, teachers provided background information on parent occupation and English-language fluency of each student. This information was used to calculate socioeconomic status (SES) and English-language fluency indices for each school.

The SES index is based on a classification of the occupations of the parents of 6th-grade pupils. Teachers identified from the following list the category that corresponded most closely to the occupation of the pupil's father, mother, or guardian:

- Unknown
- Unskilled employees and welfare
- Skilled and semiskilled employees
- Semiprofessionals, clerical, sales worker, and technicians
- Executives, professionals, and managers

The first two categories were assigned a value of 1; the third a value of 2; and the last two a value of 3. The school average of these values for all students tested was the SES index.

The percentage LES/NES was the percentage of limited-English-speaking or non-English-speaking students. Using California's state-mandated criteria, teachers classified students according to four language proficiency categories:

- English-only
- Fluent-English and a second language
- Limited-English and a second language
- Non-English speaking

Classification criteria were based on student performance on a state approved language proficiency test. The school's percentage LES/NES was the percentage of students in the last two categories.

The school's AFDC factor was the percentage of pupils whose families were receiving assistance under the Aid to Families with Dependent Children program. AFDC is awarded on the basis of financial need and is used as a measure of one aspect of SES. The figure is calculated from information provided by districts on enrollment and AFDC participation.

Sample

Initially, the population included 4089 schools. Schools without a complete set of achievement and background variable scores for 3 years were excluded because the regression analysis required a complete set of data. Thus excluded were very small schools that may not have had a sixth-grade class some years and schools that did not consistently provide background information. Complete data were obtained from 3713 schools.

Analysis

A procedure based on multiple regression was used to calculate for each school a range or band of expected achievement scores. The range indicated where the school was expected to score if background characteristics, such as parent occupation, percentage LES/NES, and percentage AFDC, were taken into account. The score bands were calculated so that one-fourth of the schools' actual achievement scores were *above* the predicted band, one-fourth were *below* the band, and one-half were *within* the band. An actual school average achievement score above the computed band was considered exceptional. If a school were above expectation one year, below the next, and within expectation the third

Table 5.1
Three-Year Summary of Sixth-Grade Multiple Regressions

Subject area	Background variables[a]	Weights		
		1980–81	1978–79	1978–79
Reading (R^2)		(.65)	(.63)	(.68)
	SES	.42	.40	.40
	AFDC	−.32	−.34	−.38
	LES/NES	−.24	−.25	−.25
Language (R^2)		(.60)	(.56)	(.63)
	SES	.41	.38	.37
	AFDC	−.31	−.31	−.31
	LES/NES	−.22	−.24	−.24
Mathematics (R^2)		(.48)	(.47)	(.53)
	SES	.43	.40	.39
	AFDC	−.27	−.29	−.33
	LES/NES	−.13	−.13	−.16

year, its performance would be summarized by the acronym, ABW, with A standing for "above," B for "below," and W for "within."[1]

Individual student scores were used to create profiles for each school. The statewide ranked distribution of student scores was divided into four equal groups by the state quartiles. The percentage of students in each school scoring in each of these four statewide groups was calculated for each content area. An average, or typical, California school scored 25% of its students in each quarter for each content area. A high-scoring school placed higher percentages of students in the higher quarters. A low-scoring school was strongly represented in the lower quarters.

RESULTS

Table 5.1 shows a 3-year summary of the sixth-grade multiple regression analyses. The table displays standardized beta weights for the back-

[1] Weighted regressions of achievement scores on the three background variables were used to obtain predicted scores. Weights were the inverse of the school achievement score standard error. A linear function of the standard error was developed that defined a band of achievement for each school, symmetric around the predicted score, such that 25% of the schools in the state fell above the band, 25% fell below, and 50% fell within. This procedure was repeated for each content area every year.

Table 5.2

Number of Exemplary Schools in Selected ABW Categories

Subject area	ABW category[a]			
	AAA	BWA	BAA	BBA
Reading or language or math	508	127	44	58
Language[b]	243	46	23	25
Math[b]	299	39	14	19
Reading[b]	244	53	12	24
Math & language	125	5	4	4
Reading & language	117	5	1	5
Reading & math	115	2	0	2
Reading & language & math	79	1	0	1

[a] A = above, B = below, W = within expected achievement range.

[b] Includes schools that improved in one or two other content areas as well as this area.

ground variables and values of R^2.[2] The weights provide a means of gauging the importance of the contribution of each background variable to the regression prediction with larger weights indicating greater importance. R^2 measures the percentage of variation in achievement accounted for by the background variables included in the regression. The closer R^2 is to a value of 1.0, the better the quality of the prediction. The values of R^2 were stable across years for all content areas. Reading and language values of R^2 were in the .6–.7 range, and were around .5 for mathematics. The weights tended to be constant across years and content areas. One exception was the weight for percentage LES/NES, which was smaller for mathematics than for the other content areas. To the extent that mathematics achievement was not dependent on language fluency this result was expected.

Counts of schools in selected ABW categories are shown in Table 5.2. The categories are defined by a 3-year sequence of ABW indices in a given subject area (reading, language, or mathematics). For example, a

[2] The stability of the values of R^2 and of the beta weights are evidence that school achievement was being measured in a consistent way during the 3 years under study. The moderate values of R^2 indicated that between 30 and 50% of the variance in achievement was not accounted for by the background factors. Other school, community, and individual background factor variables, if they had been available, would have improved the quality of the regression prediction.

Table 5.3

Mean Achievement of Schools in Selected Categories

Subject area[a]		Mean percentage correct		
		1979	1980	1981
Reading	AAA	74.5	75.2	74.5
	BWA	60.6	66.7	71.7
	BAA	64.9	74.3	76.3
	BBA	58.7	60.3	68.4
Mathematics	AAA	69.9	70.8	70.8
	BWA	52.9	58.7	66.3
	BAA	54.1	59.8	70.4
	BBA	55.6	55.7	68.1
Language	AAA	74.2	75.1	75.3
	BWA	59.6	64.5	73.1
	BAA	59.0	75.2	75.7
	BBA	59.1	59.2	71.6

[a] A = above, B = below, W = within expected achievement range.

score below (B) the band in 1979, within (W) the band in 1980, and above (A) the band in 1981 is indicated by the value BWA. Those categories are included that represent either a maintained level of exceptional achievement (AAA) or extraordinary improvement in achievement (BWA, BAA, or BBA). There were 508 schools with AAA in at least one subject area. Of these, only 79 were AAA in all three subject areas.

Fewer schools showed extraordinary improvement (BWA, BAA, or BBA) than schools with a consistently high level of achievement. There were 127 schools with BWA in reading or language or math and one school with BWA in all three subjects. There were 44 with BAA in at least one subject and no schools with BAA in all subjects. Some 58 schools were BBA in at least one subject, and one was BBA in all subjects. The total number of improving-schools (BWA, BAA, and BBA) was less than the total numbers of schools with consistently high achievement.

A summary of mean achievement for schools in different achievement change categories is shown in Table 5.3. The categories are defined, as before, by a 3-year sequence (1979, 1980, 1981) of ABW acronym-type indices. The mean percentage correct achievement of the schools for each category is given for each of the 3 years. One result shown in Table 5.3 is that the achievement of AAA schools was consistently high, and the achievement of BWA, BAA, and BBA schools consistently improved.

A method used by Klitgaard (1973) can be used here to examine the hypothesis that individual schools do have effects on achievement. The method first tentatively assumes that schools have no such systematic effects. Under this assumption it would be a matter of chance whether the actual school mean achievement was higher or lower than the regression prediction. Such would be the case if nonschool factors, such as social class, totally determined school performance. This can be called the random school effects model.

Mathematically, in the random effects model, the size of the difference between an actual and a predicted score for a school, whether positive or negative, would be randomly determined and its ABW index would be a matter of chance. The method of calculating the ABW index forced one-fourth of the schools below the band, one-fourth above, and one-half within. The probability of being above the band is $p = .25$, of being below, $p = .25$, and of being within, $p = .5$. Furthermore, classification in any one year or content area is independent of classification in any other year or content area.

Under the random school effects model, the probability of being above the band for 3 years is $p = .25 \times .25 \times .25 = .015$, and the expected number of schools is 58. The same probability and expected number is associated with the BBA and BAA categories. For the BWA category the probability is $p = .03$ and the expected number of schools is 116. The actual number of schools in the AAA category was 244 in reading, 299 in mathematics, and 243 in language. These numbers far exceed expectations under the random school effects model. The number of schools in each of the improving categories (BBA, BAA, BWA) is much lower than expected in the random school effects model. These differences are all statistically significant ($p < .01$). Because the counts of schools in the various categories differ so widely from the counts hypothesized under the model, rejection of the model is indicated. What could account for the discrepancy between the prediction of the model and what actually was obtained? A possible explanation, subject to verification by field data, is that these schools were having large systematic influences on student achievement.

Mean percentages of students in each quarter of the state distribution are shown in Table 5.4. The quarters of the state distribution are defined by the quartile points (the 25th percentile, the median, and the 75th percentile) for all students taking the test. (A percentile rank is defined as the test score below which a given percentage of students score. For instance, 25% of the students score at or below the 25th percentile rank.) If the distribution of achievement scores in a school is similar to the distribution statewide, the school will have about 25% of its students in each quarter of the state distribution. If the school mean achievement is

Table 5.4

Mean Percentages of Students in Each Quarter of the State Distribution

Subject area[a]	Percentages of students											
	First quarter			Second quarter			Third quarter			Fourth quarter		
	1979	1980	1981	1979	1980	1981	1979	1980	1981	1979	1980	1981
Reading												
AAA	15	15	17	23	23	22	29	27	27	34	35	34
BWA	34	26	23	27	27	23	22	24	27	18	24	28
BAA	26	16	19	28	25	20	25	27	27	20	33	35
BBA	36	35	27	28	28	24	21	21	24	15	16	25
Math												
AAA	12	13	14	18	18	18	26	26	24	45	46	45
BWA	33	26	17	29	27	22	23	25	27	16	23	34
BAA	32	13	12	29	19	19	23	26	25	16	44	44
BBA	29	28	15	28	30	21	26	27	26	18	16	40
Language												
AAA	15	15	17	20	20	19	28	27	28	38	39	37
BWA	31	25	20	28	29	20	23	25	28	18	22	34
BAA	35	12	14	27	23	22	22	27	30	19	38	36
BBA	31	33	23	28	26	21	22	23	26	19	19	33

[a] A = above; B = below; W = within expected achievement range.

above the state average, it will have a larger percentage of students in the top two quarters of the state distribution than in the bottom two quarters. Low-achieving schools have larger percentages of students in the bottom two quarters.

Profiles of AAA schools, those that consistently exceeded expectation, changed little over the 3 years represented. For example, in reading, 15–17% of the students placed in the first quarter, 22–23% in the second, 27–29% in the third, and 34–35% in the fourth. A similar pattern occurred for language. In mathematics, higher percentages of students placed in the top quarter (45–46%) and lower percentages in the bottom quarter (12–14%).

The higher percentages of students in the top quarter for mathematics may reflect a greater capacity for AAA schools to influence mathematics achievement, compared to reading or language achievement. Verbal skills are learned not only in school but also can be influenced by the home and community. Quantitative skills are learned mainly in school with a smaller contribution from the home environment and less opportunity for negative extracurricular influences.

The percentages of students in a given quarter for schools displaying exceptional improvement (BAA, BBA, BWA) changed from year to year. In reading, the percentage of students in the bottom quarter decreased by 7–11 points over 3 years and the percentage of students in the top quarter increased by 10–15 points. A similar pattern occurred in language. In mathematics the larger changes were noted with a 14–20 point decrease in the bottom quarter over 3 years and a 18–28 point increase in the top quarter. The greater changes for mathematics offer additional evidence of a school's capacity to influence mathematics achievement.

DISCUSSION

A main activity of this study is the replication of earlier studies by Klitgaard and Hall, Dyer, and Marco. Statistically, sets of schools that are unusually effective can be identified. This study goes beyond the earlier results in that it looks at school effectiveness over a period of 3 years, and it distinguishes consistently effective schools from those that are improving.

One troublesome result is the small percentage of schools that are consistently high-achieving over 3 years. From the initial pool of 3713 schools, about 14% were consistently above expectation in at least one subject area, and 2% were consistently above expectation in all three subject areas. The implication here is that schools with high achievement in one subject do not necessarily have high achievement in all subjects. This study did not reveal reasons for this disparity of achievement across subject areas. It might be the result of differences in teachers, in curriculum, or in some other factors. Other chapters in this book examine several possible explanations for exemplary achievement.

To some extent the small number of schools with consistently high achievement was the result of the rather strict standards applied. Only one-fourth of the schools could be above expectation in a given subject area in a given year. If the standards were relaxed so that one-third could be above, the number of qualifying schools would be larger. Another reason for the small number is the error in the predicted score resulting from unmeasured sources of change in the schools. Changes in school staff and changes in the abilities and prior achievement of students from year-to-year are two important variables not taken into account. Student and staff changes may propel school achievement up or down and thus determine whether they are above or below expectation. To the extent that this happened schools would have difficulty remaining above expectation, or similarly, remaining below. The uncertainties associated with this technique make it advisable that properly trained individuals visit school sites and validate the various interpretations of the statistical outcomes.

In all subject areas, whether examined singly or in combination, far fewer schools showed extraordinary improvement in achievement than consistently high achievement. An interpretive metaphor for this result is Newton's law of inertia: A body tends to continue in its path unless acted upon by an outside force. One reason so few schools showed improvement may be that the changes required to improve significantly are too great for most schools to undertake on their own.

This study does not examine what changes are correlated with significant improvements in achievement. Much school effectiveness research so far has restricted itself to examining the characteristics of effective schools without looking at constructive change in schools. It may not be enough to show schools a picture of what is desired. Increases in school effectiveness may best be facilitated by providing models for change.

Changes in community attitudes, school staff, curriculum, or in some combination of these may be needed to produce higher student achievement. Some writers believe enough is known but that competing interests prevent change. The fact that few schools accomplish changes may indicate that more research and assistance is needed in this area.

Results from this study indicate that achievement in mathematics does not behave the same as achievement in reading or language. The lower R^2 for the mathematics multiple regressions suggest that the home and community influences on mathematics achievement are not as strong as they are on reading and language achievement. Another indication is that about 20% more schools were consistently high-achieving in mathematics than in reading or language. Put another way, the school has nearly exclusive control over mathematics training. A final indication of this difference was that schools with consistently high achievement in mathematics placed about 10% more students in the top quarter of the statewide distribution of student mathematics scores than they did in reading or language. The home and community environments may play a larger role in preserving the status quo in reading and language achievement than they do in mathematics.

CONCLUSIONS

Regression-based methods similar to those described here have been used by researchers for locating exemplary schools beginning with Dyer's work. Nearly all of these applications have involved the selection of a set of schools that show exemplary achievement for 1 or more years. Little research has studied schools that show extraordinary improvement. Such schools are even less numerous than those that traditionally have been labeled exemplary.

How might a study of improving schools be of use? To illustrate this a distinction must be drawn between two concepts: maintaining the status quo and changing it. Studies of exemplary schools reveal practices that involve maintaining a very high level status quo. This is a worthwhile endeavor and should be continued. Many schools, though, need concrete, practical models for change to reach that high plateau of success. Once achievement has increased, they can work on maintaining it. The relatively small number of schools found in this study to exhibit extraordinary improvement indicate that necessary methods are neither very widespread nor obvious. But it can be said that this study did find that a significant number of schools are influencing their pupils favorably. This should encourage the research community to continue efforts to identify these schools and catalog their unique characteristics.

REFERENCES

Austin, G. (1981). Exemplary schools and their identification. *New Directions for Testing and Measurement, 10,* 31–48.
California State Department of Education. (1977). *California school effectiveness study, the first year: 1974–75,* Sacramento, CA: Author.

Coleman, J. S., Campbell, E. Q., Hobson, C. J., McPartland, J., Mood, A. M., Weinfeld, F. D., & York, R. L. (1966). *Equality of educational opportunity*, Washington, DC: U.S. Government Printing Office.

Dyer, H. (1966). The Pennsylvania plan. *Science Education, 50*, 242–248.

Dyer, H., Linn, R., & Patton, M. (1969). A comparison of four methods of obtaining discrepancy measures based on observed and predicted school system means on achievement tests. *American Educational Research Journal, 6*, 591–605.

Klitgaard, R., & Hall, G. (1973). *A statistical search for unusually effective schools*. Santa Monica, CA: Rand Corporation.

Marco, G. (1974). A comparison of selected school effectiveness measures based on longitudinal data. *Journal of Educational Measurement, 11*, 225–234.

CHAPTER 6

The Investigation of School Climate

Carolyn S. Anderson

INTRODUCTION

As researchers, educators, and policymakers have sought to paint a composite portrait of the effective school, a popular component has been school climate. Theorists, practitioners, and politicians alike applaud the presence of a "positive climate" in a school. Furthermore, probably no one would suggest that schools do not differ—often to a considerable degree—in atmosphere. Thus, in this construct we have a variable considered both worthy of nurturing and worthy of study. And, in fact, as one would anticipate with such a construct, the marketplace (of both scholar and practitioner) has been deluged with studies, instruments, and climate improvement packages.

How are we to make sense out of this plethora of material so that valid applications can be made to an actual school program? This chapter provides assistance to the reader by (1) defining the construct of school climate, (2) identifying the variables that consistently are associated with a positive school climate, and (3) providing a framework to evaluate the conclusions of any study of school climate.

DEFINING SCHOOL CLIMATE

Climate is a word that seems so intuitively understandable that at first glance it might appear to need no definition. In fact, it is often alluded to in the literature without even being named. For example, Jencks *et al.* (1972) in their landmark study of school effectiveness noted that "some schools are dull, depressing, even terrifying places, while others are lively, comfortable and reassuring" (p. 256). Tye (1974) observed that "when an individual visits a school for the first time, he develops, almost immediately, a feeling about that school" (p. 20).

Other authors discuss climate directly but without ever formally defining the construct. Edmonds (1979), for instance, noted that effective schools "share a climate in which it is incumbent on all personnel to be instructionally effective for all pupils" (p. 22). Vyskocil and Goens (1979) observed that "a positive school organizational climate can be developed only if there is trust, respect, and caring" (p. 176).

At other times, formal definitions exist but tend to be analogous, abstract (nonoperationalized), or example based. For instance, Halpin and Croft (1963) used a now classic analogy: "Personality is to the individual what 'climate' is to the organization" (p. 1). Nwankwo (1979) defined climate as "the general 'we-feeling', group subculture or interactive life of the school" (p. 268). Deal and Kennedy (1983) referred to climate as the culture of the school, defined as "an informal understanding of the 'way we do things around here' or 'what keeps the herd moving roughly west' " (p. 14). Hellrigel and Slocum (1974) described climate as "a set of attributes . . . induced from the way that organization and/or its subsystems deal with their members and environment" (p. 256).

Such nebulous definitions are useful for communicating a certain level of understanding and for providing a shared intuitive sense of the construct so that two persons might be able to agree that a given school possesses a more or less positive climate. However, in order to establish either the components of climate, its correlates, its causes, or its effects, the construct must be operationalized. That is, it must be defined in terms of aspects that are observable and therefore measurable.

Furthermore, the term *climate* is often used in conjunction with related terms, such as *atmosphere, ecology, ethos, environment, culture, ecology, milieu, setting, context,* and so forth. It is not always clear whether the terms are intended to be synonomous or even whether any two writers are using a given word in the same way.

For example, Tagiuri (1968) considered climate as a characteristic of the total environment, with four dimensions: *ecology* (physical and material aspects), *milieu* (social dimension created by the characteristics of groups of persons), *social system* (social dimension created by the relationships of persons and groups), and *culture* (social dimension created by belief systems, values, cognitive structures, and meaning).

On the other hand, Moos (1974) and Insel and Moos (1974) used the term *social ecology* to refer to the total human environment. They conceptualized climate more narrowly than did Tagiuri, as one of six aspects of the environment, along with *ecological factors* (geographical, meteorological, and architectural), *behavior settings* (with both material and behavioral components), *organizational structure* (such as size and span of control), *average personal characteristics* of individuals, and *functional dimensions* of specific situations (that provide reinforcing contingencies to maintain behaviors).

Some researchers have attempted to restrict the application of climate to a unit smaller than the total school, as a way of making the construct more manageable. For instance, Barker's (1963, 1965, 1968) and Gump's work (1971) focused on behavior settings, or groupings of persons within an organization or building, such as groups of students in a lunchroom or teachers in a faculty room. Other researchers have restricted their study to individual classroom climates (Coleman, 1961; Deal & Celotti, 1980; Meyer, 1980; Moos, 1976, 1979a, 1979b; Rowan, Bossert, & Dwyer, 1983; Trickett and Moos, 1973).

In this chapter, however, climate is explored as a total school construct, relying on the view of Barr and Dreeban (1981) and Purkey and Smith (1982) that schools are part of a nested organizational system. In this view the quality of the environment in classrooms or behavior settings is influenced by the school environment in which it is nested: The broader context is thus important.

MEASURING SCHOOL CLIMATE

The wide variation in the conceptualization and definition of climate is clearly reflected in the instruments used to measure the construct. Explicitly or implicitly each climate instrument claims to embody the climate of the organization to which it is applied. In the history of climate instruments (see C. S. Anderson, 1982, for an extensive review of this background), several approaches have been taken.

The pioneering work of Stern (1961, 1964, 1970) involved instruments at both college and high school levels (the College Characteristics Index and the High School Characteristics Index) that emphasize the environmental demands, or "press," of the school as perceived by the students. Persons were thought to respond differently to these salient features of the environment, based on their individual needs. Thus, student behavior was seen as a function of the interaction of environmental press, or climate, and individual needs.

Several instruments reflect a theoretical perspective similar to Stern's. These include (1) the Classroom Environment Scale (Moos, 1976, 1979a, 1979b; Trickett & Moos, 1973), which focuses on participants' perceptions of classroom interactions; (2) the Learning Environment Inventory, My Class Inventory, and My School Inventory (G. J. Anderson, 1973; Anderson & Walberg, 1974; Ellett, Capie, & Johnson, 1980; Walberg, 1969; Walberg & Anderson, 1972), which also rely on subjective ratings to describe, respectively, secondary classrooms, elementary classrooms, and elementary schools; and (3) the Elementary School Environment Survey (Sinclair, 1970), which relies on student perceptions of teacher and peer values and attitudes to build a school profile.

Astin and Holland (1961), on the other hand, viewed climate primarily as a function of the typical characteristics of participants. Their instrument, the Environmental Assessment Technique, relies on the measurement of eight variables concerned with the student body (size, average intelligence, and six personal value orientations).

A third approach defines climate as a function of teacher perceptions and attitudes. In the Organizational Climate Description Questionnaire (OCDQ), for example, Halpin and Croft (1963) attempted to classify schools on an open–closed continuum, based on teachers' perceptions of their own work orientation and their perceptions of the principal's manner of interacting with teachers and school tasks. Willower and others (Licata, Willower, & Ellett, 1978; Willower, Eidell, & Hoy, 1967; Willower & Jones, 1963) described climate as a function of teacher attitude toward discipline and structure. They measured it on a dimension called *pupil control ideology.* Licata *et al.* (1978) later looked at "robustness" as a related climate dimension using the Robustness Semantic Differential Scale. Robust schools were characterized by high pupil control ideology and were related to measures of student satisfaction with school. Similar in approach (but not in origin) is the School Description Inventory (B. D. Anderson, 1970; Anderson & Tissier, 1973), which relies on teacher perception of the bureaucracy in secondary school environments.

The most attitudinal (as opposed to perceptual) approach to the instrumentation of school climate is rooted in the concept of *quality of life,* as delineated by the U.S. Environmental Protection Agency (1973) in its environmental studies of adults. Epstein and McPartland (1976) applied this concept to schools with the Quality of School Life Scale. They considered quality of school life (predominantly in elementary schools) to be reflected in students' general satisfaction with school, their commitment to classwork, and their reaction to teachers. Williams and Batten

(1981) developed a similar instrument for secondary schools that expands the concept to include student affect (positive and negative), as well as feelings of well-being that refer to specific aspects of school.

It is clear that the measurement of climate has proceeded along a number of rather divergent lines. In some cases it has been tied to institutional demands perceived to be thrust on the student. In other cases the link has been to average student body characteristics. Still other approaches have stressed teacher attitudes or teacher perception in characterizing school climate. Finally, climate has been related to student satisfaction with school and even to students' general affect.

With such diversity in instruments, it is no surprise to find parallel differences in the climate portraits that emerge from the application of such instruments. Differences appear either at the level of factors or subscales or at the level of typology, where schools are classified as a climate type based on the pattern of subscales.

For example, the OCDQ (Halpin & Croft, 1963) includes four group subscales: Disengagement (the teachers' tendency to be "not with it," going through the motions only), Hindrance (teachers' feeling that the principal burdens them and does not facilitate their work), Esprit (teachers' feeling that their social needs are satisfied and that they have accomplished something), Intimacy (teachers' feeling of friendliness toward each other or social need satisfaction without necessarily a sense of accomplishment).

The four leader subscales of the OCDQ include the following: Aloofness (principal is seen as formal and impersonal, preferring rules to face-to-face contact), Thrust (principal is viewed favorably as task oriented and wanting to move the organization), Consideration (principal is perceived to treat teachers humanely, facilitating their efforts), and Production Emphasis (principal is viewed as directive, relying on close supervision and one-way communication).

Schools are then categorized on an open–closed continuum based on patterns of these subscales. Schools with closed climates are characterized by uncommitted teachers and principals who dictate rules, are critical, and provide for few meetings and informal gatherings. Schools with open climates, by contrast, are staffed by teachers who are interested in their work and are cooperative, and by principals who interact positively and frequently with teachers and students.

Climate dimensions reported by Brookover and others (1977, 1978, 1979) and by McDill and others (1967, 1969, 1973) expanded the relevant climate factors to include those concerning students as well as teachers and principals, although in neither case was a climate typology developed based on patterns of these factors. In addition, the teachers' role in climate creation is now tied to their perceptions of students as well as their perceptions of themselves, the principal, and colleagues.

The Brookover instruments (used with elementary schools) identified a set of factors reflecting student, teacher, and principal climate perceptions. These factors include various aspects of academic futility, evaluations and expectations, academic norms, and commitment or efforts to improve.

The McDill instruments identified six climate factors in secondary schools that reflect values manifest in a school: (1) academic excellence, (2) acquiring knowledge, (3) intellectual criteria for status in the student social system in addition to social cohesiveness, (4) scientific emphasis, (5) emphasis on the arts, humanities, social studies, and current social issues, and (6) intellectual and academic performance socially rewarded in the student social system.

In contrast to all of the previously discussed instruments, those built on the quality-of-life concept concern only student perceptions of school life (Epstein & McPartland, 1976; Williams & Batten, 1981). Such instruments link climate to students' self-reported (not observed) attitudes. The Epstein and McPartland instrument identified three factors: Student Satisfaction (students' general reactions to school), Student Commitment to Classwork (students' interest in the educational work), and Student Reactions to Teacher (students' perceptions of student–teacher relationships). The Williams and Batten instrument, on the other hand, was factor analyzed into six factors: General Affect (positive well-being), Negative Affect (experiences of depression, loneliness, etc.), Status (experiences derived from others), Identity (socialization and self-understanding experiences), Teachers (student–teacher interaction), and Opportunity (feelings of competence–success).

Similarly the Elementary School Environment Survey (ESES; Sinclair, 1970) relies on student perceptions of teacher and peer values and attitudes. Schools are classified on a five-category typology: Practical Climates (emphasizing control, procedures, personal status, and benefits), Community Climates (characterized as friendly, cohesive, group oriented, supportive, and sympathetic, emphasizing group welfare and loyalty), Awareness Climates (stressing self-understanding, reflectiveness, identity, creativity, the future, the welfare of humanity), Propriety Climates (valuing standards of decorum such as politeness, consideration, caution, and thoughtfulness, without rebellious, assertive, or risk-taking behavior), Scholarship Climates (encouraging academics, intellectual discipline, and the serious pursuit of knowledge).

Finally, some instruments have tied climate to structural and organizational variables rather than to personal behavior or attitude variables. Wynne (1980, 1981) suggested the continuum of coherent and noncoherent schools, although his observational data are qualitative and no quantifiable system exists for assigning schools to a particular point on the continuum. Coherence is described as a composite of clarity, purposefulness, good communication, consensus, and consistency.

Similarly, Willower and Licata (1975) used the construct of *environmental robustness* to differentiate the climates of schools. Environmentally robust schools are characterized by "high dramatic content," having structures that are tension producing (such as a tough discipline system, structured school activities, and distinct boundaries of propriety) so as to arouse and focus empathy among students.

At this point it should be evident that no definitive portrait of school climate has been painted. We are left with the consensus that such a construct does describe something that exists inside schools. However, its definition and delineation will vary from researcher to researcher or practitioner to practitioner depending on the school qualities that are assumed to be responsible for school climate and the instrument they use. At the very least, we are forced to conclude that the construct is multifaceted and that perhaps each approach provides a part of the truth about the nature of climate in school settings.

VARIABLES ASSOCIATED WITH SCHOOL CLIMATE

If we are willing to ignore for a moment any discomfort we may have about the ambiguity of the climate construct, it is possible to focus on some discrete and more measurable variables. They appear repeatedly in the climate literature. These variables include those that are derived from climate instruments and that show a pattern of positive association with various outcomes.

It must be emphasized that the results reported here are based on a wide variety of studies, with varying degrees of methodological and conceptual sophistication and rigor. The intent was to be as inclusive as possible in order to provide a broad picture of those variables that recur repeatedly in all kinds of research. In a sense we are trying to see what kind of picture emerges when we combine studies that vary in methodological excellence and assumptions about climate. Given the discussion concerning the variability in climate definitions, the possibility exists that we are combining apples and oranges in attempting to identify common findings. On the other hand, the broader picture of "fruit" may escape us unless we risk mixing apples and oranges.

The framework used to organize these variables is the taxonomy proposed by Tagiuri (1968) for describing an organization's climate. His categories were ecology, milieu, social system, and culture. The findings presented are abbreviated from a more complete summary that appeared in C. S. Anderson (1982) where both the findings and the sources are documented in more detail.

Ecology Variables

This category of variables in Tagiuri's taxonomy includes characteristics of the physical environment of the school. The relationship between ecology variables and student outcomes, a frequent focus of early input–output school effects studies, appears to be relatively weak or nonexistent. Such a low relationship may occur for a number of reasons. For example, it is possible that ecological variables do not operate directly on student outcomes but rather have their impact through the mediating effect of school climate. It is also possible that the wrong ecological variables have been used in previous studies and that more proximal variables within this category would show important effects. For example, school appearance is a more proximal ecological variable than age of building, in terms of its effect on student outcomes.

Studies have shown fairly consistently that, in fact, the age of school buildings has no relationship to any outcomes, including behavior, attendance, and achievement, as well as climate (McDill & Rigsby, 1973; Rutter, Maughan, Mortimore, Ouston, & Smith, 1979; Weber, 1971). On the other hand, variables such as decoration and care of school and classrooms do appear to be characteristics of high-achieving schools (Phi Delta Kappa, 1980; Rutter et al., 1979) and schools with a positive and cohesive climate (Wynne, 1980).

The influence of class and school enrollment as potential climate mediators is not clear, with some studies suggesting that "smaller is better" in terms of academic effectiveness (Duke & Perry, 1978; Edmonds & Fredericksen, 1978; Klitgaard & Hall, 1973a, 1973b; New York State Department of Education, 1976), while other studies suggest no effect on outcomes (McDill & Rigsby, 1973; Rutter et al., 1979; Weber, 1971). When climate is the dependent variable, however, smaller schools do appear to have the advantage in being more open (Flagg, 1964/1965) or friendlier and more cohesive (Morocco, 1978).

Milieu Variables

This category of variables focuses on the characteristics of persons and groups within the school environment. Findings are not conclusive, due to some discrepancies among studies. The lack of a clear picture may be the result of inadequate (poorly specified) causal models or problems in the aggregation of data. (See Blalock, 1971 and Hauser, 1970, for a detailed discussion of the aggregation problem as related to milieu variables.)

When low-inference measures of teacher characteristics, such as hours of preparation and mean annual salary, are related to student outcomes, the effect is minimal (McDill & Rigsby, 1973; Rutter et al., 1979). On the other hand, teacher stability (low-turnover rates in a building) and teacher education (both amount and quality) have been related to achievement and to aspirations, as well as to climate (McDill and Rigsby, 1973; Rutter et al., 1979; Wynne, 1980). There is some evidence that the effect of teacher characteristics may interact with student characteristics. Summers and Wolfe (1977), for instance, reported that teacher experience is positively associated with student achievement for high-achieving students, but negatively associated for low achievers.

Teacher morale, a more subjective milieu variable, has shown a consistent association with school climate, in that teachers who express satisfaction with school tend to perceive the school climate as more positive (Kalis, 1980; Sargeant, 1967). Teacher attitude, however, correlates with student perception of school climate only in elementary schools (Ellett, Payne, Masters, & Pool, 1977). The same researchers also reported a relationship between teacher morale and student attendance and achievement, a relationship confirmed by Brookover and Lezotte (1979).

The effect of student characteristics on school outcomes has been of continual interest to researchers. Aggregated student characteristics, once used as proxies for school climate, are now considered apart from more direct measures of climate and, in fact, are less important in predicting student outcomes than more direct measures of climate, such as various psychosocial variables (Brookover et al., 1979; McDill & Rigsby, 1973; Schneider, Glasheen & Hadley, 1979). On the other hand, some research indicates that there are optimal "mixes" in terms of student body composition. Murnane (1980) and Summers and Wolfe (1977) both noted that a 40–60% racial balance was best. Furthermore, low-socioeconomic-status students and low achievers both performed better in schools with a high-average socioeconomic status and achievement level respectively (Murnane, 1980).

As was true for teachers, the morale of students appears to be important both for achievement and self-concept (Brookover & Schneider, 1975; Edmonds, 1979a; Schneider et al., 1979; Weber, 1971). This finding is consistent across a multitude of definitions for morale, including sense of futility, self-concept, and alienation (Brookover et al., 1979; Licata et al., 1978).

Social System Variables

Findings in this area, Tagiuri's third category, which includes the patterns of interactions and relationships within a school, are inconsistent and difficult to compare because the constructs measured are diverse and the methods of operationalizing them differ.

Administrative organization, including bureaucratization of staff responsibilities, shows little relationship to student outcomes (Anderson & Tissier, 1973; Rutter et al., 1979). However, evidence exists to suggest that organizational structure influences teacher performance and thus may indirectly affect student performance (Anglin, 1979).

The instructional program in which a student is enrolled appears to influence several outcomes, including aspirations (Anderson & Tissier, 1973; McDill & Rigsby, 1973) and achievement (McDill & Rigsby, 1973). Opportunities for advanced placement or any kind of accelerated curriculum, as well as grading policy, are examples of important variables.

The effect of ability grouping (differentiation of students) is unclear. Some researchers report findings to suggest that effective schools use heterogeneous student groupings (Brookover et al., 1979; Edmonds & Fredericksen, 1978; Sorensen, 1970). Others report that ability grouping is associated with higher achievement (Wynne, 1980) or has no relationship to achievement or aspirations (McDill & Rigsby, 1973; Weber, 1971).

The relationship between administration and teachers can clearly influence a school's climate for achievement. Isolation of teachers and the absence of collegiality can be detrimental, while rapport and a positive perception of the principal as leader can improve climate and subsequent student achievement (Bell, 1979; Breckenridge, 1976; Ellett & Walberg, 1979; Feldvebel, 1964a, 1964b; Hale, 1965/1966; H. E. Miller, 1969; New York State, 1976).

Staff participation and leadership in decision making appears as an important social system variable in the literature. Its relationship to student achievement, cohesiveness of the school, and teacher morale has been documented (Ellett & Walberg, 1979; Phi Delta Kappa, 1980; Rutter et al., 1979; Wynne, 1980). Good communication, coupled with an atmosphere of trust and mutual respect, is closely related to staff participation and leadership. Communication has been related to improved decision making (Christie & Kurpius, 1978), school climate (Vyskocil & Goens, 1979; Wynne, 1980), and achievement (Silberman, 1970).

Good relationships and interactions of students and faculty, including joint participation in nonacademic events, can contribute to a school's climate. Shared activities can encourage students to accept school norms (Rutter et al., 1979) and can improve student behavior (Duke & Perry, 1978). Evidence also exists to suggest a relationship between this factor and academic achievement (Phi Delta Kappa, 1980).

Providing opportunities for students to participate in the life of the school can be another important social system variable. Giving students a significant role in decision making has been related to improved behavior (Cox, 1978; Duke & Perry, 1978; Rutter et al., 1979) and improved climate (Beane, 1979; Breckenridge, 1976; Urich & Batchelder, 1979). The availability of school activities, the freedom of students to use the building, and the opportunities for student success in extracurricular activities are strongly related to climate, to student satisfaction, and to achievement (Epstein & McPartland, 1976; Mitchell, 1967; Rutter et al., 1979; Weber, 1971).

Teacher–teacher relationships and socializing among teachers are both strongly related to school climate and to student achievement (H. E. Miller, 1969; Phi Delta Kappa, 1980; Rutter et al., 1979; Wynne, 1980). These studies have characterized this variable as including cooperation, concern, and friendliness among faculty.

A good relationship between community and school, usually manifested in parent–administrator or parent–teacher rapport, is critical to outcomes, including climate and student achievement (Breckenridge, 1976; New York State, 1976; Phi Delta Kappa, 1980).

Strong administrative leadership in instruction has consistently been associated with student academic success (Brookover et al., 1979; Brookover & Lezotte, 1979; Edmonds, 1979; New York State, 1976; Weber, 1971). Principal involvement in and concern for instruction also related to pupil social growth, teacher morale, and school climate (Ellett & Walberg, 1979; Licata et al., 1978; Young, 1980).

Parent involvement in the school generally has been associated with positive outcomes including climate, achievement, and aspirations (McDill & Rigsby, 1973; Phi Delta Kappa, 1980; Silberman, 1970). A study by Brookover and Lezotte (1979), however, suggested that parent-initiated involvement may be the important variable, rather than parent participation per se.

Culture Variables

This category, Tagiuri's fourth and last, which includes the values and beliefs of various groups within a school, has been related both to climate and to student outcomes.

Teacher commitment to improve students' academic performance has been clearly established as a significant variable in school climate, as measured usually by student perception that teachers care (Brookover *et al.*, 1979; Brookover & Lezotte, 1979; Phi Delta Kappa, 1980). These studies and others (Maxwell, 1967/1968; H. E. Miller, 1969) also relate this variable to student achievement.

The attitudes of a student's peer group are another important source of individual attitudes and behaviors. When academics are valued by the peer group, research shows that students have higher aspirations and a greater sense of control over their lives, which in turn relates to achievement (Brookover *et al.*, 1979; Brookover & Schneider, 1975; Coleman, 1961; McDill & Rigsby, 1973; New York State, 1976; Rutter *et al.*, 1979). These attitudes, while certainly influenced by the background and characteristics of students who attend a given school, are also influenced by (and interact with) the social system variables discussed previously.

A group or team emphasis in contrast to individual competition has been associated with positive school climate and improved academic outcomes (Brookover *et al.*, 1979; Wynne, 1980). An emphasis on helping behaviors and cooperation are also important factors in establishing positive citizenship (Wynne, 1980). There is some evidence that competitiveness has a negative component only in the academic arena (Licata *et al.*, 1978).

The level of expectations teachers and administrators hold for each other and especially for students is a recurring variable, related to both climate and other outcomes. An expectation is in one sense a "self-fulfilling prophecy" (Rosenthal & Jacobson, 1968), so that where staff express attitudes of confidence in students' ability to succeed, we would expect students to succeed. Several studies in fact have found a relationship between high expectations and high achievement, which is a stronger relationship than that which exists for race or SES and achievement (Brookover *et al.*, 1979; Brookover & Lezotte, 1979; Brookover & Schneider, 1975; Rutter *et al.*, 1979; Schneider *et al.*, 1979; Weber, 1971). High expectations of administrators for staff are also related to student outcomes (Brookover *et al.*, 1979; Brookover & Lezotte, 1979; Edmonds, 1979; Phi Delta Kappa, 1980; New York State, 1976).

An academic emphasis usually accompanies high expectations for student achievement and is clearly related to student performance and to student aspirations (Brookover *et al.*, 1978; Brookover & Lezotte, 1979; Edmonds, 1979; Mitchell, 1967; Weber, 1971). A concomitant emphasis appears to be a quiet and orderly atmosphere.

Frequent and public occasions for reward and praise tend to occur in high-achieving schools. Recognizing student achievements and providing rewards for good grades or behavior has been associated with higher levels of achievement and with good citizenship (Brookover *et al.*, 1979; Rutter *et al.*, 1979; Wynne, 1980).

The consistent application of rewards and punishments, according to established rules, is another important value in effective schools. This factor has been associated with improved climate (Breckenridge, 1976), school coherence (Wynne, 1980), academic achievement (Phi Delta Kappa, 1980), and a clear policy direction (Rutter *et al.*, 1979). A consensus on curriculum and discipline by teachers and administrators is related to consistency and has been correlated with high achievement and with a positive school climate (Rutter *et al.*, 1979; Wynne, 1980). However, this consensus must include students as well as administrators and faculty, or the peer group culture may reject the school norms.

Finally, exceptional schools are characterized by clearly defined goals and boundaries for both academics and behavior. This clarity has been associated both with student achievement (Ellett *et al.*, 1977; Phi Delta Kappa, 1980) and with school coherence (Wynne, 1980). Clearly articulated goals and objectives are also related to student satisfaction as mediated through the variable of robustness (Licata *et al.*, 1978).

USEFULNESS OF THE CLIMATE CONSTRUCT

The construct of school climate has an inherent appeal to both the practitioner and the policymaker, and by implication, also to the average citizen or parent who is concerned about schools. Even to imply that climate is not worth studying is apostasy. In fact, the wave of popular opinion is so solidly behind the idea of school climate (regardless of the diversity of intuitive or empirical definitions) that schools frequently embark on programs (which are often costly) to improve climate without critically analyzing the value of the construct for school improvement.

Numerous programs and models have been described in the literature, mostly as case studies. Synder (1983), for instance, proposed a program of team planning based on the coaching model and the rationale that "continuous collaboration among teachers, parents, students, and principals tends to produce a healthy school climate, which also influences success or failure" (p. 32). Other programs propose to improve children's self-concept or self-esteem in order to achieve a positive school climate. Mitchell and McCollum (1983), for example, described the POPS program (Power of Positive Students) in which children are encouraged to believe they can succeed. Urich and Batchelder (1979) described a program that improved climate by involving students through leadership training. Yeates (1979) proposed as a low-cost climate program holding "school climate days" in which a cross section of students, teachers, staff, administrators, parents, and community persons would spend a day identifying concerns and issues that would improve their school. Breckenridge (1976) reviewed a similar program that involved a workshop to increase dialogue among members of the school community.

In most cases the efficacy of such programs is assumed, or at best some informal evidence of improvement is offered. For example, Yeates (1979) noted that "in schools where this program is successful, it is reported that vandalism drops, attendance increases, racial problems are minimal, student–staff relationships increase, and other positive effects" [sic] (p. 14). Snyder (1983) provided no evidence that her proposed program is effective. Mitchell and McCollum (1983) pointed to undefined "measurable results" after 2 years of implementation of the POPS program, including academic gains, improved attendance, decrease in disciplinary actions and vandalism, increase in parent participation, and even a better football record. Breckenridge (1976) noted twelve positive outcomes from the workshop, including such observed changes as improved communication, more consistent discipline, more cooperation, more positive interpersonal feelings. Urich and Batchelder (1979) reported that an improved climate (the result of leadership workshops) did lead to higher test scores. In all these cases, however, no controls are discussed (e.g., could the student body or teaching staff have changed in composition and affected those outcomes?). And no evidence is presented that the increases cited were of sufficient magnitude to be attributable to the treatment rather than to chance.

Based on these few examples it is clear, as Rowan *et al.* (1983) pointed out, that we currently are not able to distinguish the relative value of programs to improve climate as compared to other kinds of programs, such as those to improve school leadership. Therefore, practitioners who choose a program to improve school climate have little guidance either in distinguishing effective from ineffective climate programs or in comparing any of them to other kinds of school improvement programs. Often, assertions are made about the value of programs for which empirical evidence simply does not exist or is seriously flawed.

The inconsistent and imprecise effects reported for such programs can be attributed to several causes. To some extent, the problem concerns the diffusion and utilization of research findings. Purkey and Smith (1983), for example, criticized as simplistic the assumption that a set of identified features of effective schools can simply be adopted by a less-than-effective school for a quick and easy transformation. They pointed out that this "recipe model" in "loosely coupled systems" often fails to show an effect because it does not recognize the culture(s) of the school. Pogrow (1983) provided an alternative suggestion that innovation diffusion is difficult to achieve because success requires the joint probability of three independent events occuring: adoption, implementation, and effectiveness improvement. The reality, as S. K. Miller (1982) acknowledged, is that we "know more about the characteristics of exemplary schools than about how to change a school to make it more effective" (p. 36).

Another possibility is that climate improvement programs show imprecise or inconsistent findings because often they are based on research that itself suffers from theoretical and methodological problems. For the practitioner and policymaker interested in utilizing the research on school climate, therefore, several cautions are in order, based both on theoretical and methodological criticisms.

Theoretical Cautions

CONSTRUCT FUZZINESS

Measures of climate are often developed without a clear conceptual framework and without careful analysis of construct validity. As a result, it is generally not clear to the practitioner using such an instrument whether or not the construct being measured truly represents an organizational attribute or an individual attribute. And even if the construct does measure an organizational attribute, it may not be clear whether the aspect of the organization being measured is even appropriate to climate.

A construct frequently confused with climate is job satisfaction. Johannesson (1973) concluded that the two constructs are equivalent because both have been based on descriptions of the work situation. Hellriegel and Slocum (1973) also acknowledged the potential for overlap between the two concepts, but they sought to distinguish them by defining climate as a measure of the work environment itself and satisfaction as the affective reaction to that environment. In another attempt to distinguish the two concepts, LaFollette and Sims (1975) reported a much stronger relationship between measures of climate and organizational practices than between climate and job satisfaction.

VARIABLE REDUCTIONISM

There can be no argument about the fact that many researchers have indeed found relationships between school climate and various person variables, situation variables, and joint person situation variables. At the same time it must be acknowledged that in all likelihood these researchers were not looking at exactly the same construct, given the wide range of operationalized (as well as nonoperationalized) definitions used and thus differences in emphasis. In all likelihood, climate results from the cumulative effect of many variables and to the extent that some of these contributory variables are omitted from the investigation or de-emphasized, bias will result.

In fact, the lack of inclusiveness becomes an even greater problem when we note that most climate instruments look at variables that fall in only one or two of the Tagiuri dimensions (C. S. Anderson, 1982). Programs that purport to change climate may in fact change only a few variables that contribute to the overall climate. Since we have little knowledge of which climate variables individually or cumulatively have the most influence on which outcomes, little basis exists for choosing one program over another.

Furthermore, it is probable that climate operates in conjunction with other school-related variables, and since we do not know the relative importance of each one, it is necessary to implement all the characteristics at once in a school improvement program to assure maximum success (Edmonds, 1982).

When we add to this picture the background and personal qualities that the individual student brings to school, the potential for misinterpretation increases dramatically. Obviously, unless some attempt is made to control for differences in these individual input variables, any association between climate and outcomes might be attributable to the personal characteristics of the students rather than the collective climate of the school. The difficulty here stems from the fact that both students and teachers self-select into schools, and it is impossible for researchers to assign them to a given "condition" or "treatment." And the longer a student is in school, the harder it is to disentangle statistical associations between background, school resources, student attitudes and achievement test results (Spady, 1973).

Although researchers have proposed different conceptual and statistical solutions to this problem with varying degrees of success (C. S.

Anderson, 1982), to some extent different solutions will yield different results. Werts and Linn (1969) suggested using one of four methods based on the researcher's hypothesis and the existing patterns of correlation among variables. Although the problem of individual background variables is well recognized in the research literature, climate improvement programs pay little attention to the issue. In fact programs frequently claim improvements either in climate or student outcomes without attempting to control for the potentially confounding influence of background and personal qualities.

A third problem concerning variables is the restricted focus on only one or two outcome variables. The most highly touted variable is student achievement, but as Levin (1970), Rowan, Dwyer, and Bossert (1982), and others have noted, multiple output variables are more appropriate for a study because schools are expected to achieve multiple goals. Again, the state of the art is such that we simply don't know which climate variables are most influential for which outcomes. Thus a climate improvement program may have unanticipated, unintended, or even undesired effects. This problem is compounded by the fact that various measures of the same outcome may be differentially responsive to school climate or other school variables. Schneider *et al.* (1979), for instance, found grade point average to be more responsive than achievement tests to the influence of attendance.

With all three types of variables (climate, input, and outcome), it is important to choose variables that are relevant, that is, those that can be influenced effectively (Bloom, 1980; McPartland, Epstein, Karweit, & Slavin, 1976). In general, these include proximal variables (e.g., school neatness as opposed to number of books in the library), variables that apply to all students rather than to a single subgroup and that provide a direct measure of the environment rather than proxies, and that concern modifiable actions.

MODEL INADEQUACIES

Of course, even the most appropriate variables remain an untapped source of information without the specification of a causal model. C. S. Anderson (1982) distinguished three kinds of models in which the causal relationships among variables are specified. *Additive models* assume that each variable directly and cumulatively influences outcomes. *Mediated models* assume that some variables affect outcome indirectly, through the influence of another variable or variables. *Interactive models* propose that climate not only influences outcomes but is also influenced by them.

Most researchers agree with Hallinan and Sorensen (1975) that "using an additive model for school effects then clearly is a misspecification of the impact of schools on learning" (p. 13). A few researchers have looked at climate from a mediated model framework (Brookover *et al.*, 1979; Dyer, 1972; McPartland *et al.*, 1976) and even fewer have struggled with the interactive model concept (Hallinan & Sorensen, 1975; Clauset & Gaynor, 1981, 1982).

The scarcity of interactive models in the literature points out that we simply do not know much about the reciprocal affects of climate, school structure, outcome, and input (background) variables. Clauset and Gaynor (1982) have argued that specific policy interventions will have limited impact until we understand the reciprocal relationships among leadership, expectations, climate, instruction, and achievement (a list that could be expanded).

We need to know, for instance, (1) what outcome variables are most influenced by climate, (2) what outcome variables in turn have the greatest impact on climate, (3) to what extent climate affects background variables, both of the individual and of the group, and (4) the relative effects of different school variables on climate.

From an even broader perspective, we need to study the effect of school climate relative to the effect of other school variables on student outcome. Since other variables and climate doubtless interact, we need an interactive model to make these comparisons. Meyer (1980) further pointed out that we should be concerned with the interactive effect of different institutional levels on student outcomes. For example, rather than look only at the classroom and school (organizational levels), he suggested looking at the effect of institutional levels such as grade, type of school, district characteristics, and curriculum characteristics. Such information gathered within an interactive model would allow practitioners and policymakers to evaluate proposed climate programs in terms of those variables that are most effective, most easily modified, and most cost effective.

Methodological Cautions

UNIT-OF-MEASUREMENT DISAGREEMENTS

Researchers often fail to specify how they think school climate is received—by pupils individually or by classes or by the entire school (Wittrock & Wiley, 1970). When the school is the focus of interest, mean scores are the appropriate outcome and the variance explained by the predictor variables is between schools. When the unit of analysis is the individual, individual student scores are the appropriate outcome and the variance explained is between individuals (Johnstone, 1981).

B. D. Anderson (1972) suggested that individual outcome could be seen as a function of (1) the individual's perceptions plus individual background, (2) the average group perceptions plus individual background, or (3) the average perception plus average background. On the other hand, grouped outcome is best conceptualized as a function of average perception plus grouped background.

Burstein (1980) pointed out that interpretations vary with the type of effect assumed to exist and that each type requires different statistical estimators of the effect. An assumption of individual effect, for instance, leads to an interpretation of achievement outcomes as due to a student's ability. An effect assumed due to context could be interpreted as the influence of group ability on instructional practice or on individual motivation. The "frog pond" effect assumes that a student's relative standing in a group affects either the allocation of resources and instructional style or individual motivation.

Interpretations as well as instrument design must follow the researcher's unit-of-measurement assumptions in order to be valid. For example, a researcher who believes that a student's individual performance is a function of milieu variables (i.e., average background characteristics) and average perception of the group about the environment will analyze a climate instrument differently than a researcher with a more individualistic bent.

By the same token, a climate improvement program that attempts to influence the attitudes of individual students will need to measure climate in terms of individual rather than average perceptions. Other programs that attempt to influence climate through a modification of school structural variables (such as the administration of rewards and punishments) or interpersonal relationship may more appropriately look at average perceptions as affecting outcomes. Unfortunately most of the research and programs to date have not specified a unit-of-measurement perspective nor related the instrument or analysis to that perspective.

INSTRUMENTATION DIFFICULTIES

Regardless of the unit of measurement used, instruments also differ in whether the included items require descriptive or evaluative perceptions (Howe, 1977) or what Sirotnik (1980) referred to as systemic or individual properties. According to Howe (1977), "Descriptions minimize, whereas evaluations emphasize the *personal* value, significance, and meaning of stimuli to the observer" (p. 107). In order for perceptions to reflect a group accurately, consensus within a group must exist, and a descriptive instrument is more likely to reflect consensus than is an evaluative instrument. So-called climate instruments with an evaluative design are more likely to be measuring satisfaction than the organizational property of climate (Howe, 1977).

Many instruments and studies fail to distinguish the descriptive and evaluative approaches, although two attempts worthy of note are Howe (1977) and Hall and Griffin (1982). To the extent that practitioners use measures of climate that confuse the two approaches, we can expect confusion as to what is actually being measured. Furthermore, such confusion may mean that individual variance will eliminate the possibility of a consensus by which to identify group climate.

Some researchers have criticized the inclusion of *any* subjective perceptions (whether evaluative or descriptive), and have called for objective measures of climate. The issue concerns whether it is more relevant to know how people perceive, for instance, the level of cooperation in a school, or to have some objective measure of the actual level of cooperation.

Subjective (or high inference) data have some serious flaws, including the fact that they are confounded with previous experiences and values (Bloom, 1976; Davis, 1963; Hellriegel & Slocum, 1974; Herr, 1965; Mitchell, 1967) and tend to create a halo effect in which perceptions of one variable influence perceptions of other variables (Soar, 1980, 1982). On the other hand, more objective measures of climate (such as size or social composition) are often either inadequate proxies or an inadequate reflection of reality because relevant behavior may not be observable to the outsider.

Research by Hall and Griffin (1982) was based on the assumption of James and Jones (1974) that both the subjective perception (called climate) and the more objective measures (called context or setting) are important. The inclusion of both the objective and subjective approaches may be an appropriate solution to this dilemma. However, we still need to specify the relative importance of each, and we need to find ways to assure that subjective ratings involve some indication of external behavior so that variance in perception is not solely a function of personal differences (Soar, 1980).

The fact that we do not have a clear picture of the relative value of objective and subjective measures, as well as their probable interaction presents problems for both the design and evaluation of climate programs. In essence, we do not know whether it is better to modify participants' perceptions or to modify their actual behavior (or some structural component of the school).

OBSERVER CONFUSION

Another instrumentation problem concerns disagreement about who should be the source of data. Whose perception of climate is most accurate? students? teachers? administrators? parents? outside observers? Neither does the literature clearly suggest which group's perception of climate is most critical in terms of outcomes for students. To the extent that these questions cannot be answered, we must remain skeptical about programs that choose one group over another as a focus of change or as a source of information about climate.

STATISTICAL MISINTERPRETATIONS

Another set of problems with climate studies concerns the issue of statistics. Not only do statistics fail to represent all of the social reality of a school, but they also are often misinterpreted even for that part that they do represent.

As noted earlier, many researchers have established a clear relationship between and among variables. However, although a pattern of association gives us an idea of possible casual relationships, correlational studies are inconclusive at best because they do not tell us how that climate or outcome came to exist (Rutter *et al.*, 1979; Austin, 1979). As Dyer (1968) pointed out, the presence of a large correlation does not mean that one variable produced the variation in the other. In fact, a high correlation can occur under any of four conditions (LaFollette & Sims, 1975): (1) *A* and *B* are redundant (i.e., they are measuring the same property); (2) *A* causes *B* or vice versa; (3) *A* correlates with *B* but neither determines the other although they may both be causally related to a third variable; (4) *A* and *B* are related by happenstance (i.e., no logical explanation exists for the statistical relationship).

DESIGN INADEQUACIES

Because correlational techniques leave us without a causal understanding of climate, we are left with the likely possibility that factors that are reported to "cause" a positive climate in one school through the application of a specific program may not work in another setting, or that a climate that is associated with positive outcomes in one school may not have the same relationship in another school.

Both policy and theory require research that specifies the levels and conditions under which differences are created. In short, "We need to know what sorts of schools have what sorts of impact on what sort of student" (Anderson & Tissier, 1973, p. 46). Furthermore, we need to know how this impact occurs. Unless we know how schools affect achievement, we cannot develop programs to modify behavior.

As a result of the inadequacy of correlational studies, researchers have consistently called for longitudinal and experimental research in place of survey research (Boocock, 1973; Brookover et al., 1979; Edmonds, 1979a, McDill and Rigsby, 1973; Miskel, Fevurly, & Stewart 1979; Phi Delta Kappa, 1980; Purkey & Smith, 1983; Rowan et al., 1982; Rutter et al., 1979; Sinclair, 1970). Longitudinal data are more suitable because the effects of school variables accumulate slowly, and measurement at one point in time may not accurately estimate those effects. Longitudinal data can also control for pupil mobility (B. D. Anderson, 1972).

Experimental studies, in which school practices are altered and the effect on children's progress measured, are also needed (Rutter et al., 1979). As programs for school improvement (climate and other outcomes) have developed, their effectiveness has seldom been determined experimentally, nor have alternative interventions been compared for effectiveness. One program in which some attempt was made to evaluate effectiveness experimentally (i.e., treatment groups compared to control groups) found disappointingly few effects, most of which suffered from admittedly confounding influences anyway (Tornatzky, Brookover, Hathaway, Miller, & Passalacqua, 1980).

An alternative to experimental design is to use outliers (schools that consistently outperform or underperform other schools) or other versions of stratification in which the relationship of school variables to outcomes is investigated for different kinds of students. By essentially blocking on some variables we counteract to some extent the self-selection bias inherent in schools. Thus, in schools that are similar in race, or socioeconomic status, any difference in achievement (or other outcomes) might better be attributable to factors other than individual background.

Outlier studies are not without problems that suggest caution in interpretation of findings. Purkey and Smith (1983) criticized them for (1) using relatively small samples that lack representativeness, (2) failing to partial out the effects of background adequately, (3) aggregating achievement data at the school level, (4) comparing positive outliers with negative outliers rather than with average schools, and (5) using subjective criteria for determining effectiveness. Furthermore, Frechtling (1982) showed that the methods of choosing outliers do not consistently produce the same group of effective or ineffective schools.

Future research with outliers should attempt to eliminate these problems. Of critical importance is the selection of effective schools, which Frechtling (1982) determined was best done with a school-level residual analysis. Given the discrepancies among selection methods, the identification of outliers might be improved by using multiple selection procedures and choosing schools that repeatedly show up on the "effective" or "ineffective" list.

SUMMARY AND CONCLUSIONS

A considerable body of research exists on the subject of school climate. The volume of material is largely reflective of the widespread interest in this concept among practitioners and policymakers.

Climate has been differentially defined, often in broad and nonoperationalized ways, and occasionally with more precision. Definitions of climate in the literature are limited by the instrument used to measure climate. Some instruments have tied climate to the press or demands of the environment on the individual. Others have defined climate by the average characteristics of the student body or by teacher attitudes and perceptions. The most personalistic definitions have related climate to student satisfaction or even students' general affect. These differences have made research on schools as learning environments "both difficult and wide ranging in its scope" (Reynolds, 1976, p. 219).

If we ignore differences in the definitions of climate, we can identify some relatively discrete variables that consistently appear to be related to climate. However, cautions are in order, both in terms of theoretical and methodological weaknesses. Theoretical weaknesses include *construct fuzziness* (i.e., the lack of clarity about whether an organizational attribute is even being measured and if so, what that attribute looks like); *variable reductionism* (i.e., lack of comprehensiveness, inclusiveness, and control of variables); and *model inadequacies* (i.e., the lack of research specifying links among variables, including the direction of effects). Methodological cautions include *unit-of-measurement disagreements* (i.e., whether to focus on the individual or the school as the unit of effect); *instrumentation difficulties* (i.e., the focus on either descriptive or evaluative perceptions, or purely objective measures of climate); *observer confusion* (i.e., who to use as a source of data); *statistical misinterpretations* (i.e., assumptions of causation with correlational data) and *design inadequacies* (i.e., the lack of experimental and longitudinal research).

The literature clearly suggests what needs to be addressed by researchers who would produce studies relevant for the policymaker and other consumers of research. Only as research becomes more sophisticated can we hope to sort through the "wash basket" of variables known to be associated with school climate and identify those that are both relevant to a given situation, easily modifiable, and cost effective.

Until that point practitioners would be well advised to approach cautiously any climate program that makes grandiose claims in terms of student outcomes. The construction of climate programs needs to be thoroughly grounded in theory, with a causal model that adequately reflects the complexity of the actual school environment. In addition, such programs should be linked to research, preferably research that is either experimental or longitudinal in design.

This is not to suggest that programs not be created until the definitive research study has been done. As Lezotte (1982) pointed out, although the research on effective schools in general is an "evolving body of research" (p. 63), we cannot expect the public sector to ignore its findings, however tentative and lacking in specificity they may be.

The sensible approach would focus, it seems, on three fronts simultaneously. The researcher is advised to design theoretically and methodologically improved research. The climate improvement program developer is advised to link programs closely to existing research (or to work with researchers). The practitioner and policymaker are advised to hold a healthy skepticism about available climate improvement programs and proposals.

REFERENCES

Anderson, B. D. (1970, March). *The bureaucracy-alienation relationship in secondary schools.* Revised version of a paper presented at the Annual Meeting of the American Educational Research Association, Minneapolis. (ERIC Document Reproduction Service No. ED 053 445)

Anderson, B. D. (1972, May). *A methodological note on contextual effects studies in education.* Paper presented to the Canadian Educational Research Association. (ERIC Document Reproduction Service No. ED 069 806)

Anderson, B. D. & Tissier, R. M. (1973). Social class, school bureaucratization, and educational aspiration. *Educational Administration Quarterly, 5*(2), 34–49.

Anderson, C. S. (1982). The search for school climate: A review of the research. *Review of Educational Research, 52,* 368–420.

Anderson, G. J. (1973). *The assessment of learning environments: A manual for the Learning Environment Inventory and the My Class Inventory.* Halifax, Nova Scotia: Atlantic Institute of Education.

Anderson, G. J. & Walberg, H. J. (1974). Learning environments. In H. J. Walberg (Ed.), *Evaluating educational performances.* Berkeley, CA: McCutchan.

Anglin, L. W. (1979). Teacher roles and alternative school organizations. *Educational Forum, 43,* 439–452.

Astin, A. W. & Holland, J. L. (1961). The Environmental Assessment Technique: A way to measure college environments. *Journal of Educational Psychology, 52,* 308–316.

Austin, G. R. (1979). Exemplary schools and the search for effectiveness. *Educational Leadership, 37*, 10–12, 14.

Barker, R. G. (1963). On the nature of the environment. *Journal of Social Issues, 19*(4), 17–38.

Barker, R. G. (1965). Explorations in ecological psychology. *American Psychologist, 20*, 1–14.

Barker, R. G. (1968). *Ecological psychology.* Stanford, Calif: Stanford University Press.

Barr, R. & Dreeban, R. (1981). *School policy, production, and productivity.* Chicago: University of Chicago.

Beane, J. A. (1979). Institutional affect in the high school. *High School Journal, 62*, 209–216.

Bell, W. E. (1979). Obstacles to urban school renewal. *Theory Into Practice, 18*, 65–72.

Blalock, H. M., Jr. (1971). Aggregation an measurement error. *Social Forces, 50*, 151–165.

Bloom, B. S. (1976). *Human characteristics and school learning.* New York: McGraw-Hill.

Bloom, B. S. (1980). The new direction in educational research: Alterable variables. *Phi Delta Kappan, 61*, 382–385.

Boocock, S. S. (1973). The school as a social environment for learning: Social organization and microsocial process in education. *Sociology of Education, 46*, 15–50.

Breckenridge, E. (1976). Improving school climate. *Phi Delta Kappan, 58*, 314–318.

Brookover, W. B., Beady, C., Flood, P., Schweitzer, J., & Wisenbaker, J. (1977). *Schools can make a difference: A study of elementary school social systems and school outcomes.* East Lansing: Michigan State University, Center for Urban Affairs. (ERIC Document Reproduction Service No. ED 145 034)

Brookover, W. B., Beady, C., Flood, P., Schweitzer, J., & Wisenbaker, J. (1979). *School social systems and student achievement.* New York: Praeger.

Brookover, W. B., & Lezotte, L. W. (1979, May). *Changes in school characteristics coincident with changes in student achievement* [Executive summary]. (Occasional Paper No. 17). Michigan State University, Institute for Research on Teaching.

Brookover, W. B., & Schneider, J. M. (1975). Academic environments and elementary school achievement. *Journal of Research and Development in Education, 9*(1), 82-91.

Brookover, W. B., Schweitzer, J. H., Schneider, J. M., Beady, C. H., Flood, P. K., & Wisenbaker, J. M. (1978). Elementary school climate and school achievement. *American Educational Research Journal, 15*, 301–318.

Burstein, L. (1980). The role of levels of analysis in the specification of education effects. In R. Dreeben & J. A. Thomas (Eds.), *The analysis of educational productivity: Vol. I Issues in microanalysis.* Cambridge, MA: Ballinger.

Christie, S. G., & Kurpius, D. J. (1978). A systematic and collaborative approach to problem solving. In D. J. Kurpius (Ed.), *Learning: Making learning environments more effective.* Muncie, IN: Accelerated Development.

Clauset, K. H., Jr., & Gaynor, A. K. (1981, April). *The dynamics of effective and ineffective schooling: Preliminary report of a system dynamics policy study.* Paper presented at the Annual Meeting of the American Educational Research Association, Los Angeles.

Clauset, K. H., Jr., & Gaynor, A. K. (1982). A systems perspective on effective schools. *Educational Leadership, 40*(3), 54–59.

Coleman, J. S. (1961). *The adolescent society.* New York: The Free Press of Glencoe.

Cox, W. B. (1978). Crime and punishment on campus: An inner city case. *Adolescence, 3*, 339-348.

Davis, J. A. (1963). Intellectual climates in 135 American colleges and universities. *Sociology of Education, 37*, 110–128.

Deal, T. E., & Celotti, L. D. (1980). How much influence do (and can) educational administrators have on classrooms? *Phi Delta Kappan, 61*, 471–473.

Deal, T. E., & Kennedy, A. A. (1983). Culture and school performance. *Educational Leadership, 40*(5), 14–15.

Duke, D. L., & Perry, C. (1978). Can alternative schools succeed where Benjamin Spock, Spiro Agnew and B. F. Skinner have failed? *Adolescence, 13,* 375–392.

Dyer, H. S. (1968). School factors and equal educational opportunity. *Harvard Educational Review, 38,* 38–56.

Dyer, H. S. (1972). Some thoughts about future studies. In F. Mosteller & D. P. Moynihan (Ed.), *On equality of educational opportunity* (pp. 384–422). New York: Random House.

Edmonds, R. R. (1979). Effective schools for the urban poor. *Educational Leadership, 37,* 15–18, 20–24.

Edmonds, R. R. (1982). Programs of school improvement: An overview. *Educational Leadership, 40*(3), 4–11.

Edmonds, R. R., & Fredericksen, J. R. (1978). *Search for effective schools: The identification and analysis of city schools that are instructionally effective for poor children.* Cambridge, MA: Harvard University, Center for Urban Studies.

Ellett, C. D., Capie, W., & Johnson, C. E. (1980, March). *Teacher performance and pupil perceptions of the social environment of learning.* Paper presented at the Annual Meeting of the Eastern Educational Research Association, Norfolk, VA.

Ellett, C. D., Payne, D. A., Masters, J. A., & Pool, J. E. (1977, May). *The relationship between teacher and student assessments of school environment characteristics and school outcome variables.* Paper presented at the 23rd Annual Meeting of the Southeastern Psychological Association, Hollywood, FL.

Ellett, D. C., & Walberg, H. J. (1979). Principals' competency, environment, and outcomes. In H. J. Walberg (Ed.), *Educational environments and effects* (pp. 140–164). Berkeley, CA: McCutchan.

Epstein, J. L., & McPartland, J. M. (1976). The concept and measurement of the quality of school life. *American Educational Research Journal, 13,* 15–30.

Feldvebel, A. M. (1964a). Organizational climate, social class and educational output [whole issue]. *Administrator's Notebook, 12*(8).

Feldvebel, A. M. (1964b). *The relationship between socioeconomic status of the school's patrons, organization climate in the school and pupil achievement level.* Unpublished doctoral dissertation, University of Chicago.

Flagg, J. T., Jr. (1965). The organizational climate of schools: Its relationship to pupil achievement, size of school, and teacher turnover (Doctoral dissertation, Rutgers, the State University, 1964). *Dissertation Abstracts, 26,* 818–819.

Frechtling, J. A. (1982, March). *Alternative method for determining effectiveness: Convergence and divergence.* Paper presented at the Annual Meeting of the American Educational Research Association in New York City.

Gump, P. V. (1971). The behavior setting: A promising unit for environmental designers. *Landscape Architecture, 61,* 130–134.

Hale, J. A. (1966). A study of the relationship between selected factors of organizational climate and pupil achievement in reading, arithmetic, and language (doctornal dissertation, University of Alabama, 1965). *Dissertation Abstracts, 26,* 5817A.

Hall, G. E. & Griffin, T. (1982, March). *Analyzing context/climate in school settings—Which is which?* Paper presented at the Annual Meeting of the American Educational Research Association, New York City.

Hallinan, M. T. & Sorensen, A. B. (1975). *School effects on growth in academic achievement* (Working Paper 75–6). Madison: University of Wisconsin.

Halpin, A. W., & Croft, D. B. (1963). *The organizational climate of schools.* Chicago: University of Chicago.

Hauser, R. M. (1970). Context and consex: A cautionary tale. *American Journal of Sociology, 75,* 645–664.

Hellriegel, D., & Slocum, J. W., Jr. (1974). Organizational climate: Measures, research and contingencies. *Academy of Management Journal, 17,* 255–280.

Herr, E. L. (1965). Differential perceptions of "environmental press" by high school students. *Personnel and Guidance Journal, 43,* 678–686.

Howe, J. G. (1977). Group climate: An exploratory analysis of construct validity. *Organizational Behavior and Human Performance, 19,* 106–125.

Insel, P. M., & Moos, R. J. (1974). Psychological environments: Expanding the scope of human ecology. *American Psychologist, 29,* 179–188.

James, L. R., & Jones, A. P. (1974). Organizational climate: A review of theory and research. *Psychological Bulletin, 81,* 1096–1112.

Jencks, C. S., Smith, M., Acland, H., Bane, M. J., Cohen, D., Gintis, H., Heyns, B., and Michelson, S. (Eds.). (1972). *Inequality: A reassessment of the effect of family and schooling in America.* New York: Basic Books.

Johannesson, R. E. (1973). Some problems in the measurement of organizational climate. *Organizational Behavior and Human Performance, 10,* 118–144.

Johnstone, W. G. (1981, April). *A technique for relating school variables to individual student achievement.* Paper presented at the Annual Meeting of the American Educational Research Association, Los Angeles.

Kalis, M. C. (1980). Teaching experience: Its effect on school climate, teacher morale. *NASSP Bulletin, 64*(435), 89–102.

Klitgaard, R. E., & Hall, G. (1973a). *Are there usually effective schools?* Santa Monica, CA: The Rand Corporation.

Klitgaard, R. E., & Hall, G. (1973b). *A statistical search for unusually effective schools.* Santa Monica, CA: The Rand Corporation.

LaFollette, W. R. & Simms, H. P., Jr. (1975). Is satisfaction redundant with organizational climate? *Organizational Behavior and Human Performance, 13,* 257–278.

Levin, H. M. (1970). *A new model of school effectiveness: A report on recent research on pupil achievement.* Standord, CA: Stanford University, Center for Research and Development on Teaching. (ERIC Document Reproduction Service No. ED 040 252)

Lezotte, C. W. (1982). A response to D'Amico: Not a recipe but a framework. *Educational Leadership, 40*(3), 63.

Licata, J. W., Willower, D., & Ellett, C. D. (1978). The school and environmental robustness: An initial inquiry. *Journal of Experimental Education, 47,* 28–34.

Maxwell, R. W. (1968). Leader behavior of princiapls: A study of ten inner-city elementary schools of Flint, Michigan (Doctoral dissertation, Wayne State University, 1967). *Dissertation Abstracts, 28A,* 2950A.

McDill, E. L., Meyers, E. D., Jr., & Rigsby, L. C. (1967). Institutional effects on the academic behavior of high school students. *Sociology of Education, 40,* 181–199.

McDill, E. L., & Rigsby, L. C. (1973). *Structure and process in secondary schools: The academic impact of educational climates.* Baltimore, MD: Johns Hopkins University Press.

McDill, E. L., Rigsby, L. C., & Meyers, E. D., Jr. (1969). Educational climates of high schools: Their effects and sources. *The American Journal of Sociology, 74,* 567–586.

McPartland, J. M., Epstein, J. L., Karweit, N. L., & Slavin, R. E. (1976). *Productivity of schools: Conceptual and methodological frameworks for research* (Report No. 218). Baltimore, MD: Johns Hopkins University, Center for the Study of Social Organization of Schools. (ERIC Document Reproduction Service No. ED 133 316)

Meyer, J. W. (1980). Levels of the educational system and schooling effects. In C. E. Bidwell & D. M. Windham (Eds.), *The analysis of educational productivity: Vol. 2. Issues in macroanalysis.* Cambridge, MA: Ballinger.

Miller, H. E. (1969). An investigation of organizational climate as a variable in pupil achievement among 29 elementary schools in an urban school district (Doctoral dissertation, University of Minnesota, 1968). *Dissertation Abstracts, 29,* 3387A.

Miller, S. K. (1982). School learning climate improvement: A case study. *Educational Leadership, 40*(3), 36–37.

Miskel, C. G., Fevurly, R., & Stewart, J. (1979). Organizational structures and processes, perceived school effectiveness, loyalty, and job satisfaction. *Educational Administration Quarterly, 15*(3), 97–118.

Mitchell, H. W. & McCollum, M. G. (1983). The power of positive students. *Educational Leadership, 40*(5), 48–51.

Mitchell, J. V., Jr. (1967). *A study of high school learning environments and their impact on students* (Report, U.S. Office of Education, Project No. 5-8032). Rochester, NY: University of Rochester.

Moos, R. H. (1974). Systems for the assessment and classification of human environments: An overview. In R. H. Moos and P. M. Insel (Eds.). *Issues in social ecology.* Palo Alto, CA: National Press Books.

Moos, R. H. (1976). *The human context: Environmental determinants of behavior.* New York: Wiley.

Moos, R. H. (1979a). Educational climates. In H. J. Walberg (Ed.), *Educational environments and effects* (pp. 79–100). Berkeley, CA: McCutchan.

Moos, R. H. (1979b). *Evaluating educational environments.* San Francisco: Jossey-Bass.

Morocco, J. C. (1978). The relationship between the size of elementary schools and pupils perceptions on their environment. *Education, 98,* 451–454.

Murnane, R. J. (1980). *Interpreting the evidence on school effectiveness* (Working Paper No. 830). New Haven, CT: Yale University.

New York State Department of Education, Bureau of School Programs Evaluation. (1976). *Which school factors relate to learning? Summary of findings of three sets of studies.* Albany, NY: Author. (ERIC Document Reproduction Service No. ED 126 613)

Nwankwo, J. I. (1979). The school climate as a factor in students' conflict in Nigeria. *Educational Studies, 10,* 267–279.

Phi Delta Kappa. (1980). *Why do some urban schools succeed? The Phi Delta Kappa study of exceptional urban elementary schools.* Bloomington, IN: Author.

Pogrow, S. (1983). Shifting policy analysis and formation from an effectiveness emphasis to a cost perspective. *Educational Evaluation and Policy Analysis, 5,* 75–82.

Purkey, S. C. & Smith, M. S. (1983). Effective schools: A review. *The Elementary School Journal, 83,* 427–452.

Reynolds, D. (1976). The delinquent school. In M. Hammersley and P. Woods (Eds.), *The process of schooling.* London: Routledge and Kegan Paul.

Rosenthal, R., & Jacobson, L. (1968). *Pygmalion in the classroom.* New York: Holt, Rinehart, and Winston.

Rowan, B., Dwyer, D. C., & Bossert, S. T. (1982, March). *Methodological considerations in studies of effective principals.* Paper presented at the Annual Meeting of the American Educational Research Association, New York City.

Rowan, B., Bossert, S. T., & Dwyer, D. C. (1983). Research on effective schools: A cautionary note. *Educational Researcher, 12*(4), 24–31.

Rutter, M., Maughan, B., Mortimore, P., Ouston, J., & Smith, A. (1979). *Fifteen thousand hours: Secondary schools and their effects on children.* Cambridge, Mass: Harvard University Press.

Sargeant, J. C. (1967). *Organizational climate of high school* (Research Monograph No. 4). Minneapolis: University of Minnesota, Educational Research and Development Council.

Schneider, J. M., Glasheen, J. D., & Hadley, D. W. (1979). Secondary school participation, institutional socialization, and student achievement. *Urban Education, 14*, 285–302.

Silberman, C. E. (1970). *Crisis in the classroom.* New York: Randon House.

Sinclair, R. L. (1970). Elementary school educational environments: Toward schools that are responsive to students. *National Elementary Principal, 49*(5), 53–58.

Sirotnik, K. A. (1980). Psychometric implications of the unit-of-analysis problem (with examples from the measurement of organizational climate). *Journal of Educational Measurement, 17*, 245–282.

Snyder, K. J. (1983). Instructional leadership for productive schools. *Educational Leadership, 40*(5), 32–37.

Soar, R. S. (1980, April). Problems and procedures of aggregating items to represent competencies. In *Issues in the Measurement of Teacher-Compentencies.* Symposium conducted at the annual meeting of the American Educational Research Association, Boston.

Soar, R. S. (1982, March). *Scoring the records—Implications for rating scales.* Paper presented at the Annual Meeting of the American Educational Research Association, New York City.

Sorensen, A. B. (1970). Organizational differentiation of students and educational opportunity. *Sociology of Education, 43*, 355–376.

Spady, W. G. (1973). The impact of school resources on students. In F. N. Kerlinger (Ed.), *Review of Research in Education* (Vol. 1 pp. 135–177). Itasca, IL: Peacock.

Stern, G. G. (1961). Continuity and contrast in the transition from high school to college. In N. C. Brown (Ed.), *Orientation to college learning—A reappraisal* (pp. 33–58). Washington, DC: American Council on Education.

Stern, G. G. (1964). B=F(P,E). *Journal of Personality Assessment, 28*(2), 161–168.

Stern, G. G. (1970). *People in context: Measuring person–environment congruence in education and industry.* New York: Wiley.

Summers, A. A., & Wolfe, B. L. Do schools make a difference? *American Economic Review, 67*, 639–652.

Tagiuri, R. (1968). The concept of organizational climate. In R. Tagiuri & G. H. Litwin (Eds.), *Organizational climate: Exploration of a concept* (pp. 11–34). Boston: Harvard University, Division of Research, Graduate School of Business Administration.

Tornatzky, L. G. Brookover, W. B., Hathaway, D. V., Miller, S. K., & Passalacqua, J. (1980). Changing school climate: A case study in implementation. *Urban Education, 15*, 49–64.

Trickett, E. J., & Moos, R. H. (1973). The social environment of junior high and high school classrooms. *Journal of Educational Psychology, 65*, 93–102.

Tye, K. A. (1974). The culture of the school. In J. I. Goodlad, M. F. Klein, J. M. Novotnew, & K. A. Tye (Eds.), *Towards a mankind school: An adventure in humanistic education* (pp. 20–40). New York: McGraw-Hill.

Urich, T., & Batchelder, R. (1979). Turning an urban high school around. *Phi Delta Kappan, 61*, 206–209.

U. S. Environmental Protection Agency. (1973). *The quality of life concept; A potential new tool for decision-makers.* Office of Research and Monitoring, Environmental Studies Division.

Vyskocil, J. R., & Goens, G. A. (1979). Collective bargaining and supervision: A matter of climate. *Educational Leadership, 37*, 175–177.

Walberg, H. J. (1969). Social environment as a mediator of classroom learning. *Journal of Educational Psychology, 60*, 443–448.

Walberg, H. J., & Anderson, G. J. (1972). Properties of the achieving urban classes. *Journal of Educational Psychology, 63,* 381–385.

Weber, G. (1971). Inner city children can be taught to read: Four successful schools (Occasional paper No. 18). Washington, DC: Council for Basic Education.

Werts, C. E., & Linn, R. L. (1969). Analyzing school effects: How to use the same data to support different hypotheses. *American Educational Research Journal, 6,* 439–447.

Williams, T., & Batten, M. (1981). *The quality of school life* (ACER Research Monograph No. 12). Hawthorne, Victoria: Australian Council for Educational Research.

Willower, D. J., Eidell, T. L., & Hoy, W. K. (1967). *The school and pupil control ideology* (The Pennsylvania State University Studies No. 24). University Park: Pennsylvania State University.

Willower, D. J., & Jones, R. G. (1963). When pupil control becomes an institutional theme. *Phi Delta Kappan, 45,* 107–109.

Willower, D. J., & Licata, J. W. (1975). Environmental robustness and school structure. *Planning and Changing, 6,* 120–127.

Wittrock, M. D., & Wiley, D. E. (Eds.) 1970. *The evaluation of instruction: Issues and problems.* New York: Holt, Rinehart, and Winston.

Wynne, E. A. (1980). *Looking at schools: Good, bad, and indifferent.* Lexington, MA: D. C. Health.

Wynne, E. A. (1981). Looking at good schools. *Phi Delta Kappan, 62,* 377-381.

Yeates, K. (1979). Low cost successful school climate program. *The Networker, 3* (Fall/Spring), 12–14. (ERIC Document Reproduction Service No. ED 190 559)

Young, B. S. (1980). Principals can be promoters of teaching effectiveness. *Thrust for Educational Leadership, 9,* 11–12.

CHAPTER 7

Effective Classroom Teaching: The Necessary but Not Sufficient Condition for Developing Exemplary Schools

David C. Berliner

It is a reasonable belief to hold that effective teachers can exist outside exemplary schools but an exemplary school cannot exist without a large number of effective teachers. This logic brings us to an enduring question in educational practice and educational research: What is an effective teacher? There are, to be sure, different answers to that question, most of which are sensible, many of which are quite complex. In this chapter an attempt is made to provide a relatively simple answer to this most salient question about effective teaching. This answer is, in part, distinguishable from other responses to questions about effective teaching because of its reliance on contemporary research on teaching as a major source of ideas for organizing this answer.

OPPORTUNITY TO LEARN

The single most important factor in predicting whether or not a teacher will be effective is whether the curriculum that is delivered to students in his or her classroom is linked logically or empirically to the outcomes that are desired. One should always be wary of simple answers to complex questions. The deceptively simple proposition offered here needs some elaboration.

The heart of the proposition presented above is a concern with what is sometimes called curriculum alignment, the congruence or overlap of the curriculum with the outcome, or as it is most commonly called, opportunity to learn (Carroll, 1963; Cooley & Leinhardt, 1980). A student must have the opportunity to learn what is expected of him or her. Thus, what is expected of the student should be made clear to that student. Continuing with this logic it is apparent that to communicate the expectations for desired behavior to students, the teacher of the students must have a clear conception of the desired outcomes for the students in a class or a course. A teacher who does not know what outcomes are desired for students at a particular grade level or in a particular course has been grievously abandoned by the administrative team of a school district. A teacher who knows the outcomes that are desired in a particular course or at a particular grade level, but does not direct his or her class toward such outcomes, has been unmonitored by the administrative staff of a school district.

More than any other members of a school system, the administrative staff is responsible for determining the outcomes of schooling, communicating those outcomes to teachers, and ensuring that the teachers of a school district engage in classroom activities likely to lead to such outcomes. Without a clear set of purposes, what is seen in classrooms more often resembles babysitting than it does education.

The issue of outcomes is one of the oldest issues faced in education. Determining what knowledge is of most worth sparks continuous debate. Because of the complexity of the issue and the difficulty of ever adequately resolving these fundamentally philosophical questions, schools and teachers within the same district may not share the belief that particular outcomes are expected for students at a given grade level or in a particular course. When schools and teachers share no common beliefs about what constitutes a desired set of outcomes for particular grades and courses, the issue of effective schooling or effective teaching is irrelevant. This is because the concept of effective teaching or schooling directly implies a criterion. Good teaching, for example, implies no such criterion. A teacher who starts a lecture on time, provides a review, gives an advance organizer, emphasizes important points, asks higher-order questions throughout, cracks a good joke and the like, may be judged to be a "good" teacher, whether or not students learn. Good (and poor) teaching and schooling is determined by values and by knowledge of the standards of good practice, independent of effectiveness. Thus, a medical doctor may have patients that die, but if best practices are used, the doctor may still be judged to be a good doctor. An effective doctor, however, has a record of many fewer deaths. Since the outcomes for medicine are clearer, effective medical practice is usually easier to judge. We in education have a more difficult time. Nevertheless, if we are determined to make judgments of effectiveness about teachers, we must make our outcomes as clear as possible.

In no way does this imply that teachers need 97 objectives for reading, 74 objectives for mathematics, and a few hundred others for science, prosocial behavior, and physical education. The behavioral objectives movement in education did foster a too molecular and rational view of classroom teaching, often trivializing teaching and learning. But one need not throw out the baby with the bathwater. It appears that the development of 10 to 15 objectives for reading, another dozen or so for mathematics, and another dozen or so for the rest of the curriculum are reasonable aspirations. For a single class, as in junior or senior high school, a dozen or more objectives is all that is necessary to proceed with any kind of study or program concerned about teacher effectiveness.

Tests and Other Outcomes

Although the outcomes of education must be specified to make any kinds of judgments about effectiveness, it is important to emphasize that not all outcomes are tests. In fact, some of the most desired and important outcomes are not even testable in ordinary ways. We have, as educators, a legitimate interest in striving to achieve some of these outcomes. We want our students to engage in cooperative behavior, to be able to make complex sensory discriminations, to evaluate aesthetic phenomena, and to solve problems in creative ways. The attainment of such outcomes is not usually measured by tests. A teacher predicted to be effective in achieving these kinds of outcomes, however, is one who can link the curriculum in use in a class to these outcomes. If cooperative behavior is a desired goal, then the infrequent use of competitive instructional methods and the frequent use of cooperative learning classroom activities (e.g., Aronson, 1978; Sharon, 1980; Slavin, 1983) is at least likely to be related to achievement of the desired outcomes. Effective teaching can be assessed by judging whether classroom processes are related to the intentions of the district, school, or classroom, even when no test is used.

If, however, tests are to be used as measures of outcomes (and state agencies, the federal government, and local parents love such instruments), then a concern for effectiveness requires that either of two conditions be met:

1. A test is created to assess the curriculum that has been chosen to produce the desired outcomes; or
2. A curriculum is created to teach the things that are on the test that has been chosen to assess the desired outcomes.

School districts or teachers caught with a curriculum and a test that are not carefully matched to each other are in deep trouble as they try to determine effectiveness. It is impossible for teachers to be found effective if they teach one thing but find themselves tested on another. If students are to take tests that will be used to judge their teachers' effectiveness then they must have the opportunity to learn what the test covers. It is unfortunate that school districts and teachers have much too frequently been foolish enough to be trapped in an untenable position. When, as is often true, tests that are poorly matched to the curriculum are accepted as indicators of the effectiveness of schools and teachers, they must necessarily vastly underestimate the effectiveness of instruction.

A study of such a mismatch between tests and teaching comes from Michigan State University (Freeman *et al.*, 1980). The researchers analyzed three leading mathematics textbook series and five commonly used achievement tests. Each test and textbook underwent an item by item scrutiny to determine its content. They found matches of test and text content ranging from a low of 47% to a high of merely 71%. In the worst case, judgments about school and teacher effectiveness will occur when students encounter tests in which 47% of the topics that are tested have been taught, and where 53% of the topics that are tested may never have been taught. Even in the best case, judgments about teacher and school effectiveness will be made from tests in which about 30% of the topics that are tested may never have been taught to students.

We started this section by saying opportunity to learn is a crucial concern. Sensible discussions of effectiveness cannot be held unless the outcomes of instruction are known, and students have the opportunity to learn the skills and knowledge that is deemed to be desirable. Any achievement tests used as indicators of the desired outcomes must sensibly represent those outcomes and be validly related to what is taught. Thus, the proposition given above appears reasonable: The effective teacher is one who links, logically or empirically, the curriculum that is delivered to students in their classrooms with the outcomes that are desired.

A DELIVERED CURRICULUM

An effective teacher, it was stated, "delivers a curriculum" that is matched to desired outcomes. The meaning of a "delivered curriculum" must also be made clear.

A curriculum is delivered to students when students have the opportunity to spend sufficient time engaged in tasks and succeeding at tasks that are related to the desired outcomes. Engagement and success are the key concepts. They are discussed next, along with the concepts of allocated time and academic learning time, ideas that help clarify this discussion of effectiveness.

ALLOCATED TIME

Some states, school districts, or schools may prescribe explicitly how much time students are to spend on each subject each day or each week. Nonetheless, teachers, and only teachers, make the final decisions about allocating time to subject matter. Teachers in their classrooms are only infrequently monitored or evaluated. Thus, school board members, superintendents of schools, principals, and parents have only the vaguest of notions about how teachers use the school day. Teachers show enormous variability in their decisions about how much time to spend on each curriculum area.

The Beginning Teacher Evaluation Study (BTES; Dishaw 1977a, 1977b) collected allocated times for instruction by various teachers of grades 2 and 5 in reading and mathematics. Five grade 2 teachers allowed from an average of 47 to 118 min daily for reading instruction for a maximum difference of 71 min per day. For mathematics instruction in five other grade 2 classrooms, the differences in time allocations across classrooms was also considerable: 35 min per day. Grade 5 teachers showed similar variation in time allotment decisions. This variability is closely associated with teacher effectiveness.

It is not surprising to find that allocated time predicts achievement, and therefore must enter into discussions about effectiveness of teaching. The variability in allocation is what is most important. Because teachers do not usually keep track of their expenditure of time, some teachers probably spend too little time per day on the subject matter they are committed to teaching. When teachers allocate too little time to a subject, the achievement scores of students will be low. The effective teacher, at a minimum, allocates sufficient time for learning a subject.

Important decisions about how to allocate time must also be made by junior or senior high school teachers. However, these decisions are concerned with content areas within a particular subject-matter area. Elementary and secondary teachers must make choices about how much time to allocate to each content area of a curriculum. For example, when teaching mathematics, how much time should be allocated to fractions? word problems? linear measurement? probability?

The BTES (Dishaw 1977a, 1977b; Berliner 1979) found unexpectedly large teacher differences in these more specific time allocation decisions. For example, one teacher spent 10 times as much time on creative writing in a school year than another teacher. Another surprising contrast emerges when the researchers noted a range of from 0 to 400 min per year in the time allotted to teaching fractions between two teachers in the same grade.

The relationship between allocated time and effectiveness is sensible and has been confirmed many times. In this same study, the data showed that the teacher of one class allocated over 50 hours to comprehension activities during reading and language arts periods while another teacher allowed fewer than 6 hours to such work. When students from the two classes take a test that requires choosing the best title for a paragraph they have just read (a common way to measure comprehension), a safe bet can be made about which class will perform better. They will therefore appear to have had a more effective teacher. In general, teachers who allocate greater amounts of time to some content area have students who perform better in that content area. Thus, in this discussion of the relationship between allocated time and judgments of effectiveness, we seem to be saying that more is better. If this rule is not adhered to blindly, it is, within limits, often true. Certainly we must remember that more is only better up to some point. When that point is reached, then more of the same thing is bound to be boring. Nevertheless, and with regard to the appropriate caveats, effective teachers seem to keep clearly in mind the fact that some curriculum areas will never be learned well if they do not allocate enough time to them. For example, most of us would not do well translating .66667 into the fraction two-thirds (2/3) or translating that value to 67%, if someone had not allocated enough time for us to learn these equivalencies in mathematics.

How much time should be allocated to each content area of the curriculum? Only a teacher can decide how much time to allocate to different content areas of the curriculum. That decision is made in cooperation with the school district personnel, with concern for the outcomes that a district values, and with intimate knowledge of the characteristics of the students in the class. Such decisions are difficult, which is why every teacher is not an effective teacher.

ENGAGED TIME

The relationship between achievement and a teacher's ability to keep students attending, on task, or engaged has been understood for centuries. Of interest are some data on the variations in engaged time in different classes that has become available (Berliner, 1979; Fisher, et al., 1978). Again, drawing on the BTES data (Dishaw, 1977a, 1977b), the percentage of engaged time in five grade 5 math classes ranged from 50 to 90%. In the class with only 50% engaged time for mathematics, a 30-min scheduled time would result in merely 15 min of actual study and learning. In such a situation, total exposure in a school year can be quite low.

It should be thought of this way. The school year really is not a calendar year. In most states it is about 180 days. If we subtract the days that teachers are absent, students are absent, the week before Christmas and the week at the end of the year (when very little gets done), the four days put aside for state testing, the days put aside for field trips, and the like, the number of days in which instruction takes place may total about 140. Now suppose 30 min of time per day is allocated for mathematics, in a class with an engagement rate of 50%. In this example, students really receive only 35 hours of mathematics instruction (140 days × 30 min per day × 50% engagement). Thirty-five hours does not appear to be very much in the way of a total school year's curriculum in mathematics. When we find large differences in engaged time with a curriculum, we also find substantial differences in achievement in that curriculum area. Data collected by Rossmiller (1982) makes this quite clear.

His data reveal that for low-ability children, the variance in reading and mathematics achievement accounted for by engaged-time variables ranged as high as 73%! Even for the highest ability groups, over 3 years, the mean variance accounted for in reading and mathematics achievement was about 10%. Thus, engaged time appears to be an important predictor of achievement and, therefore, a high rate of engagement appears to be a characteristic of classrooms managed by effective teachers. The levels of engagement within a classroom that are necessary to insure achievement are more easily attained in schools where the entire staff is concerned about these issues. It would appear easier to be an effective teacher if one is in an effective school; one that promotes safety, order, a businesslike atmosphere, and seems to hold high expectations for achievement and finds ways to reward such achievement.

SUCCESS RATE

An important instructional variable that has not received a great deal of attention in discussions of effectiveness, until recently, is the variable of success rate. Three obvious levels of success rate may be defined. *High* success rate is defined as the amount of time students spend in high success experiences, say where approximately 80% or more correct responses are made; *medium* success rate is defined as the percentage of time students spend in activities or with curriculum materials that provide them with between 20 and 80% correct responses; *low* success rate is defined as the percentage of time students spend in activities or with curriculum materials that provide for approximately 20% or fewer correct responses. High success means that a student would show a low error rate and consider the task to be easy; low success means a student has a high error rate and probably considers the task difficult. It is an important variable in a discussion of effectiveness because very high and very low success rates in classrooms appear to affect student attitudes and student achievement.

High Success Rate

Many educators had argued that teachers should work hard to develop a high self-concept for students and that a student's achievement in academic areas would develop after his or her self-concept is positive and secure. The research now supports the opposite view. The behavioral programs of instruction, such as the Becker–Engelmann Direct Instructional Program (DISTAR) is based on the notion that after a child has many successful learning experiences, he or she will develop a good self-concept as a learner (see Becker & Engelmann, 1981). Other researchers (Bridgeman & Shipman, 1978; Kifer, 1975) reached similar conclusions. It is now thought likely that a high level of success in a learning environment causes students to develop an enhanced self-concept as a learner. Thus, to build a positive self-concept, a teacher needs to design environments and make assignments so that students can have experience at obtaining high levels of success.

Besides building self-esteem, a higher-than-average success rate in instruction during the school year has been associated with higher achievement on test scores in the spring, better retention of learning over the summer, and more positive attitudes toward school (Fisher *et al.*, 1978, 1980). It should be noted, however, that the positive effects of highly successful school experiences, where very low rates occur, probably are confined to younger school-age children and to duller children of all ages. The importance of success rate in the learning process is more understandable if one thinks about the cyclical nature of learning. We may think of most learning in a classroom as a process of moving from not knowing something to knowing something. When new material is introduced the students most likely will not understand completely and will make some errors. Guided practice or explanations by an instructor help the student to understand. He or she comes to make fewer errors. Eventually, the student will perform correctly, although probably with some effort. Learning eventually becomes well established and further work may be considered practice or review. This stage of practice and review could be thought of as one of consolidation of learning. At some later point, the student knows the material so well that further practice is of minimal value. At that time the teacher would be wise to move on to something new. The results of the Fisher *et al.*, study (1978, 1980) suggest that for the learning of basic skills in the elementary grades, the stage of consolidation, characterized by successful practice, is particularly important to the thorough mastery of concepts and procedures. Teachers need, therefore, to give considerable thought to planning for a stage of consolidation in the learning process.

Rosenshine (1983) has reviewed the data from a number of studies (see particularly Marliave & Filby, 1985) and concluded that during the initial phases of learning, during recitation or small-group work, success rate in reading should be at about the 70–80% level. When students are reviewing or practicing—as in seat work—engaging in drill activities, or working on homework, student responses should be rapid, smooth, and almost always correct.

Another writer (Brophy, 1983) has emphasized the need for psychologically sophisticated sequencing of tasks by the effective classroom manager–teacher. Brophy points out that teachers should be certain that pupils are allowed to engage in independent learning activities (e.g., seat work) when, and only when, they have mastered the prerequisite skills and knowledge. He cautions that severe management and instructional problems will develop if a single important concept or skill is lacking. The observant supervisor will note that inappropriate tasks are more often too difficult for pupils than too easy.

Low Success Rate

We have discussed the importance of a high success rate in fostering achievement, and seen how effective teaching requires attention to the success rate of students. But the research also shows the important effects of a low success rate. It is not surprising to find that when students have spent large amounts of time in low success experiences their achievement is lower. We define low success experiences as those in which a student is making errors more than 80% of the time. Such work is clearly too hard for the student. The student in such a situation is experiencing excessive failure. Effective teachers are very sensitive to failure by students and take pains to avoid having a student spend too much time in such frustrating situations. Thus, most teachers see to it that students spend only 0–3% of their time in such a stressful environment. Yet, from Fisher *et al.*, (1978) we see that in some classes students were observed being assigned to activities or materials that resulted in a low success rate 10% or more of the time. It appears that some teachers are not monitoring the instructional situation carefully enough and are allowing students to spend relatively large amounts of the school day in what must be a very frustrating environment. Self-concept and achievement are bound to be lower when large amounts of time are spent in low success activities.

ACADEMIC LEARNING TIME

Academic learning time (ALT) is defined as *engaged time with materials or activities related to the outcome measures that are being used, and in which a student experiences a high success rate.* The variable of ALT is likely to become one of the more useful concepts for judging whether student learning is taking place at a particular point in time in some particular curriculum area. It is appropriate to think of ALT as a proxy variable for student learning. It is a reasonable variable to attend to when wanting to decide if a teacher is going to be an effective one or not. It is a variable we can observe and measure in the classroom, and it has known relations with student learning.

The practical importance of ALT in relation to teacher effectiveness is illustrated by an example from an analysis of reading instruction in 2nd grade (Fisher *et al.*, 1978). Consider a 2nd-grade student whose reading score in October was average in the sample of students under study. That is, the student was at the 50th percentile. If this student experiences an average amount of ALT (573 min total, or 23 min per day in reading), the student can be expected to show average reading achievement in December. That is, the student will once again be at the 50th percentile. This student would have learned quite a bit between October and December, but would not have changed his or her relative standing in the total sample. Now let us suppose that this student who begins as an average student experiences only 4 min per day of ALT (100 min total) for the time period between October and December. In this case, he or she would be expected to show almost no change in raw score and would decline considerably in relative terms. That is, the student would go from the 50th percentile in October to about the 39th percentile in December in terms of relative standing in the sample. If this average student had experienced very large amounts of ALT, say 52 min per day between October and December, then he or she could be expected to show considerable improvement in reading achievement relative to the other students in the study. The student would have started at the 50th percentile in October, and have moved to the 66th percentile in relative standing in December. Thus, the student with large amounts of ALT appears to benefit substantially. At least, these are the expectations that researchers have for groups of students who experience these differential amounts of ALT. These expectations are derived from data collected on hundreds of elementary school students.

It may appear that this range of from 4 to 52 min per day in ALT is unrealistically large. However, these were the times that actually occurred in the classes studied by Fisher *et al.* (1978, 1980). Furthermore, it is easy to imagine how either 4 or 52 min per day of ALT might come about for a particular student. If 50 min of reading instruction per day is allocated to a student who pays attention about one-third of the time, and only one-fourth of the student's reading time is at a high level of success, the student will experience only about 4 min of ALT—engaged reading time at a high success level. Similarly, if 100 min per day is allocated to reading for a student who pays attention 85% of the time and is at a high level of success for about three-fifths of that time, then that student will experience about 52 min per day of ALT.

Effective teachers seem to keep ALT in mind as they instruct, though they rarely call it by this name and rarely are that deliberate about making conscious their cognitive processes. Nevertheless, effective teachers seem to know the outcome measures used for instruction, assign activities related to those outcome measures, see to it that enough time is allocated for students, find ways to keep students engaged, and insure that the younger or less-bright students spend large percentages of time in high success experiences. In short, effective teachers have students who accumulate a good deal of ALT. Empirically, students and classes that accumulate high levels of ALT are those that are likely to achieve more than students or classes that accumulate lower amounts of ALT.

Let us return now to the initial simple statement offered about what constitutes effective teaching. We stated that the effective teacher delivers a curriculum that is linked to certain outcomes. Delivery of the curriculum requires the teacher to insure that allocated, and especially engaged, time is sufficient for learning and that the materials and activities students are engaged in lead to high success. That is, an effective teacher controls ALT. Perhaps, at this abstract verbal level, the definition of an effective teacher is as simple as I have stated it—it is simply a person who delivers to students a curriculum related to the outcomes that are valued. The only warning needed is to remind readers that outcomes need not be tests.

RELATED CHARACTERISTICS OF EFFECTIVE TEACHERS

A number of teacher characteristics have been correlated with student achievement. Given the simple view of teacher effectiveness presented, we would posit that these characteristics only work, that is, affect achievement, by increasing engaged time, or the time spent in successful environments, or by somehow increasing a student's opportunity to learn. These characteristics of teachers are now described and in a concluding section the links of these characteristics to engagement, success, and opportunity to learn are discussed.

Monitoring

A good deal of classroom work in today's schools is done by students on their own. Students may spend large segments of the elementary school day in seat work, working individually on a contract in reading, doing the ditto sheets related to a science lesson, or finishing the workbook pages associated with a topic in mathematics. In three different studies of schooling, examining hundreds of classrooms for students aged 8–11, researchers found that students worked privately about 50% of the time (Angus, Evans, & Parkin, 1975; Good & Beckermann, 1978; McDonald, 1976). Very little substantive interaction between a student and his or her teachers, classroom aides, or peers, occurs in the schools.

When students are left to work privately and are not monitored by the teacher or classroom aide, they often spend less time engaged in the activities for which they are responsible. In classes where a good deal of work is done by students on their own, the engagement rate in academic subjects usually declines if teachers do not keep their monitoring behavior at a high level. It appears that the classroom in which the teacher moves about rapidly, monitoring students and raising the number of substantive interactions with students, is the class where students do well. A substantive interaction between a teacher and student takes place when the teacher checks to see if the student is doing things correctly, asks questions, gives the student academic feedback, and so on. The greater the number of substantive interactions that take place, the more likely it is that students will achieve academically (Fisher *et al.*, 1978). Thus, monitoring is associated with effective teaching.

Structuring

An ethnographic study of more and less effective teachers (Tikunoff, Berliner, & Rist, 1975) revealed the importance of structuring. In analyzing protocols of reading and mathematics lessons, the teacher's intent sometimes could not be inferred. That is, the readers did not have a clue about why the lesson was occurring, where it fit in the scheme of things, or what they, the students, needed to focus on for success at the task. Almost invariably, the teachers that were judged to be unclear about communicating their goals and giving directions were less effective in promoting academic achievement. Through additional data collection, Fisher *et al.* (1980) concluded that students "pay attention more when the teacher spends time discussing the goals or structures of the lesson or giving directions about what students are to do" (p. 26). Further, it was noted that both success rate and attention were improved when teachers spent more time structuring the lesson and giving directions.

Structuring is especially important in classes where seat work is used frequently. In those classes children work alone a good deal of the time. Therefore, it is not surprising that children who are uncertain about goals and procedures easily find ways to do nothing. Jerome Bruner (1981) has reached a similar conclusion. In visits to schools he had seen many children unable to figure out what was expected of them. He felt that some simple attention to this basic management function would easily improve achievement in classrooms.

Structuring affects attention and success rate. Sometimes, it is not done at all, sometimes it is done only minimally, and sometimes it is overdone. The case of too much structuring was reported by Hassenpflug (1981). Her field notes documented how the directions given for many of the worksheet assignments in third grade actually lasted longer than the amount of time needed by most of the children to finish the assignment! In any case, what is worth noting is that structuring is the responsibility of the teacher; it affects performance and it can be taught to people.

Pacing

Pacing or content coverage was measured in one study as the number of pages of a textbook covered (Good, Grouws, & Beckerman, 1978). In another study it was measured as the number of mathematics problems that were taught (McDonald, 1976). In still another series of studies, it was measured as the number of words that the teacher attempted to teach in basic reading (Barr, 1973–1974; 1980). A relatively strong and consistent relationship occurs between achievement and the way a teacher paces or the amount of content that the teacher covers (cf. Armento, 1977; Rosenshine, 1971). The data reveal that the quicker the pace, the more content covered, the higher the achievement of students. The evidence for the power of pacing keeps mounting. One teacher seems to adjust the pace in the workplace to cover half the text in a semester, another finishes it all. One teacher has 20 practice problems covered in a lesson, another manages to cover only 10. One teacher has students who develop a sight vocabulary of 100 words before Christmas, another teacher's students learn only 50. A remarkable finding reported by Shavelson (1983) was concerned with the teachers' differential treatment of ability groups. Once teachers formed ability groups, they tended to pace the groups differently. That in itself sounds sensible. But the high groups were paced as much as 15 times faster than the low groups, increasing dramatically the difference in what the high and low groups would have been exposed to in the school curriculum. The choice of pace, like the choice of content and the decisions about the time to be spent learning particular content areas, determines student achievement. It therefore is a teacher behavior related to effectiveness.

Questioning

From the time of Socrates to the present day, educators have used questioning as an instructional technique. We have learned from research that elementary school teachers ask many questions—150 per hour when teaching science or social studies (Gall, 1970), and that high school teachers also ask many hundreds of questions per day.

COGNITIVE LEVEL OF QUESTIONS

We have confirmed a suspicion long held by observers of schools that the cognitive level of the questions teachers ask is very low. A question's cognitive level is that level of thought believed to be required for a student to consider and answer a question. Bloom's taxonomy is one way of categorizing questions (Bloom, Engelhart, Furst, Hill, & Krathwohl, 1956). Using that categorization system to classify questions asked by teachers in the classroom, we find that most teachers ask lower-order knowledge-level questions (such as, "When did Columbus discover America?"). Teachers less often ask higher-order questions that require application, synthesis of knowledge, evaluation, or analysis of information (for example, "Why did Columbus want to reach the East?"). Trachtenberg (1974) analyzed over 61,000 questions in the workbooks, tests, and teachers' manuals accompanying nine world history textbooks. Over 95% of those questions were lower-order questions.

Lower-order Questions.   These questions are not very appealing philosophically, since most of us value the higher-order, more thought-provoking questions. Nevertheless, the lower-order question has been found to serve some positive functions. It promotes participation, establishes a factual data base from which more relevant higher-order discussions can arise, and provides high success experiences for students. Moreover, in the case of students of lower socioeconomic standing, the effective teacher seems to demonstrate high levels of lower-order questions, and such behavior seems to correlate positively with achievement (Brophy & Everston, 1974).

Higher-order Questions.   Although it is not customary for teachers to ask many higher-order cognitive questions, when they do, another problem arises. They may receive and accept answers that do not match the level of cognitive thought required by the question. An analysis of questions and answers in hundreds of teacher–student interchanges showed that the odds are only about 50–50 that an analysis-, synthesis-, or application-level question will be responded to with an answer reflecting analysis, synthesis, or application (Mills, Rice, Berliner, & Rousseau, 1980). The effective teacher appears to have experience in more than phrasing questions; he or she appears to classify answers as well.

Perhaps the most important point about questions is that higher-order questions do facilitate learning. In a review of the effects of higher-order questions, Redfield and Rousseau (1981) found that teachers who ask more higher-order questions have students who achieve considerably more. The overall effect is such that a typical student exposed to a lesson without higher-order questions may be expected to perform at the 50th percentile on a test related to that lesson. In contrast, if that same student had been exposed to a lesson where many intelligent higher-order questions were asked, the student would be performing at about the 75th percentile on the same test! Effective teaching with questions, then, includes being able to ask questions at a high level of the Bloom taxonomy, insuring that answers given to such questions are at the level of the question, and insuring also that students with lower social-class backgrounds get many lower-order questions during instruction.

WAIT-TIME AFTER QUESTIONS

Finally, research informs us that we should consider carefully Rowe's (1974) finding that students' answers to questions are of much better quality if teachers wait longer than they usually do between asking a question and requesting a response. This increased wait-time results in increased appropriateness of the response, increased confidence in responding, an increase in the variety of responses, and an increase in the cognitive level of responses. This is not a bad return for a simple adjustment in teaching style—going from the typical 1 sec or less to the recommended 3 or more sec of wait-time. Effective teachers appear to have mastered this oldest of pedagogical forms—the question–answer episode.

CLIMATE FACTORS

For want of a better term, we shall use the term *climate* to describe characteristics of classroom environments that appear to lead to achievement, and are therefore necessary to discuss when developing the notion of the effective teacher. Four such factors seem particularly important: the communication of academic expectations for achievement; development of a safe, orderly and academically focused environment for work; management of deviancy in quick, fair and sensible ways; and development of a convivial atmosphere.

Communicating Academic Expectations for Achievement

The voluminous literature on expectancy effects in education has been reviewed by Brophy and Good (1974), by Cooper (1979), and by Good (1983). And, of course, the reader should see Anderson's Chapter 6 in this volume. The expectation literature is consistently, though not unanimously, interpreted to show that there are powerful effects on performance when teachers communicate their goals for performance to those they are teaching. Academic achievement will usually reflect teacher-set academic performance goals.

The evidence on the differential treatment accorded to high- and low-ability students is believed to provide clues to the mechanism by which expectancies about performance are communicated. Good (1983) summarized this literature as follows: In comparison to students for whom teachers hold high expectations about performance, the students perceived to be low performers are more often seated farther away from the teacher; treated as groups, not individuals; smiled at less; made eye contact with less; called on less to answer questions; are given less time to answer those questions; have their answers followed up less frequently; are praised more often for marginal and inadequate answers; are praised less frequently for successful public responses; interrupted in their work more often, and so forth. This kind of treatment differential between students for whom teachers hold high and low expectations appears to influence their performance in predictable ways.

The communication of expectations does not just create a classroom climate. The expectations of teachers and administrators can permeate a school, creating a school climate. The work of Rutter, Maughan, Mortimore, and Ouston (1979), as well as others (Brookover & Lezotte, 1977; Edmonds, 1979; Vanezky & Winfield, 1979), makes this point. Rutter *et al.* (1979) found marked differences in the outcomes of secondary schools attributable to school-level variables such as expectations. Their data revealed that "children had better academic success in schools . . . where teachers expressed expectations that a high proportion of the children would do well in national examinations" (p. 188). Furthermore, the beneficial effects of high expectations are felt in areas other than academic achievement. Better behavior, attendance, and fewer delinquent acts were reported from schools that gave pupils increased responsibility for caring for school property. Also, assigning pupils other responsibilities yielded more mature behavior (Rutter *et al.*, 1979, p. 188). Thus, the processes by which expectations about academic performance are communicated seem to be part of the effective teacher's knowledge of pedagogy, and they lead to an environment conducive to learning.

Developing a Safe, Orderly, and Academically Focused Environment for Work

The evidence on effective classrooms and effective schools is amazingly congruent. There is always an indication of higher achievement in classes or schools where there is an orderly, safe environment, a businesslike manner among the teachers, and a school-wide system that (1) reflects thoughtfulness in fostering academic programs, (2) focuses on achievement, (3) holds students accountable for achievement, and (4) rewards achievement. Where such evidence of order and focus are missing, achievement is lower. Case studies of unusually effective classes in the BTES (Fisher et al., 1978) showed this rather clearly. And Rutter and his colleagues (1979) found similar variables related to achievement when they looked between schools, rather than between classes. Purkey and Smith (1983, p. 445), after reviewing the effective schools literature, wrote a noteworthy summary. They indicate that pupils can feel pride and responsibility and suffer few behavior problems when the school maintains order and discipline through reasonable rules enforced with fairness and consistency. Such a school assumes a serious, purposeful approach to its task.

It should be noted that literal interpretation of these findings can lead to overcontrol and such a strict academic focus that it denies the arts or produces debilitating levels of anxiety among students. Thus, a literal application of these ideas actually could give rise to ineffective teaching. On the other hand, a lack of order and a lack of academic focus have been empirically determined to lead to low levels of achievement and are, therefore, a clear indication of ineffective teaching. The ability to balance these forces is the problem for the effective teacher. Effective teachers probably find ways to demonstrate that such things as playfulness and order are not incompatible.

Sensible Management of Deviancy

Jacob Kounin, in an enormously influential work (1970), has provided a set of concepts that helps us understand the process of maintaining a workplace free from deviance and in which students attend to their assignments. He gave us the concept of *withitness*, describing how effective managers nip behavioral problems in the bud; *overlappingness*, describing how effective classroom managers handle more than one thing at a time; he also described the need for *signals* for academic work; the effects of *momentum* and *smoothness* in lessons on student behavior; and the positive effects on attention of *group alerting, accountability*, and *variety* in teaching. These variables have, for the most part, been verified or appropriately qualified in the work of Brophy and Evertson (1976) and Anderson, Evertson and Brophy (1979), among others. Borg and Ascione (1982) have taken these concepts and developed training materials for teachers. So have Evertson et al. (1984) and Emmer et al. (1984). Field tests of these suggestions about management, garnered from research and practice, show that they do work. Effective teachers are good managers. They control attention and prevent deviancy. This results in increased achievement through a reduction of time lost due to management problems and by helping to foster a safe and orderly environment in which it is possible for students to learn the school curriculum that was selected for them.

Development of a Convivial Atmosphere

In a number of studies (Fisher, *et al.*, 1978; Tikunoff, *et al.*, 1975) it was found that achievement was higher in classes characterized as warm and democratic in atmosphere, where students cooperated on academic tasks, and where there appeared to be a high level of student responsibility for academic work. These positive predictors of achievement can be grouped under the heading of "conviviality." Teachers who create convivial atmospheres are more likely to be effective than teachers who do not create such environments.

Summary of Climate Factors

In this section four climate variables that affect achievement were noted. It was suggested that an effective teacher communicates high academic expectations, and when such expectations become a part of the classroom and school ethos, achievement is positively affected; effective teachers create classrooms that are safe, orderly, and academically focused; effective teachers also show sensible management of behavior problems; and, they create a pleasant place to be.

Teaching takes place in a context. It can never be decontextualized. The context—that special climate or environment for learning that must be developed in order for classrooms or schools to be judged successful—appears to require conviviality, within which is developed a press for both prosocial and academically oriented behavior.

TESTS AND GRADES

People hold strong opinions about the role of tests and grades in the schools. In recent years there have been many persuasive arguments against the use of tests and grades. Because of these often perceptive criticisms some of the proven instructional benefits of tests and grades have been overlooked. It is easy to acknowledge that tests and grades can be used stupidly, brutally, and unfairly. Nevertheless, sensible and sensitive use of tests and grades have some positive effects on students' achievement, and often help to distinguish between effective and less effective teachers.

A classic study of the positive motivational effects of tests and grades was undertaken during World War II (Hovland, Lumsdaine, & Sheffield, 1949). Soldiers were asked to learn the military phonetic alphabet (A-able; B-baker; etc.). The number of letters they could correctly pair up after exposure to different conditions of learning was investigated. The data were clear. When tests and grades were expected, performance was higher.

The positive motivational and instructional effects of tests and grades have also been shown in a study where students were tested either very frequently, infrequently, or not at all during the course of a semester (Fitch, Drucker, & Norton, 1951). The classes with more frequent testing had students that showed higher achievement. It should be noted that frequency of testing and grading is a key element in mastery learning, personalized systems of instruction, and many other successful individualized instructional programs. This lends more credence to the idea that sensible use of tests and grades have motivational and instructional effects that are beneficial.

In still another study in this area the instructors had the actual grades for students who elected to take a pass–fail grade in a course and they also had the students' grades in conventional courses where the pass–fail option could not be used (Hales, Bain, & Rand, 1971). Whether a student had been an A, B, or C student previously, when taking a pass–fail course, the student did less well than in conventionally graded courses. Once again the positive motivational effects of tests and grades seems to be demonstrated. In another study a comparison of grading and no grading of graduate student term papers in a prestigious university was undertaken (Clark, 1969). It was found that students in the graded condition read more references, discussed their papers more with their instructor, spent more time preparing and writing the papers, and completed a higher percentage of their papers. As would be expected from the above noted differences, the papers of the group who were being graded were, in fact, superior to the papers of students who expected no grade. These data seem to refute the claim by graduate students that they are already motivated enough and really do not work for grades.

Effective teachers often capitalize on the motivational aspects of tests and grades. The knowledge that a test and a grade are forthcoming seems to exert some pressure on students to perform a little better. But there are also negative effects from overuse of tests and grades. For example, students may not build internal standards for feedback. Rather, they may learn to rely on external standards only. Some students may become so anxious over tests and grades that they actually show a decrement in performance. Thus, heavy use of tests and grades for summative evaluation can also be associated with ineffective teaching. Effective teachers seem to know the difference between the positive and negative motivational effects of tests and grades.

FEEDBACK

Practice or testing with feedback has been found to affect student behavior. Feedback can take a number of forms, and includes praise, use of ideas, corrective feedback, and criticism. The first three forms of feedback have been associated with more-effective teachers, the latter form of feedback has been associated with less-effective teachers.

Praise

Dozens of studies about the relationship between praise and achievement have been analyzed (Gage & Berliner, 1984). Most of these studies show a positive effect. Nevertheless, some studies show a negative effect. The negative findings seem to point out two things: (1) too much praise can result in a loss of the effectiveness of praise, and (2) unless praise is contingent on the quality of the student's response, it is ineffective. Contingent praise means that praise should be given when and only when an acceptable response is made by students. Marginal and inappropriate responses should not be reinforced by praise.

Brophy (1981) has analyzed the kinds of praise that may or may not be useful to a teacher for promoting achievement and feelings of success by students. Effective teachers have learned to use praise differently from ineffective teachers.

Using Student Ideas

Another way teachers can provide acceptance of students' responses and thereby provide students with positive feedback is through accepting a student's ideas. The teacher may acknowledge a student's response publicly, summarize it, modify it, apply it, or compare it with others. Acceptance and use of a student's idea is considered to be a favorable reaction because it indicates to the student that the teacher considers his or her ideas worth taking seriously. Praise may be perceived as perfunctory or courteous; acceptance of a student's ideas is not likely to be interpreted in that way. The acceptance and use of ideas probably has reinforcing or motivating effects, in addition to the cognitive value of repeating and reprocessing good ideas. The experimental and correlational research summarized by Rosenshine (1971) and Dunkin and Biddle (1974) points to a moderate but positive relationship between use of student ideas and student achievement. It appears that many effective teachers provide greater amounts of feedback to students in the form of the acceptance of student ideas. This usually leads to higher student achievement.

Corrective Feedback

From virtually all learning theories we find claims that feedback during instruction is very beneficial. The major problem for teachers is how best to provide such feedback when students are making inappropriate responses. Criticism or sarcasm is not the proper way to do this. The way effective teachers appear to do this is (1) to distinguish between the student and the student's response, and (2) to provide opportunities for the student to make the acceptable response.

Distinguishing between the student and the student's response means that a teacher says or writes, "This is the wrong answer—please fix," instead of saying, "You are wrong!" Or, it is the difference between a teacher saying, "That answer's not right, anyone know why?" and, "Can anyone see Johnny's mistake?" Corrective feedback is affectively neutral. Corrective feedback provided by an effective teacher is interpreted by a student or a class to mean simply that the response, answer, test item, or behavior is inaccurate or inappropriate. It should never be interpreted by a student as meaning that a student is dumb, sloppy, or bad. Corrective feedback is meant to communicate that something should be corrected. But, it should communicate in such a way that resentment and hostility are not built up.

When corrective feedback is given to students it appears best to provide an opportunity for making the appropriate or acceptable response. It is not really fair just to say to a student that an answer is wrong. The feedback should include a comment like, "Please do this over, following the procedures on page 110 of the text." Or, the teacher may inform a student about his or her use of poor grammar in a composition, point out in a neutral way where errors had been made, and suggest that the student fix those errors.

By combining affectively neutral feedback with chances for correction of an inappropriate response, a student's learning rate and attitude toward learning appears to be enhanced. Effective teachers appear to provide higher levels of corrective feedback, which seems to help students achieve more in less time with less stress.

Criticism

One way to provide feedback when inappropriate or inaccurate responses are made is to provide criticism. Teachers can respond to students with anything from, "Your facts and logic are inane," to a simple, "No" or a curt, "Wrong!"

It is fortunate that criticism accompanied by sarcasm (e.g., "No, you dummy!") is infrequently found in classrooms. But when sarcasm is found to exist in a significant amount, it is almost always indicative of a teacher whose students achieve poorly and feel negatively toward the teacher. When a teacher is found using too much criticism and disapproval, it is an indication that something is wrong with the teacher's attitudes, methods, choice of curriculum, classroom organization, or other factors. Ineffective teachers display high rates of criticism.

SUMMARY OF CHARACTERISTICS OF EFFECTIVE TEACHERS

A set of teacher behaviors and classroom characteristics related to achievement have been described in this section. Two important things to keep in mind are: (1) this is an incomplete and highly selected set of behaviors and characteristics; and (2) no one set of behaviors or characteristics of classrooms will adequately describe all the events in an effective teacher's classroom.

The incompleteness of the list of teacher behaviors and classroom characteristics associated with teacher effectiveness has to do with the burgeoning literature in this area since 1970. Hundreds of teacher behaviors and characteristics of classrooms have now been found to distinguish between more effective and less effective teachers. Some of the findings are supported in one, some in half a dozen studies. Thus, some personal selection was called for. Moreover, studies of classrooms have revealed that there are many ways to be effective. Not all the behaviors noted above occur in every classroom of every teacher who is regarded as effective. Effectiveness as a teacher can occur by many routes. Nevertheless, if one is interested in identifying effective teachers, or training teachers in order to build exemplary schools, these behaviors and classroom characteristics are probably a sensible set to consider seriously.

As stated above, the key to effective teaching is said to be engagement and success with a curriculum that is matched to desired outcomes. Teacher behaviors and classroom characteristics that distinguish more-effective from less-effective teachers influence achievement by affecting these factors. For example, monitoring keeps engagement high, thus influencing achievement. Structuring helps students know what is expected, thus influencing success with the tasks they work at. Pacing, when rapid, insures that a maximum amount of the curriculum to be learned is provided to the student. Thus, it affects opportunity to learn. Questioning influences attending in classrooms and reveals something about the content of the tests if the questions are related to the desired outcomes and not just time fillers. This is true of questions at any cognitive level. Wait-time after questioning seems to influence attending by requiring deeper processing than is ordinarily the case, and by influencing success rate, apparently by insuring that enough time is granted to correctly answer thoughtful questions. The climate variables, such as communicating academic expectations, apparently influences motivation, positively or negatively, thereby affecting the engaged time students put into acquiring skills and information. A safe and orderly classroom where there is evidence of academic focus also allows for higher rates of engaged time in the academic tasks, presumably those related to academic outcomes. The sensible management of deviancy keeps interruptions to a minimum, insuring high levels of engagement. A convivial atmosphere develops the trust and cooperation necessary to complete academic tasks successfully. Tests and grades used as summative information for students are motivating and increase total engaged time in academic pursuits. When used as formative information, test and grades also reveal something of the nature of the outcome measure. They also help to insure higher rates of success by the nature of the feedback they provide learners. Feedback such as praise or using student ideas increases motivation, thereby insuring higher rates of engagement. Corrective feedback affects error rate, insuring higher levels of success experience.

Thus, one way to examine the many teacher behaviors and classroom characteristics said to relate to achievement is to put them through a mental screening process. They probably will be related to effectiveness if they give experience with the outcome measures, increase engagement, and increase success during learning.

CONCLUSION

There cannot be an exemplary school without large numbers of effective teachers. To be an effective teacher means more than being a good teacher. It means that achievement of certain types does take place. Achievement takes place at the classroom level when the teacher can deliver to students a curriculum that is matched to desired outcomes. To deliver a curriculum means to find ways to have students be engaged with and succeed at materials and activities that have empirical or logical links with the sought outcomes. The ways teachers find to increase engagement, success rate, or the students' understanding of the desired outcomes includes monitoring, structuring, questioning, creating environments for learning, testing, grading, and providing feedback. These behaviors give rise to academic learning time—ALT. ALT is a measurable variable derived from observations in classrooms. It is defined as a student's engaged time—at a high level of success—with materials or activities related to the desired outcomes. Other things being equal, when comparing classrooms, higher levels of ALT will be predictive of higher levels of achievement. It is not remarkable that ALT demonstrates a strong relationship with achievement. If we look into classrooms where students are engaged, succeeding, and working on tasks similar to the kinds of tasks that we have set up as criteria for them, then we should be very pleased. In this sense ALT is a measure of that very elusive concept in education called "quality instruction." It is likely that exemplary schools show high levels of ALT—high levels of quality instruction—in many of their classrooms.

REFERENCES

Anderson, L. M., Evertson, C. M., & Brophy, J. E. (1979). An experimental study of effective teaching in first grade reading groups. *The Elementary School Journal, 79*, 193–223.

Angus, M. J., Evans, K. W., & Parkin, B. (1975). *An observational study of selected pupil and teacher behavior in open plan and conventional design classrooms.* Australian Open Area Project (Tech. Rep. No. 4). Perth, Australia: Education Department of Western Australia.

Armento, B. A. (1977). Teacher behavior related to student achievement on a social science content test. *Journal of Teacher Education, 28* (2), 46–52.

Aronson, E., Blaney, N., Sikes, J., Stephan, G., & Snapp, M. (1978). *The jigsaw classroom.* Beverly Hills, CA: Sage Publications.

Barr, R. C. (1973–74). Instructional pace differences and their effect on reading acquisition. *Reading Research Quarterly, 9*, 526–554.

Barr, R. C. (1980, April). *School, class, group, and pace effects on learning.* Paper presented at the meeting of the American Educational Research Association, Boston, MA.

Becker, W. C., Engleman, S., Carnine, D. W., & Rhine, W. R. (1981). The Direct Instruction Model. In W. R. Rhine (Ed.) *Making schools more effective: New directions from follow-through.* New York: Academic Press.

Berliner, D. C. (1979). Tempus Educare. In P. L. Peterson and H. J. Walberg (Eds.), *Research on teaching* (pp. 120–135). Berkeley, CA: McCutchan.

Bloom, B. S., Engelhart, M. B., Furst, E. J., Hill, W. M., & Krathwohl, D. R. (1956). *Taxonomy of educational objectives: The classification of educational goals: Handbook I. Cognitive domain.* New York: Longmans Green.

Borg, W. R., & Ascione, F. R. (1982). Classroom management in elementary mainstreaming classrooms. *Journal of Educational Psychology, 74,* 85–95.

Bridgeman, B., & Shipman, V. C. (1978). Preschool measure of self-esteem and achievement motivation as predictors of third-grade achievement. *Journal of Educational Psychology, 70,* 17–28.

Brookover, W. B., & Lezotte, L. (1977). *Change in school characteristics coincident with changes in student achievement.* East Lansing, MI: College of Urban Development, Michigan State University.

Brophy, J. E. (1981). Teacher praise: A functional analysis. *Review of Educational Research, 51,* 5–32.

Brophy, J. E., (1983). Classroom organization and management. *The Elementary School Journal, 83,* 265–286.

Brophy, J. E., & Evertson, C. M. (1974). *Process–product correlations in the Texas teacher effectiveness study* (Final Report No. 74–4). Austin, TX: Research and Development Center for Teacher Education, University of Texas.

Brophy, J. E., & Evertson, C. M. (1976). *Learning from teaching: A developmental perspective.* Boston, MA: Allyn & Bacon.

Brophy, J. E., & Good, T. L. (1974). *Teacher–student relationships: Causes and consequences.* New York: Holt, Rinehart & Winston.

Bruner, J. (1981, August). *On instructability.* Paper presented at the meeting of the American Psychological Association, Los Angeles.

Carroll, J. B. (1963). A model of school learning. *Teachers College Record, 64,* 723–733.

Clark, D. C. (1968). Competition for grades and graduate student performance. *Journal of Educational Research, 62,* 351–354.

Cooley, W. W., & Leinhardt, G. (1980). The instructional dimensions study. *Educational Evaluation and Policy Analysis, 2* (1), 7–25.

Cooper, H. (1979). Pygmalion grows up: A model for teacher expectation, communication and performance influence. *Review of Educational Research, 79,* 389–410.

Dishaw, M. (1977a). *Descriptions of allocated time to content areas for the A-B period.* Beginning Teacher Evaluation Study (Tech. Note IV–IIa) San Francisco, CA: Far West Laboratory for Educational Research and Development.

Dishaw, M. (1977b). *Descriptions of allocated time to content areas for the B-C period.* Beginning Teacher Evaluation Study, Technical Note IV–IIb. San Francisco, CA: Far West Laboratory for Educational Research and Development.

Dunkin, M. J., & Biddle, B. J. (1974). *The study of teaching.* New York: Holt, Rinehart & Winston.

Edmonds, R. (1979, March/April) Some schools work and more can. *Social Policy, 9,* 28–32.

Emmer, E. T., Evertson, C. M., Sanford, J. P., Clements, B. W., & Worsham, M. E. (1984). *Classroom management for secondary teachers.* Englewood Cliffs, NJ: Prentice-Hall.

Evertson, C. M., Emmer, E. T., Clements, B. S., Sanford, J. P., Worsham, M. E., & Williams, E. L. (1984). *Classroom management for elementary teachers*. Englewood Cliffs, NJ: Pentice-Hall.

Fisher, C. W., Berliner, D. C., Filby, N. N., Marliave, R. S., Cahen, L. S., & Dishaw, M. M. (1980). Teaching behaviors, academic learning time and student achievement: An overview. In C. Denham & A. Lieberman (Eds.), *Time to learn* (pp. 7–32). Washington, DC: National Institute of Education.

Fisher, C. W., Filby, N. N., Marliave, R. S., Cahen, L. S., Dishaw, M. M., Moore, J. E., & Berliner, D. C. (1978). *Teaching behaviors, academic learning time and student achievement* (Final Report of Phase III-B, Beginning Teacher Evaluation Study, Tech. Rep. V–I). San Francisco, CA: Far West Laboratory for Educational Research and Development.

Fitch, M. L., Drucker, A. J., & Norton, J. A. (1951). Frequent testing as a motivating factor in large lecture classes. *Journal of Educational Psychology, 42*, 1–20.

Freeman, D., Kuhs, T., Porter, A., Knappen, L., Floden, R., Schmidt, W., & Schwille, J. (1980). *The fourth grade mathematics curriculum as inferred from textbooks and tests*. (Report No. 82) East Lansing: Michigan State University, Institute for Research on Teaching.

Gage, N. L., & Berliner, D. C. (1984). *Educational Psychology* (4th ed.). Boston, MA: Houghton-Mifflin.

Gall, M. D. (1970). The use of questioning in teaching. *Review of Educational Research, 40*, 707–721.

Good, T. L. (1983). Classroom research: A decade of progress. *Educational Psychologist, 18*, 127–144.

Good, T. L., & Beckerman, T. M. (1978). Time on Task: A naturalistic study in sixth grade classrooms. *Elementary School Journal, 78*, 193–201.

Good, T. L., Grouws, D. A., & Beckerman, T. M. (1978). Curriculum pacing: Some empirical data in mathematics. *Journal of Curriculum Studies, 10*, 75–82.

Hales, L. W., Bain, P. J., & Rand, L. P. (1971, March). *An investigation of some aspects of the pass-fail grading system*. Paper presented at the meeting of the American Educational Research Association, New York City.

Hassenpflug, A. M. (1981). *The use and understanding of school time by third graders: An ethnographic case study* (Technical Report No. 574). Madison: Research and Development Center for Individualized Schooling, University of Wisconsin.

Hovland, C. I., Lumsdaine, A. A., & Sheffield, F. D. (1949). *Experiments on mass communication*. Princeton, NJ: Princeton University Press.

Kifer, E. (1975). Relationships between academic achievement and personality characteristics: A quasi-longitudinal study. *American Educational Research Journal, 12*, 191–210.

Kounin, J. (1970). *Discipline and group management in classrooms*. New York: Holt, Rinehart and Winston.

Marliave, R., & Filby, N. N. (1985). Success rates: A measure of task appropriateness. In C. W. Fisher & D. C. Berliner (Eds.), *Perspectives on instructional time*. New York: Longman.

McDonald, F. J. (1976). *Research on teaching and its implications for policy making: Report on phase II of the Beginning Teacher Evaluation Study*. Princeton, NJ: Educational Testing Service.

Mills, S. R., Rice, C. T., Berliner, D. C., & Rousseau, E. W. (1980). The correspondence between teacher questions and student answers in classroom discourse. *Journal of Experimental Education, 48*, 194–209.

Purkey, S. C., & Smith, M. C. (1983). Effective schools: A review. *The Elementary School Journal, 93*, 428–452.

Redfield, D. L., & Rousseau, E. W. (1981). A meta-analysis of experimental research on teacher questioning behavior. *Review of Educational Research, 51,* 237–245.

Rosenshine, B. (1971). *Teaching behaviours and student achievement.* Windsor, Berkshire, England: National Foundation for Education Research in England.

Rosenshine, B. V. (1983). Teaching functions in instructional programs. *The Elementary School Journal, 83,* 335–352.

Rossmiller, R. A. (1982, September). *Managing school resources to improve student achievement.* Paper presented at the State Superintendent Conference for District Administrators, Madison, WI.

Rowe, M. B. (1974). Wait time and rewards as instructional variables: Their influence on language, logic and fate control. Part 1: Wait time. *Journal of Research Science Teaching, 11,* 81–94.

Rutter, M., Maughan, B., Mortimore, P., & Ouston, J. *Fifteen thousand hours.* Cambridge, MA: Harvard University Press.

Sharon, S. (1980). Cooperative learning in small groups: Recent methods and effects on achievement, attitudes and ethnic relations. *Review of Educational Research, 50,* 241–271.

Shavelson, R. J. (1983). Review of research on teachers' pedagogical judgments, plans, and decisions. *Elementary School Journal, 83,* 392–414.

Slavin, R. (1983). *Cooperative learning.* New York: Longman.

Tikunoff, W. J., Berliner, D. C., & Rist, R. C. (1975). *An ethnographic study of the forty classrooms of the Beginning Teacher Evaluation Study known sample* (Technical Report 75–105). San Francisco, CA: Far West Laboratory for Educational Research and Development.

Trachtenberg, D. (1974). Student tasks in text material: What cognitive skills do they tap? *Peabody Journal of Education, 52,* 54–57.

Vanezky, R. L., & Winfield, L. F. (1979). *Schools that succeed beyond expectations in teaching reading.* Final Report, National Institute of Education (Grant No. NIE-G-78-0027). Newark, DE: College of Education, University of Delaware.

CHAPTER 8

The Role of the Principal in School Improvement

Kenneth A. Leithwood and Deborah J. Montgomery

INTRODUCTION

Evidence that principals play a critical role in school improvement is considerable and mounting rapidly. The success of efforts to assist principals in becoming more effective are significantly dependent on knowledge of manageable steps principals may take in their own development. This chapter outlines what it is that exceptionally effective principals do and what constitutes growth in principal effectiveness.

Information provided about principal effectiveness here comes from a research designed to develop a principal profile (Leithwood & Montgomery, 1983). The profile is a multidimensional, multilevel, detailed description of principals' beliefs, intentions and actions, all of which are subsequently referred to as behaviors. In order to describe principal behaviors in profile form, answers were required to four questions: 1) What categories, aspects, or dimensions of principal behavior are most critical in accounting for differences in principals' effectiveness? 2) Within those dimensions, what principal behaviors appear to be most effective? 3) How can approximations to such highly effective behaviors be described and ordered according to their level of effectiveness? 4) Will the resulting whole profile of growth in principal effectiveness stand the test of empirical validation?

Most research on principals' effectiveness conceptualizes such effec-

155

tiveness in one of two related ways: impact on students or impact on school characteristics and processes plausibly influencing students. This and other research defines impact on students in terms of achievement in basic skills (Ogawa & Hart, 1983), school attendance (Stallings, 1982), amounts of vandalism (Rutter, 1979), and perceptions of school robustness (Willower & Smedley, 1981). In addition, principal behaviors are described here that are likely to facilitate student achievement of a wider range of social and intellectual outcomes—outcomes characteristic of a self-directed problem solver.

A second and closely related conception of principal effectiveness focuses on characteristics of schools and school processes likely to have an impact on staff and often on students as well. Examples of such characteristics include teacher job satisfaction (Martin, Isherwood, & Lavery, 1976), staff participation in decision making (Lipham, Dunstan, & Ranker, 1981), and implementation of innovations (Rutherford, Hord, Huling, & Hall, 1983). In earlier research, characteristics such as these were viewed as mediating variables that the principal may influence in order to have some impact on students. Since principals have limited opportunities to interact directly with students, the search for variables that both influence students and can be influenced by principals was considered a central research problem.

METHODS

The development and validation of the principal profile is described in detail in Leithwood and Montgomery (1984). The summary provided here is organized around the four questions noted in the introduction. Several qualitative and quantitative methods were used to obtain responses to each question. These methods involved both the collection and analysis of new data and the systematic review and integration of empirical research reported by others.

Identifying Dimensions of Behavior

The identification of important behaviors involved the selection of categories or dimensions of principal behavior that would (1) be meaningful to practicing principals, and (2) permit description of those aspects of behavior most likely to account for differences in principal effectiveness. To meet the first of these criteria, a series of $1\frac{1}{2}$ to 3 hour interviews was conducted with a random sample of 23 principals from four school systems. A content analysis of the interview transcripts resulted in identification of the four dimensions around which principal behavior was eventually described. Subsequent consultation with 25 principals confirmed the interview results. A subsequent review of research on principal effectiveness suggested that descriptions of behavior critical to principal effectiveness could be readily located within the four dimensions identified in the principal interviews.

Describing Highly Effective Behavior within Selected Dimensions

Three methods were used to develop a description of highly effective principal behavior. These methods included the structured application of professional judgment, collection of original opinion data, and systematic integration of extant research results.

Twenty principals (elementary and secondary), department heads, teachers, and supervisory officers from a single school system worked continuously with the researchers. Their work extended over a $2\frac{1}{2}$-year period in which they met for approximately a half-day per month and worked singly or in pairs for an equivalent period between meetings. For the first $1\frac{1}{2}$ years, they worked as two distinct groups; one focused on the elementary principal's role, the other on the secondary role. The work of the two groups was combined during the final year based on evidence suggesting that elementary and secondary principal roles were much more alike than different. The two groups are treated as one in the remaining description.

The long-term objective of the group was to develop the complete principal profile. The first step was to describe highly effective principal behavior by integrating the collective knowledge and experiences of group members with two additional sets of information; original data and the research of others.

Opinions and beliefs of the group members concerning effective principal behavior were first augmented through collection of interview data from a random sample of 28 secondary teachers, 11 department heads, and 9 secondary principals in one school system. Audiotapes of each interview were content analyzed by two independent raters and coefficients of interrater agreement were computed. The original draft of the profile explicitly incorporated features of effective principals reported in these data.

The group also integrated results of extant research with their own views and original opinion data. Two reviews of literature were carried out by the researchers (Leithwood & Montgomery, 1982; Leithwood, 1982) and subsequently read and discussed by the group. The most defensible results from these syntheses of 66 empirical studies were incorporated by the group in their description of highly effective principal behavior. Reviews conducted by others (Barth & Deal, 1982; Greenfield, 1982; Persell, Cookson, & Lyon, 1982; Yukl, 1982) were also examined.

Describing Growth in Principal Effectiveness

A tentative, unevenly detailed description of four stages of growth (subsequently reduced to three) toward the highest stage in the profile was first drafted by the group referred to in the previous section. In order to verify and add detail to these patterns of behavior, audiotaped interviews were conducted with a random sample of 63 principals from three school systems. Ratings of these interviews placed each principal at a single, predominant level on the profile. This resulted in a pool of principal interview data at each of the now four-staged profiles as follows: 4 at the highest level (Level 4), 18 at Level three, 27 at Level two, and 12 at Level one. A detailed content analysis of interviews at each level was conducted as the basis for verifying tentative descriptions developed by the group and adding detail to these descriptions.

Verifying the Growth Hypothesis

The methods already described justified two claims: The highest level in the profile described exceptionally effective principal behavior, and the other three levels in the profile described prominant patterns of behavior found among many practicing principals. That the three less effective patterns of behavior represented a hierarchy of increasing effectiveness, as arranged in the profile, was a logically plausible claim but not one justified empirically to this point, however. Four separate studies were undertaken to explore this claim.

Study 1 asked 3 superintendents, 17 principals, a consultant, 3 department heads, and 2 teachers selected from three school systems, without knowledge of the profile, to rank the effectiveness of principals using audiotaped interview data and to provide written justification for their rankings. Comparisons were made among judges ranking the same set of data and between these independent rankings and ratings of the data by the researchers based on the profile.

Study 2 compared judgments about levels of effectiveness of 12 principals from one school system based on two independent rating systems: the principal profile and a conception of principal behavior based on 12 qualities considered critical to effective administration (Ventures for Excellence Inc., 1981). The 12 qualities identified by Ventures for Excellence Inc., are encompassed primarily within two of the four dimensions of the profile.

Data for Study 3 were provided by 18 secondary principals, 29 elementary principals, 26 vice-principals, 22 teachers, 25 department heads, and 4 others who responded individually to a detailed questionnaire about the profile after a presentation and discussion of its contents.

Finally, Study 4 compared levels of principal effectiveness, as defined by the profile, with the amount of progress made by teachers in implementing a new program in their schools. The hypothesis was that teachers associated with more effective principals ought to make more progress in implementing programs than those associated with less effective principals. This study was conducted across three school systems and involved a random sample of 21 principals and 65 teachers, 2 or 3 teachers per principal. The programs to be implemented differed in each school system. Interviews were conducted to place principals on the profile prior to the beginning of the school year. Teachers' level of program implementation was assessed in the early fall and late spring of the same school year.

Considered separately, each of the four validation studies had serious limitations. For example, Study 1 permitted wide variation in how effectiveness was defined; Study 2 involved a very small sample, Study 3 allowed for collection of data concerning effectiveness from respondents ranging widely in the effectiveness of their own behavior; and Study 4 was ideally designed to extend over a longer period of time than was provided. None of the studies directly assessed the relationship between principal behavior and student outcomes. The importance of the validation studies lay in their each having different weaknesses and strengths. If the results of such widely differing methods converged, considerable confidence should be placed in such results (Campbell & Fisk, 1959).

RESULTS

The profile, summarized in Table 8.1, describes four levels of growth in principal effectiveness within four dimensions of behavior. Dimensions of behavior included (1) principals' goals, (2) factors in the school and classroom that principals try to influence in order to achieve their goals, (3) actions or strategies principals employ to exercise such influence, and (4) the nature of principals' decision-making ability concerning each of these other dimensions. The levels of effectiveness within these dimensions are labeled the *systematic problem solver* (most effec-

Table 8.1

Growth in Principal Effectiveness by Level and Behavioral Dimension

	Dimensions of behavior	
Level	Goals	Factors
4 (High) Problem Solver	Selected from multiple public sources Highly ambitious for all students Transformed into short-term goals for planning Used to actively increase consistency among staff in directions they pursue	Attempts to influence all factors bearing on achievement Expectations within factors are specific Expectations derived from research and professional judgement
3 Program Manager	Selected from several sources, some of which are public Particular focus on exceptional students Encourages staff to use goals for planning Conveys goals when requested or as particular need arises	Attempts to influence factors bearing on the school program Expectations within factors are specific Expectations are derived from personal and staff experiences and occasionally from research
2 Humanitarian	Derived from belief in the importance of interpersonal relations to effective school = happy school Goals may be ambitious but be limited in focus Goals not systematically used for planning Conveys goals to others if requested	Attempts to influence factors bearing on interpersonal relations Expectations within factors ambitious but vague Expectations are mostly derived from personal experiences and beliefs
1 (Low) Administrator	Derived from personal needs Focus on school admin. rather than students Pursuit of instructional goals considered to be responsibility of staff, not principal Conveys goals to others if requested	Attempts to influence factors bearing on school appearance and day-to-day operations (mostly nonclassroom factors) Expectations within factors are vague Expectations are derived from personal experiences

tive), *program manager, humanitarian,* and *administrator* (least effective). Higher levels or stages of effectiveness represent an accumulation of skills, knowledge, and attitudes from lower levels on the part of the principal, as well as some significant shifts in the nature of the principal's beliefs. Principals at higher levels continue to engage in many behaviors evident at lower levels but such behaviors are usually parts of

Table 8.1   *(continued)*

Dimensions of behavior	
Strategies	Decision Making
Uses a wide variety of strategies	Skilled in use of multiple forms; matches
Criteria for choice include goals, factors,	form to setting and works toward high
context and perceived obstacles	levels of participation
Makes extensive use of factor-specific	Decision processes oriented toward goals
strategies to achieve goals	of education, based on information
	from personal, prof. and research
	sources
	Anticipates, initiates and monitors deci-
	sion processes
Relies on limited number of established,	Skilled in use of several forms: selects
well tested strategies	form based on urgency and desire to
Choice based on student needs (especially	involve staff
special students), desire to be fair and	Decision processes oriented toward
consistent, concern to manage time	school's program based on information
effectively	from personal and professional sources
Uses factor-specific strategies that are de-	Anticipates most decisions and monitors
rived largely from personal experience	decision process regularly
and system direction	
Chooses strategies which focus on inter-	Uses primarily participatory forms of
personal relationships	decision making based on a strong
Choice based on view of good school	motivation to involve staff so they will
environment, view of own responsibili-	be happy
ties and desire to make jobs of staff	Tends to be proactive concerning deci-
easier	sions affecting school climate but
Makes little use of systemic factor-specific	largely reactive in all other areas unless
strategies	required to act.
Chooses strategies based on personal	Uses primarily autocratic forms of deci-
need to maintain administrative control	sion making
and remain uninvolved in classroom	Decision processes oriented toward
Strategies mostly limited to use of vested	smooth school admin. based on per-
authority and assist. staff with routine	sonal sources of information
tasks	Decision processes are reactive, inconsis-
Attends to factor-specific strategies in a	tent and rarely monitored
superficial way if required to do so	

a more extensive repertoire, rather than the whole repertoire. Results of the four validation studies converged in support of the hierarchical description of principal behavior contained in the profile.

Before describing the contents of the profile, several indirect but important findings are noted. First, most principals about whom data were collected varied, to some degree, in the level of their behaviors across the dimensions and subdimensions of the profile. Second, only a very small proportion of the principals involved in our studies worked predominantly at the highest level described in the profile (about 10%, based on data from about 200 principals across six school systems). Third, most school systems studied considered the lowest level in the profile to describe minimally acceptable, rather than unacceptable, principal behavior. Finally, the profile focuses on types of behavior that seemed to be largely acquirable given adequate school system support for the principal.

The next four sections present the results of the research. This is a selective elaboration of the information summarized in Table 8.1 and presented in much greater detail elsewhere (Leithwood & Montgomery, 1983). In some instances behavior is outlined through all four levels in the profile; in others, where the nature of change is straightforward, we simply contrast the most and least effective forms of behavior evident in our results.

Goals

Goals are the long-term aspirations held by principals for work in their schools and are the dimension of principal behavior most consistently linked to school improvement by current empirical research. Moreover, virtually no conflict exists within this research regarding the types of goal-related behaviors that are effective. These behaviors can be described in terms of the nature, sources, and uses of goals.

NATURE OF GOALS

Highly effective principals (Level 4) had an implicit or explicit philosophy of education including an image of what it means to be educated. This image was consistent with the values of the larger public served by the school and was likely to encompass knowledge, skill, and emotional student outcomes. All categories of outcomes were considered important by these principals. With this complete image as a frame of reference, effective principals' goals were to provide the best education and best experiences possible for students served by the school. Such experiences tended to extend beyond the formal instructional setting. Because the definition of the educated person evolves over time, effective principals were knowledgeable about changes relevant to goals for students and receptive to changes that might have helped to achieve such goals.

In contrast to highly effective principals, principals at the lowest level on the profile (Level 1) believed that teachers teach and the principal runs the school. Maintaining a smooth-running ship was their main goal, bringing with it a dominant concern for administrative logistics. While these principals sometimes justified their focus on the grounds that students and teachers required a tranquil environment in which to work, running a smooth ship had become an end in its own right. Change was a source of annoyance to these principals since it challenged the maintenance of established rules and routines.

As the nature of principals' goals grew in effectiveness they became increasingly based on a view of the educated person, increasingly consistent with those of the larger school community, and increasingly open to change in the face of reasonable evidence for the need to change.

SOURCES OF GOALS

Principals differed about the sources from which their goals were derived. As principals increased in their effectiveness, the sources from which their goals were selected became increasingly public in origin and greater in number. Highly effective principals (Level 4) systematically selected their goals from those espoused for students by agencies of the state (e.g., state education department or ministry of education), the local school board, and the perceived needs of the community and students served by the school. Because the least effective principals, described by the profile, valued running a smooth ship (administratively), their goals derived from a sense of the administrative tasks requiring attention in order for this to be achieved. Goals did not often spring from curricular, instructional, or interpersonal considerations.

USES OF GOALS

Internalized goals serve as a potential focus for principals in planning their actions and as a source of criteria for deciding what those actions will be. The research results suggested that as principals increased in their effectiveness, there was greater congruence between their espoused goals for school improvement and their planning and decision making. Less effective principals sometimes espoused goals very similar to those of their highly effective colleagues, but seemed to ignore them in practice.

In addition to these personal uses for goals, highly effective principals sought out opportunities to clarify goals with staff, students, parents, and other relevant members of the school community. They worked toward consensus about these goals and actively encouraged their use in departmental and divisional planning. While Level-1 forms of behavior sometimes included such clarification of goals, it was common for these principals to simply assume staff knowledge and agreement.

Factors

Goals are conceived as long-term professional aspirations held by principals for their work. The research suggested that goal attainment depended, in substantial measure, on the ability of principals to identify those elements of the school, called factors, that most accounted for what students learned. Goal attainment also depended on the principal determining those conditions within factors that had to be realized if student learning was to improve. Highly effective principals considered some 18 factors. Of these, 10 appeared to bear directly on students' classroom experiences largely through the teacher:

- which teacher teaches which students;
- the objectives or outcomes teachers work toward with students, including the emphasis teachers place on different types of objectives;
- teaching strategies including the types of learning activities these strategies are designed to provide for students;
- the types and amount of material and resources available and the nature and degree of their use;
- the ways in which teachers assess, record, and report student performance and experience;
- the way time is allocated and things teachers do to get and keep students focused on the learning task including student discipline and control;
- the subject matter, themes, or topics encountered by students in their programs;
- the organization and appearance of the physical environment of the classroom;
- the role model provided by the teacher, the nature of the relationships between the students and the teacher and between students and students in the classroom;
- the nature and degree of integration among curricular objectives within and across programs and grades.

A second cluster of factors considered by effective principals were thought to affect the experiences of students while in the school but outside the classroom:

- the functions, assignments, and roles of people in the school and classroom (including decisions about which teachers teach what grades and subjects; the role of the psychologist, the janitor, etc.);
- the form and substance of communications and relationships with the community;
- the nature and degree of organized out-of-classroom (area) experiences for the students;
- the adult role models provided by staff as individuals and as they interacted with one another; the form and substance of communications among staff;
- the form and substance of communications and relationships with out-of-school, school system staff;
- the conduct of students while the school was responsible for them;
- the nature of the relationships teachers developed with students on the playground, in the halls, and the like, and the role model provided by teachers in these relationships.

Variations in principal effectiveness concerning factors were a function of the factors principals selected for attention and the source and nature of expectations held for these factors.

FACTORS OF MOST CONCERN

As principals increased in effectiveness, the factors they attempted to influence increased in number and changed in focus. To a predominant concern for factors bearing on school appearance and the day-to-day operations of the school (Level 1, the administrator), especially outside the classroom (e.g., student behavior, material and physical resources) was added a concern for interpersonal factors (Level 2, the humanitarian). These in turn, were subsumed, but not replaced, by attention to program-related factors such as program objectives, use of time and its management (Level 3, the program manager), and at the most effective principal level, Level 4, attention to all factors. This pattern of growth toward attention to all factors seemed to be directly related to and perhaps explained by principals' goals. The more closely linked to school improvement such goals became, the greater the likelihood that factors selected for attention included those likely to facilitate school improvement.

While highly effective principals tended systematically to address all factors, they did so over an extended period of time. Short-term priorities often led to placing emphasis temporarily on a small set of factors. In contrast, the least effective principal behavior (Level 1) was characterized by long-term, consistent inattention to many factors and attention to others only when provoked by a crisis (e.g., parental complaints about a curriculum topic).

NATURE OF EXPECTATIONS

As principals became more effective, their expectations within factors also became more defensible and more consistent with prevailing professional judgment and the results of research. This suggests that such expectations, when met, stand a better chance of actually resulting in school improvement or goal achievement. Expectations also became increasingly detailed or concrete with increased principal effectiveness. Highly effective principals, for example, were better able to see which special characteristics of their schools needed to be accounted for in formulating expectations they held for factors and, specifically, how such characteristics might influence those expectations in practice.

Principals at Level 1 on this subdimension of behavior had vague expectations regarding the limited number of factors to which they attended. At Level 2, expectations tended to be high but still general; for example, staff were expected to "cooperate with one another," but what such cooperation entailed was not made clear by the principal. Program managers (Level 3), although not concerned with the full array of factors, as were the most effective principals, were quite specific in their expectations for those factors of concern.

SOURCES OF EXPECTATIONS

Information used in formulating expectations also varied with principal effectiveness and came from many sources. Increased effectiveness, however, was associated with systematic rather than incidental or whimsical attention to nonpersonal sources. Expectations at the least effective level varied according to what principals believed to be appropriate to the immediate situation. Such expectations were highly negotiable and could be swayed by staff preferences, parental demands, administrative demands, or the principals' interpretation of an educational trend. As principals became more effective, knowledge of respected colleagues, and eventually research-based knowledge, were actively sought out and accommodated in formulating expectations. These sources of information undoubtedly increased the sophistication or validity of principals' knowledge, hence the nature of their expectations.

Strategies

Having identified factors associated with the achievement of valued goals, principals still must act or intervene to influence selected factors in directions they consider most likely to assist in goal achievement. The research showed that principals employed a repertoire of both general-purpose and factor-specific strategies to accomplish goals.

General-purpose strategies were considered by principals as useful in influencing the condition of almost any factor, depending very much on circumstances in the school at the time action was taken. Such strategies established an appropriate background and climate within which more factor-specific action still had to be initiated to ensure goal achievement. Among the seven general-purpose strategies used by principals, the four that focused on keeping those involved in decision making willing to participate and well informed were the following:

- the building and maintenance of interpersonal relationships and motivating staff;
- provision of staff with knowledge and skills;
- facilitation of within-school communication, and
- facilitation of communication between school and community.

Two additional strategies that addressed the provision of adequate organizational resources for staff work were as follows:

- allowance for nonteaching time for staff;
- establishment of procedures to handle routine matters.

The final strategy was using vested authority; the purpose for its use varied significantly from ineffective to effective principals.

After appropriate background and climate were established, factor-specific strategies could begin to exercise a direct influence on selected factors. They included:

- program monitoring;
- goal setting, program planning and development;
- program implementation;
- staff supervision;
- provision of support resources;
- direct relationship with students.

Different levels of effectiveness among principals were evident in the criteria they used for choosing strategies.

CRITERIA AND EMPHASIS

As the strategic effectiveness of principals increased, and their goals expanded, the number and nature of strategies used over extended periods of time also increased. This increase could be traced back to the changes in types of goals, from a focus on administrative concerns through interpersonal relations to the school program and finally to student achievement. Achieving goals increasingly linked to student achievement eventually demanded attention to all factors. Effectively influencing all factors required the use of virtually all general-purpose and factor-specific strategies. And effectiveness also depended on principals' ability to identify strategies that would impact on weak or problem aspects of their own school's background or climate.

Principals least effective on this dimension (strategy selection) of behavior needed to feel in control of administrative matters in their school. Such control was usually assumed through the use of vested authority. These principals preferred not to be involved in decisions about curriculum or instruction, designating these as exclusively teachers' responsibilities. They also selected other general-purpose strategies on the basis of intuitive judgment about what was required to keep the school operating smoothly. For example, attention would be given to interpersonal relationships among staff when a serious problem arose in such relationships.

Principals at the next higher level of effectiveness sought out strategies that contributed to a warm, friendly climate in the school, often considering positive climate an end in its own right. They frequently gave considerable attention to such strategies as being positive, cheerful and encouraging, accessible to staff, acting as a role model, and facilitating communication within the school and between the school and community. When vested authority was used, their reasons varied from a desire to make teachers' lives easier by freeing them from decision-making responsibility to their convictions that some decisions were too specialized or important to be left to chance, such as school budgets and teacher record keeping.

A dominant concern for making fair, well-informed, consistent decisions and helping staff do the same was characteristic of program managers (Level 3). This concern motivated the systematic collection and distribution of information relevant to crucial decisions to staff. Such communication with the community was also viewed as an essential ingredient in building broader support for the school's program.

The most effective principals used a complex set of considerations in choosing their strategies, including (1) the goals to achieve, (2) the factors to be influenced, (3) characteristics of the people involved, (4) other activities already underway in the school, (5) school and school system norms, (6) past experiences, and (7) the nature of obstacles to be overcome. These concerns were used simultaneously and were viewed clearly as means rather than ends. Most general-purpose and task-specific strategies were used at some time by these principals to attain their goals.

QUALITY AND SKILL

Principals sometimes chose strategies well suited to factors in need of influence and still failed to exercise much influence. One cause was the quality of strategies used. The effect of principals' actions were partially a function of the specific procedures associated with their strategies. Principals increased in effectiveness as their procedures became relatively more efficient in influencing factors (e.g., a single strategy influencing several factors) and as they were more readily used by others (many principal-initiated strategies depended on other members of staff to complete). Strategies also were more effective as they became more adaptable to changing school conditions. For example, program planning procedures useful across all areas of the curriculum seemed to be generally more effective in stimulating subject-matter integration by teachers than strategies that were unique to subject areas. In the principal profile, differences in the quality of strategies used is particularly evident in factor-specific strategies such as program implementation. Highly effective principals had a strategy for program implementation that included well-refined, detailed steps applicable to many programs. Less effective principals either did not deal with implementation (Level 1) or had no systematic approach to the process (Level 2).

It was still possible, however, for a principal to select a strategy potentially able to influence the factor(s) of concern, possess extensive knowledge about how to carry out the strategy, and still not obtain the desired effect. This was the case when principals' actual skill in use of the strategy was flawed in a crucial way. For example, some principals knew that establishing good relationships with the community required listening carefully to parental concerns and patiently moving from such concerns, however expressed, toward a focus on how they were addressed in the school program. Yet these principals allowed themselves to be frustrated with parental inquiries and frequently became defensive in their responses. Highly effective principals, on the other hand, were skilled in most of the general-purpose and factor-specific strategies. As principals became highly skilled in their performance of a strategy, less conscious effort was required of them. This reduced the time required for them to respond to matters demanding their immediate attention (e.g., a report of drug use in the boys' washroom), and allowed them to attend to other problems for which solutions were less well known (e.g., increasing collaborative curriculum planning across departments in the school).

Decision Making

Decision making is a process that permeates the other dimensions of principal behavior and helps account for the quality of that behavior.

Differences in the way principals chose their directions, selected aspects of the school for attention, and decided to act accounted for much of the difference in principals' effectiveness. Results of this research focused on two aspects of the decision-making process. One was the context within which specific decisions were made—the forms and procedures used in decision making, principals' attitude and stance toward the process, and the monitoring of decision making. The second aspect concerned components of decision making—how decisions were defined, what criteria were considered relevant, and the use of information.

FORMS AND PROCEDURES FOR DECISION MAKING

Highly effective principals knew about and demonstrated use of a range of different forms of decision making in their schools. Sometimes they made unilateral decisions, sometimes they delegated the responsibility to others. Frequently there was extensive participation in the process with choices arrived at through consensus or, occasionally, by majority vote. The least effective principals made many more unilateral decisions. When staff participated in the process, choices were usually based on majority vote. These same principals appeared to give little conscious thought to which form of decision making to use. In contrast, the most effective appeared to arrive at a choice of form by consciously reviewing staff preferences and abilities, existing decision-making practices in the school, the nature of the decision to be made, and experiences from past decisions.

While highly effective principals were eclectic in the forms of decision making they used, they nevertheless had strong preferences toward decentralization and extensive staff participation. Unlike those who were least effective, they used many decision-making occasions as opportunities to foster conditions conducive to extensive decentralization (staff willingness, skill, and a climate in which the motives of those participating in decisions were widely trusted). Further, such principals were knowledgeable about how decisions were made in departments or divisions in their schools and worked toward compatability in decision-making processes at all levels in the school. Those least effective tended to be out of touch with decision-making processes in which they were not directly involved. Considerable diversity in such processes was typical within their schools.

Variation in procedures principals established for decision making also were uncovered. Lack of consistency in such procedures was common among principals least effective in decision making. For example, sometimes their procedures allowed for different points of view to be heard, sometimes not; sometimes criteria for decision making were made explicit, sometimes not. By comparison, those most effective in this behavior established procedures to help ensure consistent attention to alternative points of view (including competing values), criteria relevant to the decision, clarification of the decision, and collection of relevant information. These latter principals also had procedures (like the development of a calendar listing all major decision points in the year) for anticipating decisions and ensuring that needed decisions did not "fall through the cracks."

ATTITUDE AND STANCE TOWARD DECISION MAKING

Levels of effectiveness in this subdimension of behavior varied in the extent to which principals sought out decision-making opportunities or reacted to the necessity for decisions to be made. Those most effective tended to seek out decisions; they viewed even minor decisions as opportunities to move incrementally toward their goals. They seemed able to anticipate a large proportion of decisions that had to be made and used them to their advantage. Least effective principals, contrariwise, seemed unable or unwilling to forecast many upcoming decisions. As a result they found themselves continually reacting to decision-making situations within a time frame established by others. They rarely had enough time to make decisions carefully and, not surprisingly, tended to have negative attitudes toward change. Their stance toward decision making could be called crisis management.

MONITORING DECISION MAKING

Principals least effective in monitoring the process of decision making and its consequences relied on their feelings (i.e., informal observations, number of problems arising) about "how well things were going." Problems were reacted to in a piecemeal fashion with little effort to prevent them from recurring. At Level 2, staff satisfaction with decisions was frequently assessed. At Level 3, routine checks were typically made of school decision making; special attention was given to how well the process met the principals' standards of fairness and consistency and to the principals' perceptions of how well school needs were being met. In monitoring, the most effective principals systematically reviewed and refined the forms and procedures used. Information was usually sought out regarding the satisfaction of most of those affected by the decision including school staff; typically, resources or costs of the decision process (e.g., amounts of time spent by department staff in selecting a new textbook) and the contributions of decisions toward school goals (e.g., did the textbook selected seem to be the best one to contribute to program objectives?) were examined.

DEFINING DECISIONS AND SELECTING CRITERIA

Variation in how principals defined decisions and the criteria they used appeared to be closely related to variations in principals' goals. When running the school smoothly was the overriding concern, as in Level 1, principals tended to take the path of least resistance in their decision making—they responded swiftly to symptoms (e.g., placating a parent concerned about the amount of homework given to his child) but ignored underlying causes (e.g., absence of a school homework policy). The transformation of primarily administrative goals into criteria for decision making sometimes led to questionable emphases in the school. For example, some principals responded to broad pressures regarding the basics in such a way as to entirely ignore other equally important goals. In some decisions where these principals' usual criteria could not be applied, choices were made intuitively with the claim that much about education was intuitive.

An overriding concern for a broad range of student outcomes, as in Level 4, was associated with efforts to uncover and clarify the fundamental causes of problems. Criteria, directly based on the goals of education, included: the need for individual programs, students' stages of development, and the need to balance emphasis among knowledge, skill, and effective objectives. Other staff were actively encouraged to use similarly oriented criteria in their decision making.

Growth was also evident in how realistic and solvable were the decisions defined by the principal. Less effective principals had a greater tendency to portray problem solutions as inaccessible (e.g., not enough time or money, not their problem, age of staff). The same basic problems were frequently cast in much more accessible terms by more effective principals (e.g., weighing school priorities, staff motivation, and interest).

USE OF INFORMATION

Principals least effective in their use of information in decision making collected little information within the school except for that requested by central administrators. They tended to read report cards and were open to receiving other information but did not seek it. In contrast, the most effective principals accumulated information about most major functions of the school in a systematic way. They had procedures for routinely ensuring adequate information as a basis for major decisions. Further, they encouraged staff to do the same and expected them to be able to identify the sources of information for their decisions. The least effective principals only pressed staff for information sources if the decision was of special interest to them.

Information used most frequently by principals at Level 1 concerned administrative matters and their responsibilities in such matters. This information was usually available in the form of memos and policies from the board or ministry of education. Level-2 forms of behavior were characterized by seeking out information from staff particularly about such issues as student morale and relationships with parents. Frequent informal visits to classrooms was a typical method of collecting this information. At Level 3, information was also sought about curriculum development and implementation activities in the school and program requirements as outlined by the board or ministry of education. Principals at this level gathered this information through classroom visits, analyses of test results, reading of report cards, parental surveys, teacher plans, and other formal assessments of student needs.

Principals most effective in their use of information added to the behaviors described in Level 3 a general knowledge about curriculum and education gleaned from reading recent research. This information was interwoven with school-specific information during decision making. These principals also encouraged their staff to be familiar with and take account of research-based information in their own decision making. Level-4 principals attempted to keep staff well informed through, for example, the development of a handbook of procedures for school routines and carefully orienting new staff to school expectations and procedures.

SUMMARY AND CONCLUSION

The central purpose of this chapter was to describe stages of increasingly effective principals' behavior by providing a profile. It is grounded in empirical data sensitive to both the full array of outcomes for which principals are responsible and the school contexts in which they work. The profile incorporates data reflecting research using multiple designs. Additionally, it focuses on behavior meaningful to practicing principals and concentrates on aspects of that behavior that are amenable to change.

Systematic-problem-solver principals display the most effective forms of behavior described in the profile. Table 8.1 indicates there are three identifiable stages of growth or levels of effectiveness leading up to the systematic problem solver—the administrator, the humanitarian, and the program manager. The administrator stage is the least effective principal type. Principals at this level are preoccupied with running a smooth ship as an end in its own right. The humanitarian retains a concern for running a smooth ship but strongly believes that developing effective interpersonal relations in the school, particularly among staff, is his or her most important goal. Program managers, on the other hand, see interpersonal relationships as one important means to achieving student outcomes that they value. Implementing district or commercial programs and guidelines effectively is a central procedure for goal achievement. Systematic problem solvers begin with a legitimate, comprehensive set of goals for students, and seek out the most effective means for their achievement. This sometimes means coming into conflict with district administrators if the principal believes that he or she must seriously explore better program alternatives than the ones proposed in order to appropriately address the needs of students in his or her school.

What we have described as differences in levels of effectiveness corresponds closely, in general orientation, to what other researchers have described as different styles of principal behavior. For example, the "Initiator" style (Hall, Rutherford, Hord, & Huling, 1984) closely resembles some of the behavior described at the two highest levels in our profile; this is particularly the case within the decision-making and strategies dimensions. Similarly, the "Manager" style (Hall et al., 1984) overlaps a number of behaviors placed at the second and third levels in the profile. Hall and colleagues' "Reactor" style and the administrator level described here share a common orientation to school leadership (Hall et al., 1984). Such correspondence, found in other research on principals' styles (Rutherford, 1983), increases the confidence that may be placed in the generalizability of our results. In comparison with research on styles, the profile is more detailed in its description of behavior. It also offers evidence that different styles may have quite different effects on schools, an issue most of those investigating principal styles have avoided.

This chapter touched on the relationship between what principals do, their effects on students, and the conditions influencing principal behavior. Prior research focused most heavily on the first of these relationships. The profile is a reasonably valid description of principal behaviors we believe are increasingly effective in realizing desired outcomes for students. Given such a belief, attention here focuses on conditions that influence growth in principal behavior. The conditions range from those largely outside the realm of intervention (e.g., the principal's energy level and avocational interests) to those incorporated into the standard operating procedures of all school systems. Our concluding remarks concern how the profile may be used as part of three conditions: in-service education, performance appraisal, and principal selection.

As a framework for the in-service education of principals, the profile, in conjunction with suitable measurement devices, permits precise identification of the current behavior of principals. An interview schedule was developed to collect data for this purpose. Alternatively, several groups of principals involved in this study performed reasonably accurate self-assessments given thorough, prior introduction to the profile. Once such identification has taken place (using these or other methods) the profile provides a basis for realistic, individual principal objective setting. For example, a principal who judges his or her knowledge of curriculum implementation strategies to be exceedingly low because of school priorities, may set out to move up to the level above their present performance as described in the profile. When the objective for growth is clear and the amount of growth is manageable, it is realistic to expect that principals will be able to design and control their own in-service education much better than under conventional circumstances. While such individual design and control is not essential to effective in-service education, it is probably the most desirable response to extensive individual differences in needs found within most groups of principals.

The profile also addresses two components, traditionally not addressed adequately yet critical to the validity of both principal performance appraisal systems and principal selection procedures: the dimensions and subdimensions in the profile service as a core set of criteria for examining principal performance and estimating potential; the levels provide explicit standards against which behaviors in each dimension may be judged.

In-service education, performance appraisal and selection practices are among the formal, standard operating procedures of all school systems. The profile appears to be a potentially valuable resource in increasing the impact on principal performance of such formal procedures. Recent experiences in disseminating the profile to groups of principals suggests another unanticipated use, more informal in nature. While principals' specific reactions to the profile varies from accepting to skeptical, most have been stimulated to reexamine, weigh, and reflect on their work to an extent largely unprecedented in their experience. If an important long-range goal for principal development is to produce, as Shön (1983) suggests, a more reflective practitioner, the profile seems like a useful tool toward that end.

REFERENCES

Barth, R. A., & Deal, T. E. (1982). *The principalship: Views from without and within*. Washington, DC: National Institute of Education.

Campbell, D. T., & Fisk, D. W. (1959). Convergent and discriminant validation by the multitrait-multimethod matrix. *Psychological Bulletin, 56*, 81–105.

Greenfield, W. (1982). *A synopsis of research on school principals*. Washington, DC: National Institute of Education.

Hall, G., Rutherford, W. L., Hord, S. M., & Huling, L. L. (1984). Effects of three principal styles on school improvement. *Educational Leadership, 41*, (5), 22–31.

Leithwood, K. A. (1982). *The nature and development of procedural knowledge*. Paper presented at the annual meeting of The Canadian Society for the Study of Education, Ottawa, Ontario.

Leithwood, K. A. (1982, November). *The principals' role in school improvement: State-of-the-art research in Canada*. Paper presented to International School Improvement Project, West Palm Beach, FL.

Leithwood, K. A., & Montgomery, D. J. (1982). The principals' role in program improvement. *Review of Educational Research, 52*, 309–340.

Leithwood, K. A., & Montgomery, D. J. (1983). *A profile of growth in principal effectiveness*. Unpublished manuscript, Ontario Institute for Studies in Education, Toronto.

Leithwood, K. A., & Montgomery, D. J. (1984, June). *Methods used in developing and validating a profile of growth in principal effectiveness*. Paper presented at the meeting of The Canadian Association for the Study of Educational Administration, Guelph, Ontario.

Lipham, J. M., Dunstan, J. F., & Ranker, R. E. (1981). *The relationship of decision involvement and principals' leadership to teacher job satisfaction in selected secondary schools*. (Tech. Rep. No. 571). Madison: Madison Wisconsin Research and Development Center for Individualizing Schooling.

Martin, Y. M., Isherwood, G. B., & Lavery, R. E. (1976). Leadership effectiveness in teacher probation committees. *Educational Administration Quarterly, 12* (2), 87–99.

Ogawa, R. T., & Hart, A. W. (1983, April). *The effect of principals on the instructional performance of schools*. Paper presented at the meeting of the American Educational Research Association, Montreal, Canada.

Persell, C. H., Cookson, P. W., & Lyon, H. (1982). *Effective principals: What do we know from various educational literatures?* Washington, DC: National Institute of Education.

Rutherford, W. L. (1983). *Leadership styles and behaviors of elementary school principals and their relationship to school improvement*. Unpublished manuscript, University of Texas at Austin.

Rutherford, W. L., Hord, S. M., Huling, L. L., & Hall, G. E. (1983). *Change facilitators: In search of understanding their role*. (Report No. 5159). Austin: University of Texas at Austin, Research and Development Center for Teacher Education.

Rutter, M., Maughan, B., Mortimer, P., & Ousten, J. (1979). *Fifteen thousand hours: Secondary schools and their effects on students*. Cambridge, MA: Harvard.

Schön, D. A. (1983). *The reflective practioner*. New York: Basic Books.

Stallings, J. A. (1982). *How does the principals' leadership style and school policy enhance effective basic skills schooling?* Palo Alto, CA: Stallings Teaching and Learning Institute.

Ventures for Excellence Inc., Lincoln, Nebraska, 1981.

Willower, D. J., & Smedley, S. R. (1981, April). *Principals' pupil control behaviour and school robustness*. Paper presented at the meeting of the American Educational Research Association, Los Angeles.

Yukl, G. (1982). *Managerial leadership and the effective principal*. Washington, DC: National Institute of Education.

PART III

Research Impact on Policy and Practice

CHAPTER 9

Educational Policy and School Effectiveness

Stewart C. Purkey and Marshall S. Smith

EFFECTIVE SCHOOLS: A CULTURAL PERSPECTIVE

The major, and heartening, conclusion of research on effective schools is that differenes among schools do have an impact on the achievement of students. This finding, supported by research conducted primarily in urban elementary schools, describes schools whose students' scores on standardized tests in reading and math are better than would be predicted given their socioeconomic background.

Research, from about the mid-1960s on, found that factors such as marginal changes in class size, teacher salaries, the number of books in the library, and the instructional strategy used by the teacher had little relationship to academic achievement (Averch, Carroll, Donaldson, Kiesling, & Pincus, 1972; Coleman *et al.*, 1966; Hanushek, 1981; Mullin & Summers, 1981; Murnane, 1980). More recent research has identified characteristics of schools that seem to have influence on scholastic performance (see reviews by Austin, 1981; Clark, Lotto, & McCarthy, 1980; Hersh *et al.*, 1981; MacKenzie, 1983; Phi Delta Kappa, 1981; Rutter, 1983; Tomlinson, 1981).[1]

---

[1] It is easy to conclude that the findings of the new research contradict the findings of Coleman *et al.* (1966), Jencks *et al.* (1972) and others. In fact the results are consistent though the implications may differ. First, the new studies do not refute the general finding that easily measurable differences among schools (class size variation from 20 to 30 pupils, existing differences in teacher preservice training, teacher experience and salaries, number of books in the library, etc.) have little consistent relationship to student achievement. The

In an earlier paper (Purkey & Smith, 1983) we found the recent research weak in many respects with a tendency to present narrow, simplistic recipes for school improvement derived from nonexperimental data. Research, which is persuasive, suggests that academic success is heavily influenced by the school's culture (Brookover, Beady, Flood, Schweitzer, & Wisenbaker, 1979; Rutter, Maughan, Mortimore, Ouston, & Smith, 1979). The notion of school culture assumes schools are complex webs of values, norms, roles, and attitudes that exist within distinct organizational structures with differing patterns of communication, authority, and educational techniques. In short, schools have dynamic social systems made up of interrelated factors with each school having a distinctive climate or "ethos." An academically effective school is distinguished by its culture, which channels staff and students in the direction of successful teaching and learning.

The appropriateness of the school-culture notion is supported by ideas derived from organizational theory and from research on the implementation of education innovation. While empirical data on school organization are limited (Miles, 1981), there is an emerging consensus that schools are not rational, hierarchical institutions responsive to top-down command structures in which fundamental change can be mandated at one level with confidence that it will be carried out at subordinate levels (Derr & Deal, 1979; Dornbush & Scott, 1975; Meyer & Rowan, 1978; Weick, 1976). Rather, some theorists think that schools are "loosely coupled systems" (Weick, 1976) with weak linkages between administration levels and the relatively autonomous classroom.

Studies of the implementation of changes in schools also reinforce the validity of the school-culture perspective. In essence, successful implementation often requires changing the school culture—the wholesale influencing of the total school climate (Hargrove *et al.*, 1981). Though

---

new studies look at other variables. Second, they do not find overall large differences in achievement among existing schools. They generally do not even report data of the sort required for such analyses. Instead they identify especially good schools and examine their characteristics or compare the characteristics of high-scoring and low-scoring schools. They then imagine the improvement that would result, for example, if the least effective schools (the bottom 20%) improved to an achievement level equal to the most effective schools (the top 20%). For the average sixth grader the old literature estimates that this improvement would be on the order of two-thirds of a standard deviation or about one full grade level of achievement (see Jencks *et al.*, 1972, pp. 123–124). This estimate is consistent with the few new studies that report sufficient data to allow a quantitative estimate of the achievement differences between effective and ineffective schools. Third, the new studies imagine changes in schools that go beyond existing differences among schools. If our very best schools improve they will set a new standard for other schools to achieve.

specific tactics vary, the general strategy is best characterized as one that promotes collaborative planning, collegial work, and a school atmosphere conducive to experimentation and evaluation (Deal, Intili, Rosaler, & Stackhouse, 1977; Hargrove et al., 1981; Hawley, 1978; Little, 1981; McLaughlin, 1978). Miller (1980) suggests it is an approach that sees teachers as part of an entire school organization engaged in development activities that take place over time. Ongoing change is best accomplished by involving the people affected, at appropriate levels and frequency, in the decision-making process.

Thirteen characteristics of school culture that encourage academic achievement have been identified (Purkey & Smith, 1983). These characteristics are likely to be interrelated and have a cumulative effect. The first nine are relatively easy to implement and facilitate the development of the final four. With the caution that the empirical and theoretical bases for identifying each of these characteristics needs strengthening, an effective school culture is likely to include the following features:

1. School-site management: a considerable amount of responsibility should be given to each school to determine the exact means to address the problem of increasing academic performance.
2. Leadership: leadership from either the principal, another administrator, or a group of teachers is necessary to initiate and maintain the improvement process.
3. Staff stability: frequent transfers are likely to retard, if not prevent, the growth of a coherent and ongoing school personality, especially in early phases of the change process.
4. Curriculum articulation and organization: a planned, coordinated curriculum increases the amount of time students are engaged in studying basic skills and other academic disciplines.
5. Staff development: school-wide staff development should be ongoing and linked to the expressed concerns of the staff and the school's specific instructional and organizational needs.
6. Parental involvement and support: though the evidence is mixed, obtaining parent support is likely to positively influence student achievement, perhaps by increasing motivation.
7. School-wide recognition of academic success: publicly honoring academic achievement and stressing its importance encourages students to adopt similar norms and values.
8. Maximized learning time: more of the school day and of each class period should be devoted to active learning activities in academic areas; class periods should be free from interruptions and disruptions.

9. District support: fundamental change, school-level management, staff stability, and the like, all depend upon support from the district office.

The preceding characteristics set the stage for the features described next. These final four constitute the dynamic of the school's culture and seem responsible for an atmosphere that leads to increased student achievement.

10. Collaborative planning and collegial relationships: change attempts are more successful when teachers and administrators work together. Collegiality breaks down barriers between departments and among teachers and administrators; it encourages the kind of intellectual sharing that can lead to consensus, and it promotes feelings of unity and commonality among the staff.
11. Sense of community: schools can build feelings of community that contribute to reduced alienation and increased achievement.
12. Commonly shared clear goals and high expectations: schools whose staffs agree on their goals (e.g., academic achievement) and expectations (e.g., work and achievement expected of all students) are more likely to succeed because their energy and efforts are channeled toward a mutually agreed upon purpose.
13. Order and discipline: a school communicates how serious and purposeful it is through the order and discipline it maintains in its building and classrooms.

Within the framework provided by the first nine characteristics, the last four must develop over time as people begin to think and behave in new ways, working together toward common ends. It is a participatory approach based on the notion that how a school moves toward increasing effectiveness is critical to the comprehensiveness, stability, and longevity of the new culture it seeks. A political strategy that builds coalitions of support (Hargrove et al., 1981; Miles, 1981; Pfeffer, 1981) may work best for beginning the process within the school. It would engage various interest groups in a bargaining process, usually characterized by both political and social exchange (Talbert, 1980), to develop collaborative strategies leading toward a sense of ownership, commitment, and general consensus among the staff of the school.

In summation, differences among schools have an impact on students' academic performance. An examination of academically effective schools reveals school-culture characteristics that are conducive to student achievement. These characteristics, and hence the school culture, are alterable (Bloom, 1981) through faculty and administration collaboration and shared decision making directed toward whole-school change. The process by which schools are made more academically effective is crucial. A political approach that recognizes people's tendency to operate on the basis of their perceived self-interest as well as on their professional desire to educate children may work best. The remainder of this chapter explores the implications of this research for district, state, and federal policy and suggests policy approaches congruent with those implications.

SCHOOL-BASED DISTRICT POLICY

The nation's attention has been captured by a series of recently issued reports on public education. The reports generally suggest that school improvement must originate within state and local education agencies (National Commission on Excellence in Education, 1983; Education Commission of the States, 1983), from partnerships of colleges and secondary schools (College Entrance Examination Board, 1983), or through federal programs (Twentieth Century Fund, 1983). This top-down, traditional approach to educational reform runs counter to the basic point of the effective schools research summarized above.

If it is the school culture, which varies from school to school, that has a significant impact on the overall achievement of students, then school improvement logically must be directed toward manipulating the web of school-level characteristics that make up that culture. A state directive increasing the length of the school day, as proposed in *A Nation at Risk* (National Commission on Excellence in Education, 1983; Twentieth Century Fund, 1983), or the federal promotion of English literacy, as advocated by *Making the Grade* (National Commission on Excellence in Education, 1983; Twentieth Century Fund, 1983), could, even if implemented faithfully, leave untouched the norms, values, and structures that constitute the educational process of the school.

The policy implication is that the arena in which change must take place is the school building, not the state department of education or the federal government. And, if the school is the unit of change, then educational policy should be evaluated by the extent to which it locates responsibility for and facilitates change at the school level.

Furthermore, if loose-coupling theories of school organization are accurate, then the power of a policy-making body to affect the critical cultural variables diminishes in relationship to its distance from the school. This is congruent with what has been called the *backward mapping* approach to policy-making (Elmore, 1979–80).

DISTRICT POLICY

The level of government closest to the school building is the district administration. Though schools can act independently, district support is necessary to implement many of the characteristics associated with an effective school. Even though the school building is the logical locus of change, substantive reform, in the long run, requires the committment and support of the district administration. Interpreting school-site management and responsibility as license to place the burden of reform solely on individual schools without complementary changes at the district level may actually hinder the development of good schools (Purkey, 1984). Where schools do not choose to embark upon school-improvement projects the district administration is the policy-making body most able to successfully initiate the process. The following paragraphs describe one possible set of policies a district administration could use to begin an effective schools project based upon the research findings discussed above.[2]

The first district policy issue concerns balancing school authority and responsibility with district initiative and oversight. In some districts the tension generated by this balancing act may not be acceptable and is likely to be resolved by requiring schools to apply rigid formulas or follow detailed blueprints. However, research suggests that the more control of the school improvement process is removed from the school staffs the less likely fundamental alterations in staff values, beliefs, and behavior are to occur. On the other hand, there is no reason to grant schools autonomy and some reason to believe that many schools, left to themselves, would not undertake school improvement projects. One solution is for districts to use a combination of incentives and mandates. Under such a program schools would be instructed to initiate school improvement projects. All projects would be required to meet criteria such as the establishment of a broad-based school improvement committee, the creation of written school improvement plans made available to the public, special attention to the educational needs of disadvantaged students, and demonstration that the plan is comprehensive in scope. Within the guidelines various incentives would be provided: released time for staff planning and collaboration, in-service training in accordance with the expressed needs of school staffs, an improvement budget comprising the building's discretionary funds to spend as schools see fit, and staff protection from layoffs (though not from re-

---

[2] For a more comprehensive discussion of the district policy implications of the school effectiveness literature, see Purkey & Smith, (1985). See also Purkey (1984).

moval for inadequate performance) for the duration of the project. Such a blend of mandates and incentives would maximize schools' ability to respond to their unique situation at the same times that it insured school improvement would be on each school's agenda.

Once a decision to undertake a school-effectiveness project at the school level is made, the school characteristics and teacher behaviors in need of change must be determined. Though the procedure is not as simple as described here, participating schools could use the 13 variables discussed in the first section as both diagnostic tools and as guidelines in formulating their change strategies. Schools would implement as many of the first 9 as seem possible and warranted, with the final 4 process variables to be developed over time. Though, the elements of an effective school culture are interrelated, they are not invariably sequential and school improvement efforts are more likely to succeed to the extent that the entire school is affected. The 13 characteristics do not constitute a template. Room must be left for variation and experimentation as schools explore the impact various elements have within the schools' contexts.

To bring about cultural change, those most directly affected must be included in the planning and implementation process. Staff collaboration and shared decision making are essential to any effort directed toward whole-school improvement. For this to happen district policy must provide the resources that will encourage and nurture the process of collaboration and participation. Important resources might include sufficient released time for staff members to meet on school time in an atmosphere conducive to reflection and discussion, meaningful rewards for participating teachers (see Goodlad, 1983), and offering the staff expert guidance and assistance (Courter & Ward, 1983) in group skills and in finding and adapting research ideas to their school. The establishment of a supportive environment that encourages and rewards innovation and collegiality seems to contribute to the collaborative process (see Little, 1981).

Beyond training school administrators in the skills and attitudes necessary to create and sustain that environment, district policy would provide for the public recognition and reward of school staff involved in the collective effort to change the school culture. In short, though school improvement is a bottom-up process, it cannot succeed without visible, concrete manifestations of district support.

The importance placed upon staff participation in, and hence responsibility for, school improvement suggests the need for a partnership between the administration and the teachers' union. Without this partnership many changes critical to the improvement process may not take place. For example, unions may oppose a program that requires teachers to assume additional duties without receiving compensation in return. Administrators may be threatened by a reorganization of the school governance structure that expands staff authority over school policy issues.

It is unlikely that all areas of potential conflict between the teachers' union and the district can be eliminated. However, district policy can be formulated that would minimize conflict. First, negotiations can be initiated on matters having to do with the school-improvement project. Second, select items might be written into the collective bargaining agreement requiring the two parties to discuss pertinent issues and serving to document agreements. Third, district policy could mandate a "union seat" on school improvement committees and on oversight bodies at the district level. Such actions could help foster an administration–union partnership.

A number of other issues must be addressed by district policy if school improvement projects are to take root and grow to fruition. These issues include the following:

1. District goals must be determined that encompass all schools but leave enough room for schools to devise building-specific goals. The effective schools research points to the power generated by a staff and student body who share a common, clear understanding of the school's purpose. While unity on goals may be easier to reach for elementary schools, secondary schools, with their broader curriculum and more divergent interests, may find unity more elusive and may choose to compromise between goal clarity and goal consensus.

2. Means to evaluate the school improvement process and to measure change must be agreed upon by all the parties involved. While criticisms about the use of standardized test scores as a measure of school effectiveness are well taken (in particular see Rowan, Bossert, & Dwyer, 1983), quantitative data are relatively objective and carry a certain amount of face validity and acceptability with parents, the media, the politicians. Teachers, however, tend to be suspicious of using test scores as sole measures of school effectiveness. Therefore, room must be left for schools to develop their own indicators. Negotiated district policies on evaluation and measurement profitably include both norm- and criterion-referenced tests, various quality-of-school-life indicies (see Epstein, 1981; Moos, 1979), and organizational climate measures (see Halpin & Croft, 1963).

3. Changing a school's culture is a long-term project that involves hard work over many months. Substantial change may not occur for 2 or

3 years. The length of time needed makes particularly relevant the institutionalization of whatever changes are attempted and, most importantly, of the process of self-analysis, collaborative planning, and shared decision making (see Berman, 1981; Fullan, 1982; Hage & Aiken, 1970; Rosenblum & Louis, 1981).

As a matter of policy, districts must insure that a flywheel exists that can deal with the decay of enthusiasm and generate continuation of the change process (O'Toole, 1981). Examples of such a mechanism include: (1) contracts with negotiated items monitored, renegotiated, and so on, (2) ongoing staff development activities tied to building staff needs and interests and carrying rewards for participation, and (3) competitive grants of discretionary funds that are renewed at established times and upon the completion of previously agreed upon tasks.

In summation, district policies can be devised that build upon the findings of the effective schools research. Such policies rely upon staff collaboration and balance the necessity of district responsibility with the need for school flexibility. In the sections that follow, state and federal policies that complement these district policy recommendations are discussed.

STATE AND FEDERAL POLICY FOR BOTTOM-UP PLANNING

Even though the effective schools research is most applicable at the district and school level it suggests directions for state and federal policy. State and federal policy should encourage school-level, school-specific change—change from the bottom-up. This poses a familiar conundrum. How can top-down state and federal policy foster bottom-up planning and initiative? What state and federal policies will permit diversity, stimulate schools to change, and encourage, at the building level, the kinds of activities that the effective schools research suggests happen? Though the dilemma is real enough, answers are suggested by policy literature.

STATE POLICY: COMPETITIVE FUNDING

State policy for school effectiveness can take different forms. Most responsive to the bottom-up recommendation is backward mapping from the school level whereby policies are selected that stimulate and support local school-based improvement projects. Other approaches, while not without merit, are based upon different assumptions about school reform. Though they do not always or inherently contradict the logic of bottom-up participatory school improvement, they usually seek to impose change in a top-down manner rather than placing responsibility for a school's educational program on the shoulders of the school's staff. Such policies include the establishment of uniform standards that all schools and districts would be accountable for, such as increased graduation requirements. Other top-down policies provoke change in institutions, such as schools of education and teacher training, that have an impact on the quality of education, or they establish evaluation, monitoring, and preparation standards to regulate the quality of school personnel.

The situationally unique organizational, normative and valuative aspects of a school's culture that act as important determinants of student performance can be lost in top-down policy setting. Policies like the last three mentioned are likely to treat all schools in identical fashion and fail to address the elements of an individual school's culture. While political pressure on state governments to make a visible and dramatic response to the alleged crisis in public education is real, the less glamorous, longer-range solutions suggested by effective schools research should be at the heart of educational reform efforts.

States could stimulate school-based improvement projects in a manner congruent with the effective schools literature by holding funding competitions for schools. Local schools, through their districts, could develop proposals and apply for grants to be used for school-wide improvement. The state would establish minimum criteria to assess the proposals and certain goals or outcomes that must be addressed in each school or district plan. For example, criteria for schools might include the creation of a representative school improvement committee responsible for plan development and implementation and the requirement that each plan contain strategies for meeting state goals such as improved achievement in math and science. Within the given criteria schools could tailor their plans to fit local conditions. While proposals would have to meet the minimum state criteria, schools would be encouraged to go beyond that minimum: one might include a strategy for using computers in the classroom; another might adopt a dropout prevention program; still another might choose to emphasize attendance and student behavior. Schools would also be required to state specific, objective outcome goals that meet or go beyond those specified by the state. State panels would judge each submission. Selected proposals would be funded for at least a 3-year period. At the end of that time the schools would be reevaluated to determine if they had reached stated goals and outcomes. Successful schools would be eligible for renewed funding subject to the preparation of another plan that would be exempt from the competitive process but still subject to state criteria. The unsuccessful schools might develop new proposals and would also be eligible for special technical assistance funds from the state to enable them to seek outside help in redrawing their proposals. Schools not selected previously and schools entering the competition for the first time could submit new proposals each year.

A number of funding strategies could be used. Each school could receive the same funding amount, or all schools could receive so many dollars per student, or, schools with high numbers of disadvantaged students could receive supplementary aid beyond that available to less needy schools. The selection process itself could be weighted in favor of schools serving low-income populations or having greater than average numbers of special-needs students. The primary purpose of the money would be to stimulate school improvement, not to support additional services.[3]

States could also extend the program to districts to insure district support of individual school improvement efforts. A district-based program would work in a similar fashion as the school-based funding. Competitive awards would be made to districts with the size keyed to a preset formula such as so many dollars per school or per number of disadvantaged and special-needs students in the district. The amount of the grant could be linked to a ratio of the district's tax base to the degree of school improvement effort going on in the district, enabling hard-working poorer districts to receive a disproportionate amount. Such a formula would serve the dual purpose of stimulating school improvement and reducing inequities in district finances. In this case, however, the more complicated evaluation of outcomes might necessitate giving districts more latitude.

Competitive grants would both stimulate and support the process of school improvement. They would encourage school-wide improvement efforts, involve the schools' staff in the process and thereby promote a sense of ownership and responsibility, and tangibly reward schools whose staffs worked hard to prepare and implement their proposals. By disseminating research and providing expert advice and assistance state education agencies could help schools focus on and obtain achievement gains and higher standards without imposing them from above in a mechanistic fashion. School-based strategies that rely upon staff initia-

---

[3] To provide funds for 10% of Wisconsin schools under this program would cost roughly 15 million dollars—this is less than 1% of the total elementary–secondary budget in the state.

tive, collaboration, and shared decision making will also, in the long run, do more to attract and keep quality educators in teaching than merit-pay proposals or upgraded entrance requirements (see Freedman, Jackson, & Boles, 1983; Shulman, 1983; Weinshank, Trumbull, & Daly, 1983).

States in which competitive funding is neither politically nor economically feasible might use school accreditation as a vehicle for stimulating research-based school improvement. Accreditation is typically awarded to schools whose staffs possess acceptable academic credentials, that keep student records containing specified information, whose physical plant and school facilities meet certain standards, or in which instructional media and materials are deemed educationally adequate. None of these criteria have a significant impact on student achievement.

Without abandoning such minimum qualifications states might tie accreditation to the characteristics of effective schools. The state would establish a point or star system for school accreditation. Basic accreditation—one star—would be given to schools meeting existing standards such as those just described. Having reached that level, schools could then elect to try for a higher rating. To receive two stars, for example, a school would be required to have the following: a broadly representative school improvement committee; yearly, written plans that address the school's weaknesses in areas presently thought to be associated with achievement (e.g., order and discipline, clear school mission, etc.); evidence of staff collaboration in the change process and in their daily work; and, school-wide, staff-initiated staff development activities.

The approval and support of the central office may be necessary in many districts for these characteristics to exist. Therefore, as a by-product this method of accreditation would align the central office with a school-based approach to educational change.

Three stars could be reserved for schools that meet all of the previous requirements and whose students achieved predetermined outcomes determined by the school and the accrediting agency. Uniform standards would not be set by the state to avoid penalizing schools with high concentrations of disadvantaged students or schools that have experienced severe demographic or economic dislocations. Once reached, however, the outcomes must be sustained for 2 years before the school is awarded the top accreditation.

As an incentive to schools' participation, states would publicize those receiving two- or three-star ratings, perhaps through an annual "Michelin Guide" to good schools. Public award ceremonies could be held and symbols (e.g., flags, markers) used to designate the recipients. Further incentive would stem from the availability of the accreditation teams to assist schools in the improvement process. It is reasonable to assume that most schools would be under a considerable amount of pressure to move beyond the basic accreditation level.

While the accreditation approach has merit, two weaknesses suggest favoring competitive funding. First, some schools, by virtue of their student-body composition, their institutional history, or their environmental chemistry, will be harder to change than others; a very few schools may be impervious to substantive improvement. The former may be unfairly judged, while options for the latter may be limited to closing them, an unrealistic alternative in most cases. Second, over time, the accreditation bureaucracy could expand to such a degree as to become prohibitively expensive. Competitive funding would be more equitable and could be implemented by a leaner, less-costly mechanism.

The few states that may choose not to adopt either approach should, at minimum, examine their policies and weed out those that impede schools' effectiveness. For example, state-mandated textbooks and course content guidelines might easily discourage districts from tailoring curriculum to their students' needs and interests. Both policies, far from raising student achievement, may actually serve to allow schools to avoid responsibility for their students' performance. School staffs can logically argue that the state curriculum policies are not responsive to their students' abilities or to the talents of their teachers.

State graduation policies could also undermine school improvement. Some states have proposed significantly increasing the number of credits a student must earn in specific subjects. While we support a credit–subject floor, extreme requirements could diminish schools' flexibility and further depress staff willingness to accept responsibility for students' success. More importantly, such policies may create the illusion of change without affecting achievement and distract districts from undertaking more comprehensive changes.

The point is that if the school is to be the focus of change, then state policies that conflict with school-based reform must be removed. Policies having no clear relationship to student achievement or to equity and civil rights and that interfere with local responsibility serve no useful purpose.

Two final issues are offered for discussion. The first concerns the current distribution among schools of characteristics associated with high student achievement. Part of the attractiveness of the effective schools analysis is that all schools, whatever their social–economic composition, can develop and possess the 13 features salient to improved academic performance. Nevertheless, some of those characteristics may be more apt to exist spontaneously in more affluent schools. If so, the state may have an ethical responsibility to provide additional resources to low-income districts that are trying to implant or generate factors such as order and discipline, a revamped curriculum and so forth.

The second issue has to do with teacher preparation and the role of schools of education. The literature indicates that teachers will bear the greatest responsibility for the success or failure of school-improvement programs. These projects will be school-based, staff-designed comprehensive efforts to alter the structure and process of the school. If teachers are to play such a major part, their training must include increased emphasis on courses in the humanities and on the organizational character of schools, the nature of school culture, and the social context in which education takes place. Such a course of study—professional education classes, subject-matter emphasis, liberal arts background, and advanced study in organizational theory, problem-solving skills, and the like—cannot be accomplished in a 4-year program. A fifth year, combined with higher beginning and end salaries, may be warranted.

Finally, schools of education should conduct continuing education or in-service programs in partnership with local schools and school districts. Ongoing, whole-staff in-service training responsive to school-identified needs contribute to successful school reform. At the present time, university and college courses for practicing teachers emphasize an individualistic, piecemeal approach seldom linked to school or district needs and interests. Locally initiated, school-wide continuing education, therefore, will not happen unless (1) professors are assured of recognition and credit for tailoring classes to the expressed needs of schools, (2) colleges and universities expand efforts to offer evening, weekend, and summer courses, and (3) rewards are provided for teachers (especially on a whole-staff basis) who participate in the courses.

FEDERAL POLICY: ENDS NOT MEANS

One concern here is the past tendency for federal policy to lead to schools focusing on compliance with financial regulations at the expense of concentrating on program-quality issues (McLaughlin & McDonnell, 1982). Future programs should be developed that encourage schools to take advantage of education research and educationally effective practices adaptable to their specific conditions and environment (see Turnbull, Smith, & Ginsburg, 1981).

Education history in the United States demonstrates that disadvantaged students in general, and particularly in some states, are in need of federal assistance and, at times, protection (Kaestle & Smith, 1982).

While it makes sense to leave overall academic quality to the province of the states, federal policy is rightly concerned with issues related to basic constitutional rights and social justice (Kaestle & Smith, 1982). This suggests that the federal government might well use funding, and accompanying regulations, to enhance the educational opportunities of disadvantaged students by stimulating schools and districts to address certain issues and integrate specified goals into the overall school program.

A possible model might be the ill-fated Youth Act of 1980 proposed by the Carter administration. If passed and funded, it would have targeted funds to secondary schools with the highest percentages of needy students while encouraging program quality through competition.[4] Following this model, formula funds to stimulate effective schools could be provided to eligible districts based on the number of disadvantaged students. Schools interested in participating would have to develop a school-wide plan that would set out locally developed goals for reducing dropouts, raising low achievement, assisting non-English-speaking students, and the like, and planning-procedures would be required such as school-wide committees and school–community collaboration. Other goals and processes most likely to lead to school improvement for all would be stressed: school-site management, staff stability, district support, collaborative planning, and so on. Schools would be selected by the quality of their plans. Successful plans would receive funding for a set length of time, with continuation based upon meeting their stated goals.

How the money would be used would not be monitored once the initial grant recipients were determined—instead, the test would be whether improvement in outcomes is seen at the end of a specified period of time. Such noninterference would help insure that educationally sound practices are not lost in regulatory thickets and that school-specific strategies more likely to generate change would result.

The federal policy outlined above closely resembles the recommendation for states. Overlapping policies may be advantageous because of the likelihood of variation among states in promoting school effectiveness. Moreover, many states have less leeway than the federal government to target their funds geographically (e.g., isolated rural areas or inner cities) or demographically (e.g., low income or non-English speaking). Finally, a federal competitive program would not replace existing

---

[4] For a description and discussion of the Youth Act of 1980, see U.S. House of Representatives, HR 6711, 96th Congress, 2nd sess., Title II (Washington, DC: 5 March 1980); and U.S. House of Representatives, *Youth Act of 1980*, Report to Accompany HR 6711, Committee on Education and Labor, 96th Congress, 2nd sess., Report No. 96–1034 (Washington, DC: 16 May 1980).

federal programs. Therefore it could be viewed as responding to the "crisis" discovered by several of the national reports on education and meeting their demands that increased resources be devoted to improving schooling in America. Its combination of school-based, bottom-up initiative, competition, and emphasis on serving disadvantaged students (excellence *and* equity), could have political appeal.

Other federal policy approaches to promoting effective schools might include differential treatment of the states or the use of matching funds (McLaughlin & McDonnell, 1982; Turnbull, Smith, & Ginsburg, 1981). The purpose behind each of these approaches is to maximize the flexibility of the states while retaining accountability for the expenditure of federal funds where it is needed most. The flexibility allowed some states might encourage them to experiment with school-improvement strategies.

Differential treatment recommendations stem from recognition that states differ, often dramatically, in their capacity and will to serve disadvantaged students. The recommendations maintain tight fiscal and programmatic requirements for states that have demonstrated incapacity or lack of will, and they allow considerably more discretion by those states with a legislative history of responding to the needs of disadvantaged students. One proposal (Turnbull, Smith, & Ginsburg, 1981) suggests keying exemptions on the existence of state laws fulfilling federal criteria. For example, states with legislation or policy providing for effective schools programs for disadvantaged children would receive funds and be subject to outcome evaluation only. States that had yet to address the issue would have their federal dollars tracked to the school level. As a side benefit such a policy might encourage states to pass education legislation to gain relief from the burden of close monitoring.

Another alternative, the use of matching-funds, has the same incentive intent. Matching-funds would reward states that had already initiated programs aimed at general school improvement with special provisions for disadvantaged students. Again, the funding would continue as long as stated goals were met.

CONCLUSION

The effective schools research and past experience with federal and state education programs suggest that (1) school differences do have an effect upon student achievement, (2) it is the culture of the *whole* school that creates that effect, (3) district, state, and federal policy would best focus on instigating school-specific, whole-school improvement efforts, and (4) outcomes are the preferable means of monitoring and evaluating such efforts. The question remains whether in an era of financial retrenchment, fiscal conservatism, lingering unwillingness by the Republican administration in Washington to invest in educational programs, and the politically motivated desire to "do something quickly," the political will exists to act on the basis of what is known about improving schools and the policies that will take us there.

There is some indication that school improvement programs of the type indicated by the effective schools literature are not politically attractive. Stimulating school staffs to evaluate the learning climate and academic culture of their school and providing them with the resources necessary for the long-haul process of school improvement is not dramatic. It does not attract publicity, offer a quick-fix solution, or involve some new technological breakthrough that will revolutionize education. Instead, school-based reform requires hard, sustained work. Fundamental school improvement demands the educational equivalent of "patient money" that is invested with the expectation of seeing results 3 or more years in the future. While the concept of school culture may sound soft to the technocratic ear, evidence shows that it is precisely this culture that accounts for the impact differences schools have on student achievement. The question now is whether educational policy will reflect that conclusion.

REFERENCES

Austin, G. R. (1981). *Exemplary schools and their identification.* Unpublished manuscript. University of Maryland, Center for Educational Research and Development, College Park, MD.

Averch, H. A., Carroll, S. J., Donaldson, T. S., Kiesling, J. J., and Pincus, J. (1972). *How effective is schooling? A critical review and synthesis of research findings.* Santa Monica, CA: Rand Corporation.

Berman, P. (1981). Educational change: An implementation paradigm. In R. Lehming & M. Kane (Eds.), *Improving schools* (pp.253–286). Beverly Hills, CA: Sage.

Bloom, B. S. (1981). "The new direction in educational research and measurement: Alterable variables." Chicago, IL: University of Chicago. Paper presented at meeting of the American Educational Research Association, Los Angeles.

Brookover, W. B., Beady, C., Flood, P., Schweitzer, J., & Wisenbaker, J. (1979). *School social systems and student achievement: Schools can make a difference.* New York: Praeger. (Original work published 1977 under title, *Schools can make a difference*).

Clark, D. L., Lotto, L. S., & McCarthy, M. M. (1980). Factors associated with success in urban elementary schools. *Phi Delta Kappan, 61,* 467–470.

Coleman, J. S., Campbell, E., Hobson, C., McPartland, J., Mood, A., Weinfeld, F., & York, R. (1966). *Equality of educational opportunity.* Washington DC: Government Printing Office.

College Entrance Examination Board. (1983). *Academic preparation for college: What students need to know and be able to do.* New York: Author.

Courter, R. L., and Ward, B. A. (1983). Staff development for school improvement. In G. A. Griffin (Eds.), *Staff development. Eighty-second yearbook of the national society for the study of education* (pp.185–209). Chicago: The National Society for the Study of Education.

Deal, T. E., Intili, J., Rosaler, J. A., & Stackhouse, A. (1977). *The early childhood education program: An assessment of its impact and implementation.* Sacramento, CA: California State Department of Education.

Derr, C. B., & Deal, T. E. (1979). Toward a contingency theory of change in education: Organizational structure, processes, and symbolism. In E. King (Ed.), *Education for uncertainty* (pp.39–70). London: Sage.

Dornbush, S. M., & Scott, W. R. (1975). *Evaluation and the exercise of authority.* San Francisco, CA: Jossey-Bass.

Doss, D., & Holley, F. (1982). *A cause for national pause: Title I schoolwide projects.* (ORE Publication No. 81.55) Austin, TX: Office of Research and Evaluation, Austin Independent School District.

Education Commission of the States. (1983). *Action for excellence: A comprehensive plan to improve our nation's schools.* Denver, CO: Education Commission of the States.

Elmore, R. F. (1979–80). Backward mapping: Implementation research and policy decision. *Political Science Quarterly, 49,* 606–616.

Epstein, J. L. (Ed.). (1981). *The quality of school life.* Lexington, MA: Lexington Books.

Freedman, S., Jackson, J., & Boles, K. (1983). Teaching: An imperiled "profession." In L. Shulman & G. Sykes (Eds.), *Handbook of teaching and policy* (pp.261–299). New York: Longman.

Fullan, M. (1982, February). Implementing educational change: Progress at last. Paper presented at the National Institute of Education Conference on the Implications of Research on Teaching for Practice. Arlie House, VA.

Goodlad, J. L. (1983). The school as workplace. In G. A. Griffin (Ed.), *Staff development. Eighty-second yearbook of the National Society for the Study of Education* (pp.36–61). Chicago: The National Society for the Study of Education.

Hage, J., & Aiken, M. (1970). *Social change in complex organizations.* New York: Random House.

Halpin, A. W., & Croft, D. B. (1963). *The organizational climate of schools.* Chicago: University of Chicago, Midwest Administration Center.

Hanushek, E. A. (1981). Throwing money at schools. *Journal of Policy Analysis and Management, 1,* 19–41.

Hargrove, E. C., Graham, S. G., Ward, L. E., Abernethy, V., Cunningham, J., & Vaughn, W. K. (1981). *Regulations and schools: The implementation of equal education for handicapped children.* Nashville, TN: Vanderbilt University, Institute for Public Policy Studies.

Hawley, W. D. (1978). Horses before carts: Developing adaptive schools and the limits of innovation. In D. Mann (Ed.), *Making change happen* (pp.224–260). New York: Teachers College Press.

Hersh, R. H., Carnine, D., Gall, M., Stockard, J., Carmack, M. A., & Gannon, P. (1981). The management of education professionals in instructionally effective schools: Toward a research agenda. Unpublished manuscript. University of Oregon, Center for Educational Policy and Management, Eugene, OR.

Jencks, C. S., Smith, M. S., Ackland, H., Bane, M. J., Cohen, D., Gintis, H., Heyns, B., & Michelson, S. (1972). *Inequality: A reassessment of the effect of family and schooling in America.* New York: Basic Books.

Kaestle, C. F., & Smith, M. S. (1982). The federal role in elementary and secondary education, 1940–1980. *Harvard Educational Review, 52,* 384–408.

Little, J. W. (1981, April). *School success and staff development in urban desegregated schools: A summary of recently completed research.* Paper presented at the meeting of the American Educational Research Association, Los Angeles.

MacKenzie, D. E. (1983). Research for school improvement: An appraisal of some recent trends. *Educational Researcher, 12*(4), 5–17.

McLaughlin, M. W., & McDonnell, L. M. (1982). *Education policy and the role of the states.* Santa Monica, CA: Rand Corporation.

McLaughlin, M. W. (1978). Implementation as mutual adaptation: Change in classroom organization. In D. Mann (Ed.), *Making change happen* (pp.19–31). New York: Teachers College Press.

Meyer, J. W., & Rowan, B. (1978). The structure of educational organizations. In M. Meyer et al. (Eds.), *Environments and organizations* (pp.78–109). San Francisco, CA: Jossey-Bass.

Miles, M. B. (1981). Mapping the common properties of schools. In R. Lehming & M. Kane (Eds.), *Improving schools: Using what we know* (pp.42–114). Beverly Hills, CA: Sage.

Miller, L. (1980). BYTES: Implications for staff development. In C. Denham & A. Lieberman (Eds.), *Time to learn* (pp.159–172). Washington, DC: U.S. Department of Education.

Moos, R. H. (1979). *Evaluating educational environments.* San Francisco: Jossey-Bass.

Mullin, S. P., & Summers, A. A. (1981). *Is more better? A review of the evidence on the effectiveness of spending on compensatory education.* Unpublished manuscript. University of Pennsylvania, Philadelphia.

Murnane, R. J. (1980). *Interpreting the evidence on school effectiveness* (Working Paper No. 830). New Haven, CT: Yale University, Institution for Social and Policy Studies.

National Commission on Excellence in Education. (1983). *A nation at risk: The imperative for educational reform.* Washington, DC: U.S. Government Printing Office.

O'Toole, J. (1981). *Making America work.* New York: Continuum.

Pfeffer, J. (1981). *Power in organizations.* Marshfield, MA: Pitman.

Phi Delta Kappa. (1980). *Why do some urban schools succeed?* Bloomington, IN: Author.

Purkey, S. C. (1984). *School improvement: An analysis of an urban school district effective schools project.* Unpublished doctoral dissertation, University of Wisconsin, Madison.

Purkey, S. C., & Smith, M. S. (1983). Effective schools: A review. *The Elementary School Journal, 83,* 427–452.

Purkey, S. C. & Smith, M. S. (1985). School reform: The district policy implications of the effective schools literature. *The Elementary School Journal, 85,* 353–389.

Rosenblum, S., & Louis, K. S. (1981). *Stability and change: Innovation in an educational context.* New York: Plenum.

Rowan, B., Bossert, S. T., & Dwyer, D. C. (1983). Research on effective schools: A cautionary note. *Educational Researcher, 12*(4), 24–31.

Rutter, M. (1983). School effects on pupil progress: Research findings and policy implications. In L. Shulman & G. Sykes (Eds.), *Handbook of teaching and policy* (pp.3–41). New York: Longman.

Rutter, M., Maughan, B., Mortimore, P., Ouston, J. & Smith, S. (1979). *Fifteen thousand hours: Secondary schools and their effects on children.* Cambridge, MA: Harvard University Press.

Shulman, L. S. (1983). Autonomy and obligation: The remote control of teaching. In L. Shulman & G. Sykes (Eds.), *Handbook of teaching and policy* (pp.484–504). New York: Longman.

Talbert, J. E. (1980). *School organization and institutional change: Exchange and power in loosely coupled systems.* Stanford, CA: Stanford University, Institute for Research on Educational Finance and Governance.

Task Force on Education for Economic Growth (1983). *Action for excellence: A comprehensive plan to improve our nation's schools.* Denver, CO: Education Commission of the States.

Tomlinson, T. M. (1981). *The minority student in public schools: Fostering academic excellence.* Educational Testing Service, Office of Minority Education, *3*, 95–117.

Turnbull, B. J., Smith, M. S., & Ginsburg, A. L. (1981). Issues for a new administration: The federal role in education. *American Journal of Education, 89*, 396–426.

Twentieth Century Fund Task Force on Federal Elementary and Secondary Education Policy. (1983). *Making the grade.* New York: Twentieth Century Fund.

Weick, K. E. (1976). Educational organizations as loosely coupled systems. *Administrative Science Quarterly, 21*, 1–19.

Weinshank, A. B., Trumbull, E. S., & Daly, P. L. (1983). The role of the teacher in school change. In L. Shulman & G. Sykes (Eds.), *Handbook of teaching and policy* (pp.300–314). New York: Longman.

CHAPTER 10

Models, Media, Method: Research on Exemplary or Effective Schools as a Psychological Experience

Herbert Garber

In this concluding chapter I attempt to summarize what has gone before. I recap what the other contributors have said and fill in a few gaps. Then, I offer some suggestions on where research on effective schools ought to turn and why, in order to sustain and accelerate its progress.

As a way to accomplish the summary, I share with the reader the guiding thoughts the editors sent the authors before they prepared their manuscripts. Next, I describe how they succeeded in using these five guideline statements. Finally, I offer the suggestions mentioned above for continuing and improving effective schools research.

WHAT THE AUTHORS WERE TOLD

The contributing authors were told that this book would make the following five points:

1. America's schools are very complex human organizations with no two alike. Those who condemn them are guilty of prejudiced thinking.

Therefore, the researcher needs to define the terms *exemplary* and/or *effective* with care to guard against the error of overgeneralizing.

2. Although prominent political voices espouse commonsense, quick-fix solutions, more useful information for school reform will come from studying examples of successful schooling.

3. Current critics of the knee-jerk variety focus contempt on schools as if they alone were the cause of poor pupil achievements. This book suggests that the schools will produce what their sponsors really want, even though they say they want something different—such as citizenship as measured on a competency-based examination.

4. Amidst the smoke and dust of controversy exist instances of exemplariness. Some schools are exceptionally successful. However, the prescription for improving lagging schools and classrooms has not been recorded. Nevertheless, ways exist that enable us to learn how individual schools do manage to succeed. From a careful study of such cases, bits of knowledge and facts can be found that can be helpful in other school settings.

5. Finally, exemplary and effective are slippery terms. The values of the user are what determine their meaning just as much as the behaviors and achievements of the pupils in a given school. It is wise for one to maintain a healthy skepticism when one is told to emulate any particular exemplary schoolroom, school, or district.

WHAT OUR AUTHORS SAID

The Problem

These central problem concepts seem to compel one common method of solution; that is, the problems all require the collection of dependable data and facts. This stands to reason although there exists another school of thought that emphasizes maintaining a state of uplifting good feeling as a path to success. Robert Ebel in his forward to a book on testing (Austin & Garber, 1982) points out the reality we must face. "Both achievement and adjustment are good . . . but they compete for the same time and energy" (p. xii). For me, a survey of this book and other writings on the subject suggests a choice must be made between two principal values. The choices may be described by such constructs as medical versus patient advocacy, top-down versus bottom-up, authoritative versus authoritarian (Fromm, 1956), or Ebel's distinction cited above—achievement versus adjustment (Austin & Garber, 1982, p. xi) or to use the pair of terms he used, "excellence versus equality."

If I were a superintendent of a large school system I would be bewildered by the reports, articles, and papers produced in very recent years on effective schools research. The consistent constructs listed by reviewers along with their fuzzy, overlapping conclusions lead to confusion (MacKenzie, 1983, p. 8). Maybe, after reading a dozen or more of the better reviews, I might get the idea that this movement arose as a defense against the perception generated by the Coleman study (Coleman, et al., 1966) that one public school is the same as the next so far as pupil achievement is concerned. Also, I might begin to think that this movement arose as a rebuttal to sweeping indictments in the media brought on by Scholastic Aptitude Test (SAT) score declines (Garber & Austin, 1982, p. 1). In any event, it is fair for the reader to ask now, "What do I know that I didn't know before reading this book's first nine chapters?"

Complex Organizations

The first point this book addressed, that schools are complex organizations, should be clear from what most of our authors had to say. In particular, Hannaway and Abramowitz (Chapter 2) certainly showed that clear differences exist in the tasks emphasized by public school principals as compared to those emphasized in private schools. These authors surmise that the Avis model (We try harder!) exists in public schools exclusively because of a cultural difference. They explain this, in part, as caused by the freedom to choose to associate on the part of both the private school and its clients. Donovan and Madaus (Chapter 3) make it quite clear that the differences between Catholic and public schools are undeniable and have caused reciprocal problems.

Politics Is No Solution

The second point this book was supposed to discuss is the notion that exhortation by political voices are of uncertain help in developing school improvements. Political acts underlie much that is described in various chapters. In particular, the Great Society legislation of the mid-1960s to 1970s inspired by President Lyndon B. Johnson, changed the conduct of American schooling with varying results. However, these programs were supposed to create equality of outcome. Unexpectedly, exemplary programs emerged and they did so despite, not because of, federal aid. The Office of Education eventually needed to institute an exemplary programs dissemination activity. We live in a fairly sophisticated age. We really are disinclined to believe in magic and do not readily harken to shamans despite certain accusations (Rowan, 1984). Our authors also never cite instances when a political speech or press conference resulted directly in improved learning by school students—probably because none exist. Any positive effects would necessarily come from the direct efforts of involved professionals, parents, and pupils at the individual school level. Measurement technology has yet to develop an instrument that can trace and measure the amount of inspiration variance from political vocalizing contained in pupil achievement scores. Indeed, prominent professionals are voicing concern over the expressed need for more time to allow high school teachers to emphasize the personal educational goals of their students (Goodlad, 1984, p. 311–312).

Faulting Schools Fails To Help

Accusations that schools alone cause poor pupil achievement proved difficult for most of our contributors to discuss directly. Stephen Miller (Chapter 1) addressed it indirectly but successfully. To be sure, Admiral Hyman Rickover and others critical of the schools were cited directly in a press interested in blaming schools for America's failure to beat the Soviets into space. But we come to learn of the accusation that the schools bear the responsibility for America's problems from other evidence, too.

Purkey and Smith (Chapter 9) point out that the loosely-coupled (nonconformity of school to district office orders) concept of school district structure matches the popular notion of unresponsive school teachers and principals. The superintendent of the local district or the state commissioner can issue directives, legislatures can pass minimum competency laws (Jaeger & Tittle, 1980; Wise, 1979), but the schools just seem to go on as before. They point out, too, that the effective schools research approach is seldom advocated by political elements. It offers no dramatic, quick-fix solution. Politicians like to advocate the dramatic in order to appear competent and potent to their constituents.

Why Some Schools Are Exceptions

Our authors paid little attention to our fourth concern: the fact that no coherent theory exists to explain the rare but real exemplary school that produces surprisingly high-level student outcomes. Austin (Chapter 4) makes us aware that several researchers during the 1960s and 1970s have worked, however, to identify and later explain these outliers. And, of course, Fetler and Carlson (Chapter 5) describe in some detail a creative way by which the California Department of Education was able, at slight cost, to identify reliably the exceptionally effective elementary schools throughout the state. But these efforts fail to explain much.

What Are We Talking About?

The contributors to this book were conscious in nearly every case of the need to be clear about such terms as effective or exemplary. Miller's Chapter 1 on the history of the movement certainly shows how the schools have moved nimbly between providing equity (equal opportunity and equal outcome goals) and social efficiency (finding and nurturing excellence). His concern is that interests exist in America that will express dissatisfaction with schools that succeed in producing self-reliant, confident, good citizens among most of their pupils, but fail to raise SAT scores for their college-bound students.

Carolyn Anderson's Chapter 6 on school climate can serve as a model of terminology classification and description. Her target subject was one aspect of an exemplary school but one so crucial in the minds of many people as to make it the defining characteristic of an exemplary or effective school. She defines an effective school climate in empirical terms: we come to understand such a climate from the actions used in measuring it. What is left for the researcher, practitioner, and policymaker to ponder and debate is the perplexing philosophical question of whether to pursue a deliberate "climate improvement" program or a "renewal-of-academic-success-for-all-pupils" program that will yield a positive climate as a valued outcome. Again, the excellence versus equality issue.

David Berliner (Chapter 7) argues persuasively that the issue has been resolved. A school needs excellent teachers and the more there are in a school, the better. They are bound to create an exemplary school via the renewal-of-academic-success modality. To spend time in a deliberate effort to convince pupils they are worthy human beings while withholding the opportunity to acquire the basic skills and knowledge that an educated person needs "out there" would be a profound disservice. Also, the pupils would be aware of and irritated by such duplicity. Such a school surely would be of dubious exemplariness; but we will learn about an instructive exception later.

Kenneth Leithwood and Deborah Montgomery (Chapter 8) show us also that an exemplary and/or effective school will in all probability be led by an above average effective principal. She or he will be recognizable to most of us. Such a person can be characterized as competent, intelligent, experienced, energetic, mentally healthy, zestful, and warm and compassionate. This effective principal will be, most important of all, a consummate educator. He or she is interested in making the staff of the school become scholar–teachers who can and will think deeply about what they are doing individually and collectively as members of a small but important culture–community: in short, a person who resembles the nineteenth-century superintendent described by Cuban (1984).

This educator–leader consciously or intuitively knows that young people tend to model themselves on adults with whom they spend time. If the adults in this school are interested in broad inquiry, like to use rational methods to solve problems, prefer to tackle rather than avoid small irritations to an otherwise smooth social order, and like to listen to what the pupils want to say, then, probably, the pupils in this school will grow up to use the same sorts of approaches to problems outside school. They will also, incidentally, likely get higher achievement test scores than the children in a school with a Level 1, least effective but adequate, principal. But this conceptualization is a hunch, merely. Effective schools research rarely uses an experimental method (i.e., we cannot prove or disprove this simple, attractive theory).

WHAT OUR AUTHORS LEFT UNSAID

Media

Journalists of either print or electronic media in the United States operate under many constraints. One dominant limitation is the need for brevity. They cannot possibly take the time or space to philosophize when doing a story on schools and education. One does not expect such a writer to describe, discuss, and defend the purposes and history of schooling when reporting on a controversial topic, and most headlined reporting on schools is controversial. If such writers did present a careful background introduction to their stories it is likely the sensational component of the pieces would nearly vanish. But this book was not written by journalists. What attention to a theory of schooling should one expect from scholars using the medium of a printed scientific symposium?

Except, perhaps, for Stephen Miller (Chapter 1), the contributors to this book give scant attention to a theory of schooling. They really did not need to raise the philosophical question of why schools should exist in any society (Stephens, 1967). The typical reader shares with all others a faith that they are a necessary aspect of modern society and that whatever function they perform must, necessarily, take place in a separate institution distinct from the family and others that serve children and youth.

In this section I want to show the reader that both scholars and journalists work under various constraints. I try to show how meanings of terminology vary between scholars and how a journalist, under the right circumstances, can do commendable field research and add insight to the literature on effective schools research that might never have come from more conventional academic research efforts.

For the discussion to follow, I must remind the reader of the principle of multiple meanings. It is easily expressed in the proverbial saying, One man's meat is another man's poison. In this book some authors describe an exemplary and/or effective school as one that obtains higher than expected state achievement test scores for 3 years running or shows increasing scores. Others conceptualize it as one that sends a large percentage of its graduates (high school) on to higher education. Still others consider strict rules, steady homework, an emphasis on a basics curriculum, a compliant staff, and the like, to be the current, popular perception of such a school. And still others tell us what the teachers and principals in such schools do and allow us to assume that successful outcomes necessarily will be determined from such adult behavior.

When a rare positive picture is presented by newspaper, magazine, and television writers, the test score model or the testimony of local political or business figures is presented as evidence of effective schooling. One outstanding exception is the publication of the *Journalism Research Fellows Report* by the Institute for Educational Leadership (Brundage, n.d.). Especially notable is the section of that report by Robert Benjamin of the *Cincinnati Post, Towards Effective Urban Schools: A National Study* (Benjamin, n.d.). In this study, the skills that mark an experienced, able journalist were allowed full expression during an extended period of visiting, interviewing, and observing in several schools across the country. He was able to publish a series of newspaper columns (reprinted in the above publication) that seem to resemble closely the genre of an anthropologist of recent times. Mr. Benjamin shows an understanding and almost an advocacy for the schools and people he lived with and studied. His prescriptions for parents and citizens, put in the form of separate question boxes called "Looking at your school," reflect the set of indicators he learned were the signs of an effective school. Many of them overlap those produced by the professional writings in this volume. Some of Benjamin's topics included: changing achievement test scores in the basics, priority for math and reading, a plan for improving basic achievement, time spent on reading and math, homework, class behavior code, ability groupings on a permanent basis, and the like. For Robert Benjamin, then, an effective school is one that is sensitive to the unique needs of its community and, with deliberation and skill, proceeds to answer those needs. In short, it is like the level-headed, rational person who knows how to judge life's challenges, put them in proper order, and tackles them in a systematic, successful way. We might add that when the adults set a goal of efficiency rather than equity for the children, the climate will improve because pupils start to feel better about themselves and their school as they sense their increase in competence.

Our authors seldom told us of how important community events and perceptions of the school are to the aims, values, and outcomes of the school. Robert Benjamin studied a school in Louisville, Kentucky that was propelled into a position of high regard by a series of decisions outside its control (court-ordered combination of inner-city and suburban districts, etc; Benjamin, n.d., p. 95). The success enjoyed by this elementary school was a tribute, also, to a very competent principal. Even though test score differences continued between the two races and socioeconomic groups within the school it was regared by its clients as an effective school because the staff wisely emphasized the life adjustment or equality side of the school rationale issue. That's what was needed in a city threatened with violent reactions to forced-busing. Parents continued to want their children bused there even though academic outcomes were lower than elsewhere. At least their kids were safe! Under such conditions it was reasonable to expect equity, not efficiency or excellence, to be emphasized.

Our scholar-authors would find it difficult to squeeze a school like that into the accepted definitions of exemplary schools. The scientific community would huff and puff and blow them away, academically. But once we switch over to the journalistic medium, this school story can be admitted to our scholarly knowledge and used to broaden our understanding. It will justify the inclusion in some multivariate equation of a term for "forced-busing." It helps us appreciate that the weights or coefficients that are attached to each of the many terms in such an equation will need to be changed according to what state or county or city or, indeed, neighborhood is served at what point in history by the schools in question.

Also, lest we forget, the equation will need alteration as economic or political circumstances change. And yet, paradoxically, the image of an exemplary school can be altered by the uttering of eloquent words in well-modulated vocalizations, on television or radio, by a personality regarded as authoritative by a national or local audience. That in itself is paradoxical because one might be led to believe that Americans are well educated, which ought to mean hardheaded skeptics immune to propaganda. So, a useful model for exemplary schools research must include provisions for dealing with changing political purposes held by current office holders and the commissions and study groups that issue reports on the conditions of American education.

Models

I have shown that just as journalists work with contraints imposed by their craft, so, too, do educational researchers. I also have shown that educational researchers can benefit fairly directly sometimes from journalistic products. I have tried to show that an outside observer of schooling—a newspaper reporter—can find an exemplary school where professional school people might miss it because it did not fit a rigid definition or model they all shared. That can be bad for the effective schools research movement and for improving schooling generally. Therefore, I would like to show that the effective schools researcher ought to study how journalism and the advertising industry cause directed change in human perceptions and desires. I hope to show that a conscious, deliberate, reflective image of the changed school the researcher wishes to create can be an effective tool. Such modeling is the same process used by the media people to create a desired effect in readers and customers. Later I try to show how effective school researchers can use an instructional design system to bring about desirable change in a given school. It might even be possible in the near future to do a quasi-experiment with adequate controls using such a technique.

Our authors said more about other concerns than the print and electronic media as factors influencing American schools. I have mentioned in the last section the part played by the press as a tool of the politician. The communications industry does more than print papers and magazines, or operate television and radio transmitters.

Despite McLuhan's dark innuendo about the medium being a message, the effective designer of a media product aims to create predictable interpretations in the heads of readers and viewers. The audience will make such meaning from language symbols and carefully selected graphics provided by the message designers, not from the medium itself. Those interpretations can be predicted accurately because the writer–designer has enough psychological savvy to do so. He or she has a model of human, cognitive behavior as a guide to a successful cognitive product. Instructional systems designers do the same thing in creating a successful teaching sequence with some certain skill, knowledge, or understanding as the goal. But more about that later.

Few Americans, for example, have sufficient knowledge, leisure, and critical-thinking skills to reject exaggeration in the various media surrounding them. The professional writer knows that. Anthony Downs presented a succinct summary of the phenomenal success of word manipulation in a newspaper column, "They sell sizzle but their predictions fizzle," in the *Wall Street Journal* (Downs, 1983). He wrote on what he calls "exagger-books"—trendy publications that claim to foretell the future of the nation, the world, and the universe! We are told that some of the techniques used to persuade the unwary millions are *proof by assertion, proof by anecdote, exaggertrend* and so on. The term most appropriate to my present argument is *revelation by relabeling* (Downs, 1982). He cites Marily Ferguson, who reveals that an ancient practice, keeping in touch with people we share interests with, was renamed *networking* and thus, magically it was transformed into a new discovery in human behavior.

In our desire to analyze and explain schooling that proves that schools can make a difference, I believe too many education researchers and writers fail to use media techniques themselves and fail to take account of the ways in which practitioners, pupils, and parents are affected by television, newspapers, magazines, and books. But, mainly, they fail to select and use a workable, effective model of a school in a context. They need to take the media professional's approach: What are the needs, wishes, and other characteristics of the target audience? Or, the educator should say, "What kind of school is this and how can I help change it for the better?"

I have no certain creed to offer, but it seems imperative that the effective schools research practitioner or researcher must somehow keep a model in conscious awareness; he or she must remain alert to the fact that perceptions of the school by its public(s) and its members are what matters. I think our authors showed an appreciation of this fact in most instances. But, it bears repeating for the benefit of all concerned since it is a plain fact that mental models are just that. They can easily fade in the hurly-burly of daily life. They are not cast in concrete.

The meaning of a model needs considering from another angle. Quite often people will become possessed by the belief that a new medium of communication will solve persistent teaching–learning problems. No one knows for sure why this belief takes hold and is so hard to shake. Radio, the phonograph, the tape recorder, television, and now, the microcomputer, each has had its day. Each, in turn, except for the computer (so far), has faded from center stage. The road to an effective school depends on the quality of curriculum planning and delivery method. The communication channel will need to be varied depending on the instructional analysis and plan. No magic nor irrational explanation describes why a computer sometimes effectively brings about a desired learning outcome. It is not the computer that should get the credit. That belongs to the designer–developer who created the program

(Clark, 1983; Garber, n.d.). Again, the model must be the living, psychologically and sociologically complex organism called a school.

In a similar vein, one must guard against the uncritical, satisfied feeling one gets from merely relabeling an activity as "effective schools research." Most of what has been said in this book and elsewhere on the topic is not new (MacKenzie, 1983, p. 6). Some of each chapter conveys news about peoples' perceptions from various roles and settings. A small percentage of the writing tells of new confirmations of old hypotheses. What is important, and possibly new, is the sense of optimism that seems to accompany direct contact between researchers and school people when an effective schools case-study research project gets underway (Brookover, 1981; Cooley, 1983; MacKenzie, 1983, p. 7). This difficult-to-measure but hard-to-deny change in perception of the familiar school and its people, purpose, and future is real and probably is from the same species of human behavior that accounts for the positive phenomena emerging from expectancy theory research (Rosenthal & Jacobson, 1968; Anderson, Chapter 6, this volume). So, it is not enough to announce that we are doing a collaborative research in a school. Unless the research team knows clearly what its role should be and is expert at performing the tasks such researcher–consultants need to perform, they stand little chance of helping that school or adding to useful knowledge on effective and/or exemplary school research.

I will leave, at this point, the discussion on what the authors may have or may not have emphasized to turn to a suggestion on what I think will help keep this movement alive and growing.

FACILITATING EXEMPLARY SCHOOLS RESEARCH: AN EMPIRICAL MODEL

William W. Cooley in his article "Improving the Performance of an Educational System" (1983) describes in good detail the positive outcome of a long-term collaboration between a city school district and university educational researchers. The aim of the project was two-pronged. Both the school system and the researchers were to derive appropriate benefits. Evidently these goals are being attained. Cooley mentions that the previous work of "the past decade on effective teaching and effective schooling," was a cause for optimism that such a collaborative effort could succeed (Cooley, 1983, p. 10). Cooley's article was concerned with an entire school system and a large university in a major city. Moreover, the project has the added responsibility and purpose of studying and reporting on the evaluation process itself (1983, p. 5). Cooley points out that a cornerstone of the enterprise is the "systems approach" (1983, p. 10).

In this book on research on effective and/or exemplary schools, I sense that many readers may not be familiar with the systems approach or may be hostile to the very name. The previous chapters have dealt with the history, selection methods, characteristics, and contexts of exemplary and/or effective schools. Now, to answer the question: "What conceptualization or model of school improvement held in the minds of researchers has the highest likelihood of improving the academic achievement in a given school and adding useful knowledge to the research field?" My answer follows.

For sustaining the effective and/or exemplary schools research approach, I take as my model that of the instructional system designer. To save space and time, let me say that instructional systems design (ISD) is the logical and historical product of the scientific study of human learning applied by practitioners in many fields to real-life (as contrasted to academic) situations. ISD is to the psychology of learning as engineering is to various branches of physics and chemistry. The basic premise or creed of the ISD designer or developer is "The learner–user can do no wrong. If the outcome is not satisfactory, find and correct the flaw in the design or materials." (Please note, I am assuming that the equity versus excellence debate has been resolved in favor of equity. Those holding to the excellence side will concede that it is likely no harm will come to the gifted child or society in efforts to improve a given school academically.) I find it comforting to note that an eminent scholar in the effective schools research field who happens to be a sociologist seems to subscribe to the same creed and has done so for several decades. Wilbur B. Brookover (1981) states emphatically that the focus on failure of pupils to learn should have required school people to begin studying and improving *the school*. But, instead, he notes, the spotlight, with no improvement likely, was put on the pupil. Miller (Chapter 1, this volume) discusses this issue from an historical perspective. Brookover uses the business–agricultural analogy and explains that when production fails to reach expected levels in quantity and quality the successful entrepreneur looks at the conditions of production. Presumably, that is where the fault lies and by proper changes in the proportions of the fertilizers, moisture, and other controllable variables, production can be brought to or above the desired level. Human relations variables, too, are manipulable in industrial settings where they play a determining role in production of some desired outcomes. The same is true of a school setting as well.

This leads directly to the crucial variable I believe we must study in order to understand this phenomenon called the exemplary school. It is a state of awareness about the purpose of the school or as the ISD designer would put it—a statement of the problem in the most concrete, empirical terms possible. The effective construct, the one that accounts best for observed outcomes, is what every researcher tries hard to identify. Psychological theory building always depends for its usefulness on statements in operational terms about hypothesized constructs. To the extent that the predicted behaviors emerge from the manipulations the experimenter performs and not other nonpredicted or inconsistent behaviors, the construct is better defined. The theory in which it serves as an explanatory principle becomes that much stronger. In similar fashion, the school that sets out to study itself in collaboration with professional researchers becomes the object of study and certain constructs are selected as explanatory principles such as, a positive school climate enhances student academic achievement. The problem that preceded this selection would lead directly to it. The problem most likely was similar to this: Our 4th-grade students' reading achievement is below a desirable level. What can we do to raise average reading achievement for 4th graders by X percentile points (other than exhorting everyone to try harder)?

In stating such a problem and then analyzing the school conditions and then selecting variables (some are constructs) that theory and experience suggest are important for solving the problem, a state of awareness is created in that school, different from what had existed before.

The staff, students, and parents perceive the school as committed to a new, added purpose: self-improvement. The school has acquired, if you will, a new level of consciousness and for now, at least, what had been background (teaching, learning) becomes foreground or figure. Please note, we are now describing a school as if it were a person with a perceptional apparatus, purposes, and other personality characteristics. I believe the analogy is appropriate since a school does comprise a collection of people and groups of people. Also, the underlying principles, constructs, and theory for schooling are built very largely on psychology and particularly, the psychology of learning (Stephens, 1967).

Another suggestion comes to mind when thinking in an ISD frame of reference: documentation (Cooley, 1983). The authors of the preceding chapters have made clear many times that effective schools research projects take time to produce results. Purkey and Smith (Chapter 9), in particular, mention this as a possible obstacle to political support. In the process of change that a school is undertaking, it is reasonable to expect that people will lose some of the images and goals that existed when they began the project. To refresh and sustain the sense of purpose, careful documentation in the form of a semiannual report ought to take place. The staff can then periodically review the past conditions and compare them to the new changed conditions and thus have a clear sense of progress.

Every quality-built instructional system provides for evaluation. Formative evaluation, of course, serves to discover gross design or development errors at once. Such errors are revealed in a feedback-loop manner and usually are quickly corrected and then retested (Miller, Galanter, Pribram, 1960). In the school that has embarked on an effective schools research self-study, corrective action would take place when students fail to show gains in, say, measured self-concept. An in-service training program for teachers might be used if analysis suggested it to be a suitable response to the need.

The exemplary and/or effective school probably already engages in formative and summative evaluation activity. The summative evaluation process is that mechanism that informs the staff, again in a feedback loop, of the outcomes of their instructional efforts. Please note that by feedback loop I mean that the faculty know, diagnostically, which instructional strategies, materials, or learning activities failed to produce the desired pupil behavior. Now, effective corrective action can be taken since the instructional activities were designed in an ISD framework and therefore provisions have been made ahead of time to detect and correct systems faults and failures. As a consequence, mastery learning occurs with an increased probability (Bloom, 1976).

The model presented here in abbreviated form, may be a useful one for researchers in this very important field. It avoids some of the fuzzy ambiguities that can muddy straightforward efforts to understand how one can reform a given school or even a school system. Carolyn Anderson (Chapter 6) mentioned in her section on "Model Inadequacies" that few solutions, let alone plans, have appeared as yet to deal with that chicken and egg problem: Which variable should we tackle first? She addressed only one variable, though a complex one—school climate. It seems to me that scholarship ought to be allowed to blossom in a place called school. If not for the pupils sake, where else? And what could be handier than to study schooling itself in a school building or system.

The ISD is economically efficient. It allows the organization to maximize learning in *all* students at minimum cost. The equity model is inefficient and ineffective because it focuses on individual instances of failure to learn (which is really a *faulty design* problem) instead of failures to teach. The ISD model never blames the victim. That makes it fit both the excellence and equity requirements at once. All we need in America now is the will to get the job done.

REFERENCES

Austin, G. R., & Garber, H. (Eds.). (1982). *The rise and fall of national test scores*. New York: Academic Press.

Benjamin, R. (n.d.). Towards effective urban schools: A national study. In D. Brundage (Ed.), *The journalism research fellows report: What makes an effective school?* (pp. 69–104). Washington, DC: The Institute for Educational Leadership.

Bloom, B. S. (1976). *Human characteristics and school learning*. New York: McGraw-Hill.

Brookover, W. B. (1981, April). *Productivity of school social systems*. Paper presented at the meeting of the American Educational Research Association, Los Angeles.

Brundage, D. (Ed.). (n.d.). *The journalism research fellows report: What makes an effective school?* Washington, DC: Institute for Educational Leadership.

Clark, R. E. (1983). Reconsidering research on learning from media. *Review of Educational Research, 53*, 445–459.

Coleman, J. S., Campbell, E. F., Hobson, C. J., McPartland, J., Mood, A. M., Weinfeld, F. D., & York, R. L. (1966). *Equlity of educational opportunity*. Washington, DC: U.S. Office of Education.

Cooley, W. W. (1983). Improving the performance of an educational system. *Educational Researcher, 12*, (6), 4–12.

Cuban, L. (1984, May). Transforming the frog into a prince: Effective schools research, policy, and practice at the district level. *Harvard Educational Review*, pp. 129–151.

Downs, A. (1983, June 6). They sell sizzle, but their predictions fizzle. *The Wall Street Journal*, p. 30.

Fromm, E. (1956). *The art of loving: An inquiry into the nature of love*. New York: Harper, Row.

Garber, H. (n.d.). *Proposal to the Maryland School for the Deaf: Computer literacy*. Baltimore: University of Maryland Baltimore County, Center for Educational Research and Development.

Garber, H., & Austin, G. R. (1982). Learning, schooling, scores: A continuing controversy. In G. R. Austin & H. Garber (Eds.), *The rise and fall of national test scores* (pp. 1–8). New York: Academic.

Goodlad, J. (1984). *A place called school*. New York: McGraw-Hill.

Jaeger, R. M., & Tittle, C. K. (Eds.). (1980). *Minimum competency achievement testing: Motives, models, measures, and consequences*. Berkeley, CA: McCutchan.

MacKenzie, D. E. (1983). Research for school improvement: An appraisal of some recent trends. *Educational Researcher, 12*, (4), 5–17.

Miller, G. A., Galanter, E., & Pribram, K. H. (1960). *Plans and structure of behavior*. New York: Holt, Rinehart, and Winston.

Rosenthal, R., & Jacobson, L. (1968). *Pygmalion in the classroom*. New York: Holt, Rinehart.

Rowan, B. (1984, April). *Shamanistic rituals in effective schools*. Paper presented at the meeting of the American Educational Research Association, New Orleans.

Stephens, J. M. (1967). *The process of schooling: A psychological examination*. New York: Holt, Rinehart.

Wise, A. (1979). *Legislated learning: The bureaucratization of the American classroom*. Los Angeles: University of California Press.

AUTHOR INDEX

Number in italics show the page on which the complete reference is cited.

A

Abernethy, V., 182, 183, 184, *198*
Abramowitz, S., 33, 34, 35, 38, 40, *44*
Ackland, H., 98, *123*, 181, 182, *198*
Aiken, M., 189, *198*
Airasian, P., 47, *62*
Anderson, B. D., 100, 106, 115, 117, 118, *120*
Anderson, C. S., 99, 104, 112, 113, *120*
Anderson, G. J., 100, *120, 126*
Anderson, L. M., 144, *151*
Anderson, L. W., 21, *25*
Anglin, L. W., 106, *120*
Angus, M. J., 138, *151*
Armento, B. A., 140, *151*
Arnove, R. F., 8, *25*
Aronson, E., 129, *151*
Ascione, F. R., 144, *152*
Astin, A. W., 100, *120*
Austin, G. R., 20, *25*, 33, *44*, 67, 71, 73, 74, 79, *81, 82*, 85, *95*, 117, *121*, 181, *197*, 202, 203, *215*
Averch, H. A., 16, *25*, 181, *197*

B

Bailey, S. K., 52, *62*
Bain, P. J., 146, *153*
Bane, M. J., 98, *123*, 181, 182, *198*
Barash, D. P., 16, *25*
Baratz, J. C., 19, *25*
Baratz, S. S., 19, *25*
Barker, R. G., 43, *44*, 99, *121*
Barnett, W. S., 81

Barr, R. C., 99, *121*, 140, *151, 152*
Barth, R. A., 158, *176*
Batchelder, R., 107, 110, *125*
Batten, M., 100, 101, 102, *126*
Beady, C., 101, 106, 107, 108, 109, 114, 118, *121*, 182, *197*
Beamer, L., 22, *25*
Beane, J. A., 107, *121*
Becker, W. C., 134, *152*
Beckerman, T. M., 138, 140, *153*
Bell, D., 16, *25*
Bell, W. E., 106, *121*
Benjamin, R., 207, 208, *215*
Berger, P. L., 10, *25*
Berliner, D. C., 22, *25*, 132, 133, 135, 136, 137, 139, 141, 144, 145, 147, *152, 153, 154*
Berman, P., 189, *197*
Berrueta-Clement, J., 81, *81*
Besag, F. P., *25*
Bickel, W. E., 22, *25*
Biddle, B. J., 148, *152*
Biniaminov, I., 16, *27*
Blalock, Jr., H. M., 105, *121*
Blaney, N., 129, *151*
Blau, P., 16, *25*
Bloom, B., 66, 71, *82*
Bloom, B. S., 113, 116, *121*, 141, *152*, 184, *197*, 214, *215*
Blum, J. M., 8, *25*
Blust, R. S., 19, *28*
Boles, K., 192, *198*
Boocock, S. S., 118, *121*
Borg, W. R., 144, *152*
Bossert, S. T., 99, 110, 113, 118, *124*, 188, *199*

217

SUBJECT INDEX

A

Ability, as significant factor in educational research, 16
Absenteeism, 43
Academic emphasis, school climate variable, 108–109
Academic learning time, 183
  definition, 136
  effective teachers' application of theory, 137–138
  relation to teacher effectiveness, 136–138, 150–151
Accountability, and exemplary schools, 81
Accreditation, as a tool to encourage improvement, 192–193
Achievement
  across subject areas, in exemplary schools, 93–95
  change categories, for schools, 90
  differences between school types, 39–40
  effect of expectations, 69, 184
  effects of time and isolation, 20–21
  encouraged by pacing, 140
  improvement, 94–95
  and low-success rate, 136
  nonschool effects, separate from school effects, 84–85, 91
  in public, private, and Catholic schools, 47
  in public vs. private schools, 31–32, 75–76
  related to allocated time, 131–132
  related to success rate, 135–136
  rewarding, 109, 183
  and school culture, 182–196
  and staff changes, 94

and student changes, 94
teacher variables, 105–106
and use of student ideas, 147–148
validity of test scores in, 84
Action for Excellence, 65
Administrative organization, school climate variable, 106–107
AFDC factor, 87
A Nation at Risk, 185

B

Backward mapping, 185, 189
Beginning Teacher Evaluation Study, 131–132
Behavior variables, in effective teaching, 144
Benjamin, Robert, report on schools, 207–208
Blaming the Victim, 15
Busing, effect on Catholic school enrollments, 53–54

C

California Assessment Program (CAP), as standard for identifying exemplary schools, 84, 86
Catholic elementary schools
  enrollments, 51–52
  relationship to public schools, 48
Catholic schools
  achievement norms, vs. public schools', 47
  effect of Catholic church practice in, 55
  enrollment, effect of Catholic church, 55–56